The Gap in Shakespeare

THE GAP
IN SHAKESPEARE

The Motif of Division
from *Richard II* to *The Tempest*

by

Colin N. Manlove

VISION
and
BARNES & NOBLE

Vision Press Limited
11–14 Stanhope Mews West
London SW7 5RD

and

Barnes & Noble Books
81 Adams Drive
Totowa, NJ 07512

ISBN (UK) 0 85478 444 6
ISBN (US) 0 389 20111 1

Printed and bound by
Mansell Bookbinders Ltd.,
Witham, Essex.
Phototypeset by Galleon Photosetting,
Ipswich, Suffolk.
MCMLXXXI

Preface

I initially wrote this book simply to try to establish, shorn of preconceptions and bardolatry, my own interpretations of some of Shakespeare's major plays. Not surprisingly, I subsequently found anticipations of several of my ideas in other writers—particularly on *Hamlet* and *Troilus and Cressida*—and these chapters had to be condensed. No doubt there are other instances which I have not seen: to them my respects. No doubt too the concomitant of what originality the book possesses has been a certain provocativeness, even eccentricity. But I would prefer it to raise objections and even outrage or scorn rather than the complaisant nod of academic acceptability. Thought is free, and truth is various: to my mind Shakespeare himself can only be set free when he is encountered without any prior assumptions about his greatness or his infallibility—and also when each approach we make to his plays is recognized to be only one approach. This book, while it seeks to prove its arguments, does not emerge out of settled convictions, nor out of any wish to be definitive: it was written from the mere pleasure of intellectual adventure and exploration, which it is the writer's hope that his reader may perhaps come to try for himself.

When I looked back over the various interpretations, I saw that there was a common motif running through them—namely, one of division. Shakespeare, it seemed, was continually preoccupied with this theme: it appeared in the form of a split between mind and body in many plays from *Richard II* to *Measure for Measure*; two of his greatest plays, *King Lear* and *Macbeth*, depended upon the use of division as a technique or as an analytic tool; and *Timon*, *Antony and Cleopatra* and *Coriolanus* were founded on explorations of division between the individual and the state. The motif also appeared in less intentional modes—particularly in Shakespeare's portrayals of love-relationships, in the instability of some of his judgments and in his attempts to write tragi-comedy. Further, the broad character of the divisions changed with the development of Shakespeare's plays, forming what could be seen as a coherent psychological pattern.

There have been a number of studies dealing with the centrality in Shakespeare's plays of his use of opposites, contraries, dualities, antitheses and paradoxes. Among these are Theodore Spencer, *Shakespeare and the Nature of Man* (1943), Marion Bodwell Smith, *Dualities in Shakespeare* (1966), Rosalie L. Colie, *Paradoxia Epidemica* (1966), Norman Rabkin, *Shakespeare and the Common Understanding* (1967), Bernard McElroy, *Shakespeare's Mature Tragedies* (1973) and Robert Grudin, *Mighty Opposites: Shakespeare and Renaissance Contrariety* (1979). While these works testify to the peculiar prominence of dividedness in Shakespeare's plays, they none of them treat the fact of division itself: they are concerned more to isolate the items that are opposed and to view them as being in a continuous dialectical state, than to consider the actual tension which their being divided causes, or the origins of their division, or how the gap between them may alter during a given play. Part of this difference stems from the fact that the kinds of opposites which interest these writers are on the whole of a different type from those which I discuss. They tend to concern themselves with opposed concepts, themes or visions: with, for example, youth and age in *Romeo and Juliet*, rigour and laxity in *Measure for Measure*, Iago's and Desdemona's antagonistic views of love in *Othello*, the dual view of the universe as meaningful and meaningless in *King Lear*, Macbeth as hero only by being a criminal,[1] the total oppugnancy of Rome and Egypt in *Antony and Cleopatra*. I am more interested in the relations of lovers in Shakespeare's plays, or the presence of divided judgments and attitudes, or Shakespeare's ability with tragi-comedy, or his use of disjunctions in behaviour (in *King Lear*), or his employment of division itself as a theme (*in Macbeth*). Where I do see the opposites in conceptual terms, as between mind and body in the second history tetralogy, *Hamlet, Troilus and Cressida* and *Measure for Measure*, my actual analysis is concerned not so much with the terms themselves as with the causes and consequences within the works of their severance: and beyond that I am interested in the fact that the theme is recurrent in the plays of this period.

All the writers I have mentioned see Shakespeare's use of opposites as an expression of the essentially dual or contrary character of reality. Spencer, Smith and Grudin, in particular, make that reality Shakespeare's Renaissance environment, in which views of life in terms of contrarieties were particularly prevalent; Spencer argues for the influence of a Jacobean 'dissociation of sensibility' but is rather superseded by the weight of evidence amassed by Grudin showing that 'the idea that experience derives from the interaction of opposing forces'[2] is to be found in philosophers throughout the sixteenth century—among them Cornelius Agrippa, Castiglione, Paracelsus, Montaigne and Bruno. In general therefore these writers argue that Shakespeare's use of opposites in his plays is more or less conscious and deliberate, and that, while exceptionally prominent in his work, it expresses a view of the nature of reality common in his time. (This approach to Shakespeare as the mouthpiece of his age has been convincingly challenged.[3]) The opposites and divisions I am concerned with are often far less intentional, and point rather towards an essential dividedness in the character of Shakespeare himself. Several of them are recurrent motifs rather than polarities applicable only to single plays. They also depend on an irretrievable divorce from an original unity, whether it be of mind and body, self and state, man and woman or literary expectations and experience: the opposites of Smith, Rabkin, McElroy and Grudin, on the other hand, are either implicitly to be fused in a *discordia concors* (Smith) or conjoined in an antithetical but complementary vision.

What I am engaged on here, then, can ultimately be said in large degree to be exploration of Shakespeare himself: first the plays, then the recurrent themes, then the psychological and even biographical inference.[4] The risks are obvious; the guesses will most of them be in the dark. But it seems worth trying to trouble that darkness a little: it has been too long a Bluebeard's room of literary criticism.

NOTES

Abbreviations of academic journals used:

E in C   *Essays in Criticism*
ELH   *English Literary History*
RES   *Review of English Studies*
SEL   *Studies in English Literature, 1500–1900*
SQ   *Shakespeare Quarterly*
SS   *Shakespeare Survey*

Unless otherwise stated, place of publication is London.

1. For the last two in particular, see McElroy, op. cit. (Princeton, N.J., Princeton University Press, 1973), pp. 8–9, 161–63, 203.
2. Grudin, op. cit. (Berkeley, Los Angeles and London, University of California Press, 1979), p. 15.
3. By Howard Felperin, *Shakespearean Representation: Mimesis and Modernity in Elizabethan Tragedy* (Princeton, N.J., Princeton University Press, 1977); see, in summary, pp. 194–95.
4. *Pace* C. J. Sisson ('The Mythical Sorrows of Shakespeare', *Proceedings of the British Academy*, 20 (1934)). But what Sisson was objecting to was what he saw as unjustified inference of the dramatist's views from those expressed by his characters, and construction of spiritual biography from the sequence of Shakespeare's plays, on the assumption that he should write tragedies after his middle comedies because he became darker in mood. The kinds of evidence we shall be dealing with—recurrent themes and habits of treatment, changes in the form of a given topic over many plays—will hopefully provide alternative pointers.

   But it should also be said in this context that we suffer from a kind of critical myopia. We tend to assume that if we have found a possible answer to a given 'heresy' that heresy is finally exploded. Sisson did not destroy the case for a biographical reading of Shakespeare: he only introduced a caveat, and posed an approach other than the biographical to the changing genres in which Shakespeare wrote. It is the ignoring of this general truth that makes so much academic criticism often merely academic.

1

The Second History Tetralogy

Richard II

In *Richard II* Shakespeare begins to explore a theme which is to preoccupy him again in *Hamlet* and *Troilus and Cressida*—that of psychic and conceptual disunity, whereby any one man has only part of the equipment of humanity. Thus, on the whole, Richard thinks, and Bolingbroke acts: neither is versed in the other's ability. When Richard stops the tournament between Mowbray and Bolingbroke, his doing so indicates as much his distaste for action as his desire to save one of his henchmen; and the whole patterned quality of ritual defiance and challenge in these first scenes, whereby violence is contained within formality, is an emblem of Richard's nature, with its feudal love of ceremony and the static tableau. When Richard has banished Mowbray and Bolingbroke, and Gaunt, father to the latter, bids his son comfort himself in exile by imagining (*à la* Coriolanus) that he banished the king rather than the king him, or that he has been sent abroad by his father in quest of honour, or that he is fleeing a plague at home, or that he is going in search of what his 'soul holds dear', Bolingbroke answers him,

> O, who can hold a fire in his hand
> By thinking on the frosty Caucasus?
> Or cloy the hungry edge of appetite
> By bare imagination of a feast?
> Or wallow naked in December snow
> By thinking on fantastic summer's heat?
>
> (I, iii, 294–99)[1]

(It is typical of Bolingbroke that he should speak in terms of transforming a physical rather than a mental event into its opposite.)

Richard is capable of entertaining his imagination as Bolingbroke is not, if in the service rather of a more gloomy than a more joyous picture than the facts warrant. Before he has even encountered the returned Bolingbroke he has given up: 'of comfort no man speak./ Let's talk of graves, of worms, and epitaphs,/ Make dust our paper, and with rainy eyes/ Write sorrow on the bosom of the earth' (III, ii, 144–47). Here is delusive fancy indeed, and this in the face of only a few discouragements. He bids the land rise up against Boling-broke: to him it is not physical, but conceptual earth, at one with the furtherance of lineal kingship. Then, despite the pleas of Carlisle and Aumerle that he take practical military steps, he goes further in expecting concepts to win for him, in the belief that the rightness of his cause must necessarily expel the wrong that is Bolingbroke's, which for him goes against the grain of reality: thus, 'Not all the water in the rough rude sea/ Can wash the balm off from an anointed king' (III, ii, 54–5), and 'heaven still guards the right' (ibid., 62). There is no psychological reason for Richard's behaviour here—he has not been paralysed by his past sins, for example. Nor, finally, could it be said that Shakespeare is analysing the nature of feudal as against Renaissance kingship, for without being unwarrantedly extraliterary we are well aware that there were many highly vigorous and active 'feudal' kings (Richard I, Edward I and Edward III, for example); and in any case Henry IV will still be a medieval monarch, more politic than Richard though he may be. We can say that Shakespeare is showing a moment of historical cycle, where an old culture which has grown effete, inept and stupidly rapacious is shown being overthrown by a new and more pragmatic one. But the ultimate landscape of the analysis is that of division between mind and body, to the final frustration of both categories; and it is in terms of this that we should most accurately view the fact that Richard is associated with the metaphysics and Bolingbroke with the physics of power.

The procedure of the play is one whereby Richard moves deeper into the nature of his own passive intellectuality. His refusal to act in his own defence puts him in Bolingbroke's power, and he sees why: 'They well deserve to have/ That know the strong'st and surest way to get' (III, iii, 200–1). Gradually we become aware that trying to fight for one's kingdom with metaphysics is ultimately to settle for an intellectual rather than a real kingdom—'You may my glories and my state depose,/ But not my griefs; still am I king of those' (IV, i, 192–93)—and also that to be so passive is in the end to desire the ultimate passivity, death:

> what'er I be,
> Nor I, nor any man that but man is,
> With nothing shall be pleas'd, till he be eas'd
> With being nothing.
>
> (V, v, 38–41)

This anticipates the death-wish of another intellectual, Hamlet.

Richard's mind has only an increasingly confused connection with the outside world, even with psychological fact, from which he often launches into intellectual embroidery quite disconnected from any immediate feeling or experience in his life. Before his second interview with Northumberland at Berkeley Castle, he asks Aumerle whether he must now submit, and says he will do so, even to be deposed and lose the name of king: the mood is one of self-pity, stemming from the occasion, but it becomes steadily more ornate until the initial stimulus is lost. Noticing Aumerle weeping at the miserable picture he is painting of himself, Richard suggests that they join their tears to drown 'this revolting land', but then, as if realizing the futility of this conceit, he moves away from the predicament and cause altogether:

> Or shall we play the wantons with our woes,
> And make some pretty match with shedding tears?
> As thus to drop them still upon one place,
> Till they have fretted us a pair of graves
> Within the earth, and therein laid—there lies
> Two kinsmen digg'd their graves with weeping eyes!
> Would not this ill do well? Well, well, I see
> I talk but idly, and you laugh at me.
>
> (III, iii, 164–71)

At the end, however, even as Richard has given utterance to his long soliloquy attempting, for no obvious reason, to compare his prison to the world (rather than, say, the other way round), lapsing continually from self-condemnation into filigree conceits, he is suddenly roused to action by the attack of Exton and the murderers. Perhaps Shakespeare is suggesting that, as with Hamlet before his return to Elsinore, the only way in which Richard could act was when he was assailed without time for thought. Certainly this serves to tone down a too-stark contrast between Richard and Bolingbroke: nevertheless we note the special circumstances necessary for this.

If Richard is cut off from events, Bolingbroke seems divided from thought. What his motives are neither he nor we fully know: he simply acts as opportunity offers, and when Richard makes over the crown to him, he willingly takes it. At the beginning of *1 Henry IV* we find him guilty at this act; but he never speculates on it in *Richard II*, and we may consider that he does not at any time really know what to think or feel about it.[2] He never soliloquizes. He comes back to England to fight for his lands and rights as Duke of Lancaster, taken from him by the king after his father John of Gaunt's death; if he is to recover them, he has small alternative but to fight, since the use of the legal process is denied him. He takes on himself the authority to seize and execute the king's favourites Bushy and Green on the grounds that they have harmed King Richard and the commonwealth, and because of their being behind the seizure of his inheritance. Whether the altruistic national motive is at all a real one, and if so, just how much it weighs with him, it is impossible to tell, and, one feels, impossible for Bolingbroke too, because he is not introspective. The king gives everything to Bolingbroke before the latter has formulated any ambition that he might have, and Bolingbroke simply takes what is offered, without comment; if he thinks anything of Carlisle's remarks on the impious sacrilege he has committed in ascending the throne, we do not hear of it.

When Exton, obeying Bolingbroke's suggestion, ' "Have I no friend will rid me of this living fear?" ', kills Richard, Bolingbroke changes the 'friend' to enemy, and attempts to shuffle the guilt on to Exton:

They love not poison that do poison need,
Nor do I thee. Though I did wish him dead,
I hate the murtherer, love him murthered.
The guilt of conscience take thou for thy labour.
                                    (V, vi, 38–41)

This shows Bolingbroke's confusion whenever he has to deal
with the inner life of feeling and conscience (of which we have
previously had a sight in his mixture of barely-suppressed rage
and lamb-like reasonableness before and during his meeting
with King Richard at Berkeley). Here it is not really a question
of whether he loves or hates Exton, but of whether he is
indebted to him for murdering Richard as he wished—which
he must be: if he wished for murder, he wished for a murderer.
As for conscience, Bolingbroke initially describes the reputation that will accrue to him from the deed as slander—'thou
hast wrought/ A deed of slander with thy fatal hand/ Upon my
head and all this famous land'— and puts the guilt on Exton,
dissociating himself from him. Yet he ends by admitting
complicity, and vowing to atone for it:

I'll make a voyage to the Holy Land,
To wash this blood off from my guilty hand.
                                    (ibid., 49–50)

The evidence thus suggests that Bolingbroke simply does not
know his own mind, or at least has no steady and continued
mental life. His lack of fixity here seems mirrored not only in
the fact that he is always active, but that he is continually
mobile, ever-changing, from England to exile and back again,
on the long march of rebellion over the land, and in title from
Hereford to Lancaster to king. Richard, on the other hand, is
more fixed: he does nothing to help himself, he stands before
Bolingbroke and melts, he is the king still though he unkings
himself, he has the stasis for introspection; and when he
reflects, he speaks of the cessation of movement in his death, or
laments that his face has not changed although he has
dethroned himself, or talks of himself as a sunken bucket of
water, where Bolingbroke is 'The emptier ever dancing in the
air' (IV, i, 186).

The dualism is therefore quite clear-cut: those who think too
much cannot act, and those who act too much cannot think; or,

to put it in less prescriptive terminology, this play shows a split between inner and outer lives, whereby those who give themselves to the former are incapable of the latter, and vice versa. Actually they are not in effect very 'capable' within their specialist fields either: in the context of the whole tetralogy neither Bolingbroke's actions nor Richard's thoughts are pleasure-giving or finally productive (to repeat, it is Richard's passivity more than anything else that gives Bolingbroke the throne): excess is seen to be ultimately as sterile as total deficiency.

This theme of psychic division is continued with Henry IV's son Hal, but now it is also internalized in one mind.

Hal from 'Henry IV' to 'Henry V'

In past assessments of how far Hal is involved with Falstaff, there have been many comments on his first soliloquy, but very little detailed analysis.[3]

> I know you all, and will awhile uphold
> The unyok'd humour of your idleness.
> Yet herein will I imitate the sun,
> Who doth permit the base contagious clouds
> To smother up his beauty from the world,
> That, when he please again to be himself,
> Being wanted he may be more wonder'd at
> By breaking through the foul and ugly mists
> Of vapours that did seem to strangle him.
> If all the year were playing holidays,
> To sport would be as tedious as to work;
> But when they seldom come, they wish'd-for come,
> And nothing pleaseth but rare accidents:
> So when this loose behaviour I throw off,
> And pay the debt I never promised,
> By how much better than my word I am,
> By so much shall I falsify men's hopes;
> And like bright metal on a sullen ground,
> My reformation, glitt'ring o'er my fault,
> Shall show more goodly, and attract more eyes
> Than that which hath no foil to set it off.
> I'll so offend, to make offence a skill,
> Redeeming time when men least think I will.
>   (I, ii, 190–212)[4]

16

Politic, of course: yet there is also self-delusion here. The sun does not, except by pathetic fallacy, permit itself to be covered by clouds, nor does it determine when to break free of them once more. The image works only in the sense of something rich, being concealed, becoming the more striking when rediscovered. And could Hal really mean his argument? His reform might strike the gazers, but might they not be the more surely taken with him if he had not needed to reform? What he is saying sounds more like strained self-justification than a politic plan of campaign. It is worth noting here that Hal's father (unknowingly) contradicts just this line of reasoning in a later interview, when he tells him that he has so mixed with the populace that he has become common and unregarded:

> Had I so lavish of my presence been,
> So common-hackney'd in the eyes of men,
> So stale and cheap to vulgar company,
> Opinion, that did help me to the crown,
> Had still kept loyal to possession,
> And left me in reputeless banishment,
> A fellow of no mark nor likelihood.
> By being seldom seen, I could not stir
> But like a comet I was wonder'd at.
>
> (*1*, III, ii, 39–47)

The last two lines ironically echo Hal's own speech on the subject. The king goes on to liken Hal's performance to that of Richard II, whom he supplanted in the people's affections, and who

> gave his countenance against his name
> To laugh at gibing boys, and stand the push
> Of every beardless vain comparative,
> Grew a companion to the common streets,
> Enfeoff'd himself to popularity,
> That, being daily swallow'd by men's eyes,
> They surfeited with honey, and began
> To loathe the taste of sweetness, whereof a little
> More than a little is by much too much.
>
> (65–73)

The issue raised with this first soliloquy is how far Hal is really or only apparently corrupted by Falstaff and his followers. The sun and cloud image suggests that he does not have so much control over his destiny as he claims; and the 'base *contagious* clouds' can only further this. Later, of course, he speaks of his 'reformation' and his 'fault'. Do we then have someone who is detached from Falstaff throughout, or someone whose rejection of Falstaff is going in large part to be rejection of what he himself is? If he is simply politic, then the reasons for staying with Falstaff seem rather thin: what a deal of besmirching for one striking reformation! The ambiguity seems continued in that image of 'holidays': almost any reader would take the 'If all the year were playing holidays' as a reference by Hal to his time with Falstaff, but in fact it refers to the holiday he would take from Falstaff. The oddity is heightened by contrast with the previous scene, in which Hal's father spoke of him as a dissolute hedonist, a holiday-maker amid the cares of the time. In short, what this speech shows is someone who is radically confused about his motives, someone who is a mixture of policy and folly, of detachment from Falstaff and involvement with him, and who tries to make one side of the division explain away the other. The result must be that Hal does not know exactly where he stands in relation to Falstaff even when he says he does: and that when he finally throws him off, that rejection is not part of a cunningly-engineered plan brought into effect when the time is ripe, but another over-simplifying decision forced on him by the demands of state and respectability. Thus, when Warwick tells the king that

> The Prince but studies his companions
> Like a strange tongue, wherein, to gain the language,
> 'Tis needful that the most immodest word
> Be look'd upon and learnt; which once attain'd,
> Your Highness knows, comes to no further use
> But to be known and hated. So, like gross terms,
> The Prince will, in the perfectness of time,
> Cast off his followers, and their memory
> Shall as a pattern or a measure live
> By which his Grace must mete the lives of other,
> Turning past evils to advantages.
>
> (*2 Henry IV*, IV, iv, 68–78),

the truth is nothing so organized or carefully foreseen as

18

this—not least in the fact that this description of Hal's purpose is quite different from Hal's own account of it (here it is prole-knowing, there it was contrast-making).

Of course, as has often been pointed out, whenever we see Hal, he is at some remove from Falstaff or his companions, at whose expense he often enjoys a joke (though it may well be that he is allowed such expensive jokes only because of who he is, and from anyone else they might produce a less pacific, less amusing response). The Gadshill episode, where Hal and Poins, disguised, set on Falstaff and the others while they are robbing some travellers, and later bait them about it, illustrates Hal's stance; there is also the later episode with the drawers:

> *Prince.* Ned, prithee come out of that fat room, and lend me thy hand to laugh a little.
> *Poins.* Where hast been, Hal?
> *Prince.* With three or four loggerheads, amongst three or fourscore hogsheads. I have sounded the very base-string of humility. Sirrah, I am sworn brother to a leash of drawers, and can call them all by their christen names, as Tom, Dick, and Francis. They take it already upon their salvation, that though I be but Prince of Wales, yet I am the king of courtesy, and tell me flatly I am no proud Jack like Falstaff, but a Corinthian, a lad of mettle, a good boy (by the Lord, so they call me!), and when I am King of England I shall command all the good lads in Eastcheap. They call drinking deep 'dyeing scarlet', and when you breathe in your watering they cry 'Hem!' and bid you 'Play it off!' To conclude, I am so good a proficient in one quarter of an hour that I can drink with any tinker in his own language during my life.
>
> (*1*, II, iv, 1 ff.)

He then proposes that he and Poins bait the drawer Francis. What we have to ask ourselves here is how far we feel happy at someone who has just been together with people laughing at them behind their backs: we have the involved followed by the mocking Hal, and we are naturally tempted to see him as a hypocrite. But really he can be seen as simply confused. And his confusion is abetted by the very people with whom he mixes: knowing that he is the heir to the throne, they give him alike the privilege of joining them and laughing at what he

19

discovers through his joining them. Because of what he will be, he is allowed to exist in a no-man's land of indecision, both enjoying and mocking what they are, when if he had been anyone else commitment and decision for one side or the other would have been demanded.

The *Henry IV* plays are in part about uncertainties of identity. The fact that Hal is both prince and tavern-haunter means that he has no fixed self. At one point he and Falstaff play King Henry IV and the Lord Chief Justice (*1*, II, iv, 371 ff.), Hal's father, as a usurper, is king *de facto* but not *de jure*, and the rebellions against him, both private and political, are expressions of his unsure condition. On the battlefield of Shrewsbury at the end of *1 Henry IV* several of his barons appear disguised as the king. Even death can be uncertain: at Shrewsbury Falstaff feigns death and Hal utters a needless obsequy over him, as he does later over his apparently dead father. There is much imagery of counterfeiting and of giving fair outside to the vile throughout both parts of *Henry IV*.[5] The rebels use dynastic or religious issues to give fair countenance to revolt in order to draw popular support: they are frequently described as frauds or counterfeiters. In Prince John's betrayal of Worcester and Westmoreland, the roles of traitor and truster are switched. Character is unstable, extreme or confused. Hotspur, who in his obstinacy anticipates Coriolanus, is unyielding and ultimately self-destructive in his insistence on his self-hood and on taking stands; Hal, on the other hand, refuses to be one thing, and dislikes commitment—a dislike which explains his distance both from Falstaff and the king. (This ambiguity of character makes Hal resemble Shakespeare's Antony, but where Antony finally abandons the public world for the private, Hal is to turn from Falstaff (his Cleopatra) to the duties of state.) From the make-up of the two *Henry IV* plays it might seem that Hal is meant to be 'placed' and identified by contrast with Hotspur, Falstaff and Prince John, as someone not hasty, but not cold, and with a common touch, and yet there is a strangely null centre, a vacancy, where Hal should be. When he is characterized by both Falstaff and his father within the space of a few lines in IV, iii and iv of Part 2, we feel that this sudden attempt to 'fix' him reveals the dramatist's own uncertainties. Falstaff sees him as a flower opened in alcohol—

> Hereof comes it that Prince Harry is valiant; for the cold blood
> he did naturally inherit of his father he hath like lean, sterile,
> and bare land manured, husbanded, and tilled, with excellent
> endeavour of drinking good and good store of fertile sherris, that
> he is become very hot and valiant.
>
> (iii, 115–21)

—an explanation which will suffice only for Falstaff, and a
characterization which catches at only one aspect of Hal; and
as for the hotness, we must think too of the coldness of
attempted calculation which Falstaff does not see. But the king
gives us a Hal totally hidden from us:

> he is gracious, if he be observ'd,
> He hath a tear for pity, and a hand
> Open as day for melting charity:
> Yet notwithstanding, being incens'd, he's flint,
> As humorous as winter, and as sudden
> As flaws congealed in the spring of day.
>
> (iv, 30–5)

It may be true, but we have not seen it.[6] Without the
knowledge of Hal which might justify it, we can only see it as
a last ditch attempt to give reality and tangibility to a figure
who has so conspicuously lacked them.

This uncertainty is also evident in the scene where Hal,
approaching his father asleep on his death-bed, thinks he is
dead and leaves the room with his crown. When the king wakes
and finds his crown gone, he has Hal found and rebukes him
for his apparent indecent haste and his indifference to the loss
of his parent: Hal protests however that he was heartbroken
at the supposed death, and that he took the crown only as a
heavy burden. Yet there is in fact only sketchy evidence of these
reactions in the 'crown-talking' scene itself, and rather more
emphasis on the crown as a debt paid by his father to Hal, and
as a 'lineal honour' he is overjoyed to have gained (2, IV, v,
40–6); the words of misery and the feelings to which he says
he gave vent are scarcely present. On the other hand Warwick
tells the king that he found Hal weeping in the next room
(82–7). Clearly Hal is not simply 'a most princely hypocrite':
he is an uncertain mixture of contradictory motions unknown

21

to him and unfathomable to us, a mixture of which his account is an evasive simplification.[7]

The uncertain position that Hal has comes to final trial in *Henry V*. He has rejected Falstaff and accepted his kingly office, and in so doing has attempted to simplify himself. Yet he still distances himself from the commitment he has largely accepted. Having led his army to France and to Agincourt, he disguises himself as a common soldier on the night before the battle to go among his men: that is, he temporarily puts off his regal identity. There seems no particular reason of policy for this: we may suppose that he would wish to learn of any disaffection (though he might better learn of this by other means), but more obviously the scene presents a simple desire on his part to come back from the other side of the fence. But now, to do it, he has to be a counterfeit: and so, we are shown, is any assumed relation of equality between the king and his subjects. At first he argues that the king shares all that they do:

> I think the king is but a man, as I am: the violet smells to him as it doth to me; the element shows to him as it doth to me; all his senses have but human conditions: his ceremonies laid by, in his nakedness he appears but a man; and though his affections are higher mounted than ours, yet when they stoop, they stoop with the like wing. Therefore when he sees reason of fears, as we do, his fears, out of doubt, be of the same relish as ours are. . . .
> (*Henry V*, IV, i, 101–10)

The soldiers to whom he is speaking put the king in a relation to them not of equality but of responsibility, whereby he must answer for all that they do or that befalls them; they, in short, reject his bid for equality with them as he did Falstaff's for equality with him:

> *Bates.* . . . we know enough if we know we are the king's subjects. If his cause be wrong, our obedience to the king wipes the crime of it out of us.
>
> *Will.* But if the cause be not good, the king himself hath a heavy reckoning to make; when all those legs and arms and heads, chopped off in a battle, shall join together at the latter day, and cry all, 'We died at such a place'; some swearing, some crying for a surgeon, some upon their wives left poor behind them, some upon the debts they owe, some upon their children rawly left. I am afeard there are few die well that die in a

22

battle; for how can they charitably dispose of any thing when blood is their argument? Now, if these men do not die well, it will be a black matter for the king that led them to it, who to disobey were against all proportion of subjection.

The king's answer to this, as it must be, is to dissociate himself altogether from them and their plight. He maintains that he is not responsible, 'the king is not bound to answer the particular endings of his soldiers . . . for they purpose not their death when they purpose their services' (IV, i, 159–63). Again, he argues that many of his soldiers are sinful men for whom war is God's chastisement: 'if they die unprovided, no more is the king guilty of their damnation than he was before guilty of those impieties for the which they are now visited' (ibid., 179–82). The specific arguments Hal uses are actually questionable,[8] but the point here is their drift, which is to separate the king from his subjects in terms of responsibility where they cannot do so from him: 'Every subject's duty is the king's; but every subject's soul is his own.'

But now, left alone, Hal can think only of the unwelcome distance between subject and king, the different kind of burden which he must carry for them: he sees that ceremony and pomp, which is all that kingship gives him, cannot make him sleep as soundly as the meanest peasant:

> And, but for ceremony, such a wretch,
> Winding up days with toil and nights with sleep,
> Had the fore-hand and vantage of a king.
> The slave, a member of the country's peace,
> Enjoys it; but in gross brain little wots
> What watch the king keeps to maintain the peace,
> Whose hours the peasant best advantages.
> (284–90)

In view of all this his call the next morning to his army—

> We few, we happy few, we band of brothers;
> For he to-day that sheds his blood with me
> Shall be my brother
> (IV, iii, 60–2)

—can only have limited foundation: and only the fact that he happens to win the battle with minimal losses allows Hal to escape having to face the distance he has previously set

23

between his own soul and the next man's. But the night interview with his soldiers has taught him more about the limits of sharing and equality between a king and his subjects, and more about what it is to be a king. Early in the play we were told of the suddenness of his reformation:

> Never was such a sudden scholar made;
> Never came reformation in a flood,
> With such a heavy currance, scouring faults;
> Nor never Hydra-headed wilfulness
> So soon did lose his seat—and all at once—
> As in this king.
>
> (I, i, 32–7)

What we have seen through this play is the full removal of Hal's desires to be one with the common people: he has taken the change finally to himself.[9] By the end of the play he has settled for a manufactured common touch of his own rather than one dependent on and validated by commoners; the awkward heartiness of the scene in which he woos Kate, daughter of the King of France, in bare prose, presenting himself as a 'plain soldier', 'such a plain king that thou wouldst think I had sold my farm to buy my crown' (V, ii, 153, 125–26), expresses the limitations of this. Nevertheless, as Hal and the play see it, this degree of exclusion from common humanity and shared experience is the acceptable price of kingship, military success, peace and (temporary) national prosperity.

In keeping with this theme of the necessary ceremony that distances a king from his subjects, and the need for him to construct a self, the play is full of images of various orders of show. The Chorus continually laments that the show on the stage is so poor a representation of the great events portrayed: 'pardon, gentles all,/ The flat unraised spirits that hath dar'd/ On this unworthy scaffold to bring forth/ So great an object' (I, Prologue, 8–11); 'And so our scene must to the battle fly;/ Where, O for pity! we shall much disgrace/ With four or five most vile and ragged foils,/ . . ./ The name of Agincourt' (IV, Prologue, 48–52); 'Thus far, with rough and all-unable pen,/ Our bending author hath pursu'd the story;/ In little room confining mighty men,/ Mangling by starts the full course of their glory' (Epilogue, 1–4). The Chorus constantly

24

asks the imaginations of its hearers to work to make up for the deficiencies of the presentation. Hal wishes to have a show of just cause for invading France and has the Archbishop of Canterbury rehearse at length the justification for claiming the French throne through descent from the female side of the French royal house (I, ii, 9–100). At Harfleur Hal describes what he wants of his soldiers in terms of an imitation as much as a reality:

> In peace there's nothing so becomes a man
> As modest stillness and humility:
> But when the blast of war blows in our ears,
> Then imitate the action of the tiger;
> Stiffen the sinews, conjure up the blood,
> Disguise fair nature with hard-favour'd rage;
> Then lend the eye a terrible aspect . . .
>> (III, i, 3–9; see also 15–17, 22–7)

This is a show which will awaken the reality it copies.

All these shows are necessary. There are others that one cannot avoid. Though Hal puts off his kingship to go among his soldiers, he is still only a show of himself. And he cannot himself wear the glove by which, while 'unceremonied', he arranged that Williams the soldier could later recognize and challenge him, for that would be to have a subject strike his king: instead the glove 'show' is given to Fluellen, where it becomes mere show, since Fluellen is not the man.

Then, by contrast, there are the kinds of show which are wholly reprehensible. The traitors Grey, Cambridge and Scroop (unlike the rebels of *Richard II* and *Henry IV*) were hypocrites who showed themselves the king's friends while plotting to slay him: of Scroop in particular Hal says that his betrayal has cast a blight on the fair-seeming of all men (II, ii, 126–42). Nym, Bardolph and Pistol are corrupt fakes, thieves and cowards under a show of soldiership. The French in war are show with very little substance. They appear an army but are in fact in dissension, the noblemen disdainful both of the commoners and of each other; and they think to win the battle with the enormously superior numbers they have rather than by any actual worth or by tactics. The English on the other hand are tired and have lost all their fine show, as their king himself acknowledges to his enemies (III, vi, 148–61; IV, iii, 108–12), and seem to the French mere food for their swords—the Constable says, 'Do but behold yon poor and starved band,/ And your fair show shall suck away their souls,/ Leaving them but the shales and husks of men' (IV, ii, 16–18): yet that same army is to defeat the French completely.

Thus, through these various kinds of show the play constructs a picture of the sort of show that, with all its limitations, is both proper and necessary to true kingship and to life generally. Nevertheless, show it still in part remains, artificial and forced rather than natural and free. And if in *Henry V* it is possible for Hal to make his own peculiar accommodation with the public and ceremonial world, this is not to be the case in Shakespeare's later plays, where there is far less scope for compromise between the individual and the state, and alienation of the self from society becomes a continuing theme.

NOTES

1. References are to the Arden *Richard II*, ed. Peter Ure (Methuen, 1961).
2. See also Alvin Kernan, 'The Henriad: Shakespeare's Major History Plays', *Yale Review*, 59 (1969–70), 17.
3. Perhaps the most detailed is William Empson, 'Falstaff and Mr. Dover Wilson', *Kenyon Review*, 15 (1953), 227–28: he points out the contradiction in the idea of a 'fault' where the rest of the speech insists there is none, but does not relate this to Hal's uncertain character.
4. References for *Henry IV* Parts 1 and 2 and for *Henry V* are to the Arden editions, ed. A. R. Humphreys (Methuen, 1960, 1966) and J. H. Walter (Methuen, 1954), respectively.
5. James Winny, *The Player King: A Theme of Shakespeare's Histories* (Chatto and Windus, 1968), ch. 3; James L. Calderwood, *Metradrama in Shakespeare's Henriad: 'Richard II' to 'Henry V'* (Berkeley, Los Angeles and London, University of California Press, 1979), esp. pp. 47–67.
6. See also S.C. Sen Gupta, *A Shakespeare Manual* (Calcutta, Oxford University Press, 1977), p. 41.
7. For other readings of this scene, see Sigurd Burckhardt, *Shakespearean Meanings* (Princeton, N.J., Princeton University Press, 1968), pp. 161–63, and John W. Blanpied, ' "Unfathered heirs and loathly births of nature": Bringing History to Crisis in *2 Henry IV*', *English Literary Renaissance*, 5 (1975), 223–30. See also W. M. Thackeray's suspicion of Hal's motives, in *Vanity Fair*, ch. 47.

8. See e.g. John Palmer, *Political Characters of Shakespeare* (Macmillan, 1945), pp. 238–40; Ralph Berry, *The Shakespearean Metaphor: Studies in Language and Form* (Macmillan, 1978), pp. 57–8.
9. For similar conclusions, see D. A. Traversi, *Shakespeare: From 'Richard II' to 'Henry V'* (Hollis and Carter, 1958), pp. 166–73, 187–91, 197; Marilyn L. Williamson, 'The Episode with Williams in *Henry V*', *SEL*, 9 (1969), 275–77, 281–82. For the view that Henry is completely reformed at the outset of the play, see J. H. Walter's introduction to the Arden edition of *Henry V*, pp. xviii–xxiii.

2

Twelfth Night

Comedy often portrays development towards a marriage of
lovers: and certainly almost all of Shakespeare's 'middle'
comedies end in such unions. Shakespeare, however, has a
particular fondness for joining opposites in the marriages of his
comedies. Sometimes he uses the hermaphroditic image of the
woman disguised as a man, as in *As You Like It* or *Twelfth Night*;
or of the woman who takes over a male role, as Portia the
lawyer in *The Merchant of Venice*. In *The Taming of the Shrew* the
initial dominance of Katherina over Petruchio is reversed in
their marriage. In *Much Ado About Nothing* Beatrice and
Benedick express their love for one another through their
apparent mutual detestation. The puritanical Angelo in
Measure for Measure is sexually aroused by Isabella's purity.
The low-born Helena marries the aristocratic Bertram in *All's
Well That Ends Well*. Throughout the plays there is eventual
'reconciliation' of such opposites as reason and imagination
(*A Midsummer Night's Dream*), civilization and nature (*A
Midsummer Night's Dream, As You Like It*), justice and mercy
(*The Merchant of Venice, Measure for Measure*), base and noble
(the lead casket in *The Merchant*, the marriage in *All's Well*).

The comedies from *A Midsummer Night's Dream* to *As You
Like It* end in a marriage or *discordia concors* which has been long
anticipated. *Twelfth Night*, however, possibly the last of the
'middle' comedies, is distinctive in that the resolutions it
proposes are not generated from within the play, are implied
negatively rather than presented, and are imposed and
theoretic in character. In *A Midsummer Night's Dream* the flower
Love-in-Idleness has the power to heal delusion when applied
to the right person's eyes; it is only from error, which itself
reflects the temporary antagonism of Titania and Oberon,

28

the young lovers and their elders, or, more conceptually, fancy and judgment, that discord among the lovers occurs. Throughout the play we have, as it were, the sense of its ending: we know that the disputes that exist will be overcome, that all lovers will come together in right relationship, and that the more abstract opposites will no longer be disjoined. In *Much Ado About Nothing* the comic movement towards marriage between Hero and Claudio, Beatrice and Benedick, is present from the beginning of the play, and is interrupted only from without, by the stratagems of Don John to make Claudio distrust Hero's faith: although some question is made of a man who could so readily doubt his beloved as Claudio, this is forgotten as the schemes of Don John inevitably come to light. In *As You Like It*, too, the plotting against the comic world is on the whole external, in the form of the usurper Frederick who first banishes the true Duke, his court and eventually the lovers Orlando, Rosalind and Celia to the Forest of Arden, and later sends Orlando's brother Oliver to hunt them down there. For most of the play after the initial banishment, we are scarcely aware of this antagonism, being thoroughly immersed in the doings of the various lovers in the forest: we do not feel their joys under a constant cloud. We are not told that Duke Frederick himself set out against the exiles with an army until he has repented his design; and as for Oliver, he is first transformed to charitableness by being saved from death by his brother and then falls under the spell of love himself, with Celia. In *The Merchant of Venice* again we have an external threat in the form of Shylock's bond, and we feel that the existence of the seemingly omniscient Portia will confound his hopes. What we have in *Twelfth Night*, however, is a condition in which the protagonists themselves are portrayed as spiritually diseased throughout, and in which the eventual solution is imposed.

In *Twelfth Night* love has gone stale. Orsino's love for Olivia is fruitless, but he continues to please himself with it; Olivia has pledged years of devotion to a dead brother. Each is shut in on the self. Orsino's love is self-feeding, requiring little external stimulus:

If music be the food of love, play on,

29

Give me excess of it, that, surfeiting,
The appetite may sicken, and so die.

(I, i, 1–3)[1]

This is love in a nutshell: enamourment, indulgence, satiation and rejection, with no woman present; the whole is a recurrent, closed cycle. Though Orsino will employ Caesario to further his suit, he is content to keep aloof himself. Here he first wishes the music to stimulate love, and then the pleasure tips into its reverse, and he demands excess in order that love may drive out love. But this is only a disconnected fancy, for when the music does in reality become too much he will have none of it:

That strain again, it had a dying fall:
O, it came o'er my ear like the sweet sound
That breathes upon a bank of violets,
Stealing and giving odour. Enough, no more;
'Tis not so sweet now as it was before.

(4–8)

The synæsthesia of mixing sound and smell, and the curious typicality given to an occurrence which is only occasional or singular suggest that while the Duke may once have experienced something of what he describes, it has become so domiciled in his fancy as to become taken for a standard and generally-known happening in the external world. His severance from this world is shown also in his response to Curio's request that he will go hunt 'the hart': he says that he already does so, since when he first saw Olivia, 'That instant was I turn'd into a hart,/ And my desires, like fell and cruel hounds,/ E'er since pursue me' (21–3). His desires have so turned in on themselves that when he hears of Olivia's self-dedication to love of her dead brother, he is in no way dismayed, but considers only that if she can love a brother thus much, she will love him much more. He concludes, 'Away before me to sweet beds of flowers!/ Love-thoughts lie rich when canopied with bowers' (40–1). It is not so much Orsino who is to lie on these beds, but love-thoughts: the interior world is all that matters to him, and in this rhyming couplet he seems to close himself further in. This is not very far from the amorous condition of Shakespeare's Troilus.

As for Olivia, she is cut off from the world for equally self-indulgent reasons. Valentine, the Duke's servant, learns from her handmaid that

> The element itself, till seven years' heat,
> Shall not behold her face at ample view;
> But like a cloistress she will veiled walk,
> And water once a day her chamber round
> With eye-offending brine: all this to season
> A brother's dead love, which she would keep fresh
> And lasting, in her sad remembrance.
>
> (I, i, 26–32)

When Orsino portrays himself as the helpless victim of her passion, she acts decisively out of self-will: each, however, is excessive. She will water her sterile chamber round, not a garden, and she will do it with brine, which would kill plants anyway. It is 'a brother's dead love', not 'a dead brother's love'. Orsino found the spirit of love 'quick and fresh' in making everything else stale; and Olivia will keep the love of her dead brother fresh like killed meat, with salt tears.

The suggestion of some healthy counter to this is made in the next scene, in Viola's arrival on the coast of Illyria after being shipwrecked and the conversation she has with the captain about the fate of her brother, now missing. She, unlike Olivia, has just left salt-water behind, and external, not internally-generated brine at that: she has been fully exposed to the 'element' from which Olivia has just shut herself off. She, unlike Orsino, talks to other people rather than to herself: there is a sudden sense of fresh air and activity. She, like Olivia, may have lost her brother Sebastian, but unlike Olivia or Orsino she does not linger over grief or speculation, since, not knowing for sure, either is a waste of time. At this point in the play there is insistence on chance:

> *Viola.* My brother he is in Elysium.
> Perchance he is not drown'd: what think you, sailors?
> *Captain.* It is perchance that you yourself were sav'd.
> *Viola.* O my poor brother! And so perchance may he be.
> *Captain.* True, madam, and to comfort you with chance,
> Assure yourself, after our ship did split,
> When you and those poor number sav'd with you
> Hung on our driving boat, I saw your brother,
> Most provident in peril, bind himself

(Courage and hope both teaching him the practice)
To a strong mast that liv'd upon the sea;
Where, like Arion on the dolphin's back,
I saw him hold acquaintance with the waves
So long as I could see.

(I, ii, 4–17)

Chance, of a singular order, is finally to unravel the plot of the play. Sebastian, at once yielding himself to the sea and seeking to preserve himself, also fuses and transcends the passivity of Orsino and the self-will of Olivia. He is associated with a mobile element, while they are given over to stasis. The sea, too, images his total exposure to and involvement with the flux and chance of the world: in his predicament, masts *live* upon the sea, he becomes like Arion, master of the sea-beast, and 'hold[s] acquaintance with the waves'; he is in harmony with an element which has no fixed boundaries or limits.

But this is all we hear for the time. Sebastian's behaviour here, insofar as it suggests a resolution to the deep divisions between characters and the world in the play, does so only at a conceptual or symbolic level, and all too briefly. For most of the rest of the play we are at best left to guess at the ideal harmony, the *discordia concors*, negatively, from the perverted behaviour of the characters. Nor is Viola herself a norm of virtue or of reconciled opposites throughout the play. Having heard of the conditions of Olivia and Orsino, she suddenly and for no clear psychological reason expresses a longing to enter Orsino's service disguised as an eunuch: but at a symbolic level we see that she has been forced to act in the perverted idiom of the play, cutting herself off from the world, here in the form of disguise. She then becomes absorbed by the chaotic spiritual landscape, prosecuting Orsino's absurd suit with Olivia while she loves him herself (and has to keep her love cut off from the world—II, iv, 111–16), and being fallen in love with by Olivia in mistake for a man.

In Sir Toby Belch, the shutting in of the self that we see in Olivia and Orsino is turned upside-down. To Maria's 'you must confine yourself within the modest limits of order,' Sir Toby replies, 'Confine! I'll confine myself no finer than I am' (I, iii, 8–10), and later he mockingly remarks, on Sir Andrew Aguecheek's assertion of his dancing abilities,

32

Wherefore are these things hid? Wherefore have these gifts a curtain before 'em? Are they like to take dust, like Mistress Mall's picture? Why dost thou not go to church in a galliard, and come home in a coranto? My very walk should be a jig; I would not so much make water but in a sink-a-pace. What dost thou mean? Is it a world to hide virtues in?

(ibid., 122–29)

Much of Sir Toby's energy in the play is devoted to the exposure of the prim steward of Olivia, Malvolio. Certainly his position is a healthy corrective to that of Orsino and Olivia, but it is hardly an alternative line of conduct. The disproportion with which he behaves in opposing the proportion embodied in Malvolio, and the violence first of his festivities and later of his behaviour towards Viola/Caesario and Sebastian speak for themselves, quite apart from the disfavour he falls into with Olivia. What we have are two contrasted kinds of excess: excessive isolation from the world and excessive exposure, and there is no suggestion of a resolution between them, as in other comedies. And where in earlier comedies the resolution is long anticipated and prepared for, here the two poles are left in a state of extreme opposition until the end of the play.

A similar case prevails in the portrayal of Malvolio. Here is someone who has lived by a rule of cold proportion and decorum, suddenly tricked by Sir Toby and the others whom he disdains into a totally opposite mode of behaviour: he is persuaded by a forged letter that Olivia his mistress will favour him with her love if he appears before her in yellow cross-gartered stockings (which in truth she detests) and with a fatuous leer stamped on his features. Malvolio is like Orsino and Olivia in that he lives in an enclosed world,[2] imagining that his impertinent love for Olivia could possibly be reciprocated. This is figured in the way he construes the letters M.O.A.I. on the message he thinks is from Olivia, as an anagram of his name; and also in the form of the darkened room supposedly for madmen in which he is later shut for his 'correction'. And Olivia herself is like Malvolio in her indecorum: for just as Malvolio, her serving-man, aspires to the hand of his high-born mistress, so Olivia courts an apparent serving-man, Caesario. The norm with Malvolio would presumably be a reconciliation of decorum and indecorum, but we are left at best to construct such a marriage for ourselves, and in truth are more conscious of the irreconcilable extremity of each pole, the malevolence of Malvolio's decorum and the grotesqueness of his indecorum, than of any possibility of bringing the two together. In *A Midsummer Night's Dream* we are continually aware of the desirable reconciliation of reason and imagination in true love, the nature of which is the central subject of the play (as in *As You Like It*), but here the conjunction of the opposites is not canvassed—and indeed at the end Malvolio refuses to be reconciled with the company.

Throughout the play, too, till the close, there is emphasis on dislocation, physical and mental. Words, the basis of communication, are seen, as Feste puts it, as 'very rascals, since bonds disgraced them' (III, i, 20–1). This recalls the same motif in *Hamlet*. So it is that Caesario addresses people in high courtly language or coarse slang; that Sir Andrew Aguecheek seeks to learn the idiom of polite society not in order to communicate but to advertise himself; that Malvolio is tricked by a letter and tricks himself with the letters in it; and that Sir Andrew by letter and Sir Toby Belch orally on his behalf deliver challenges to Caesario couched in empty rhetoric or jargon. Only in the end are words restored to 'health' in the bond of marriage between Sebastian and Olivia 'Attested by the holy close of lips' (V, i, 156), and in Viola's avowal of constancy to Orsino (ibid., 267–70).

And what happens in this late resolution of the discords of the play? Sebastian, Viola's identical twin, is married by Olivia in mistake for Caesario. When she finds out her error, Olivia is left seeming quite content to remain married to someone she has never met before; and similarly Sebastian raises little question at suddenly having been married to a stranger. No amount of theory, of statements such as 'nature to her bias drew in that' (V, i, 258) can overcome these divisions. Again, Orsino, faced by Olivia's apparent marriage to Caesario accepts it without much repining, and on finding out the true sex of Caesario, at once offers himself as a husband to her.

All this is hard enough to take: but more than this, we have to believe that these people are now cured of their spiritual diseases, in order that the happy resolution may be effected. Yet Orsino has in no way been altered: he has remained in the same infatuated attitude throughout the play. As for Olivia, although brought out of her formerly isolated self to the extent that she falls in love with Caesario, this love is in its way as absurd and sterile as her previous refusal, because, unknown to her, her beloved is a woman. Nor is she punished in her mistake, for she does not find out about it until married to Sebastian. At any convincing level she cannot be said to have learned or reformed: any 'changes' are merely theoretic. It is Malvolio who is loaded with the burdens the other characters ought still to be carrying. His refusal to repent or make up—'I'll be reveng'd on the whole pack of you!' (V, i, 377)—is simply an easily-condemned version of their own irreconcilability. We may note that his name contains a partial anagram of 'Olivia' (not to say 'Viola'). In his violent departure we see the failure of the play to face the problems it has raised: the only course is to jettison them. Here we are not far from what happens at the ends of *Measure for Measure* and the significantly-named *All's Well That Ends Well*.

With this imposed end to the play a note of dark melancholy that has made itself felt throughout, not only in the predicaments of the lovers but in such a song as Feste's on death to Orsino, becomes the last tone that we hear, in the plaintive helplessness of the Clown's parting lyric:[3]

> When that I was and a little tiny boy,
> With hey, ho, the wind and the rain,
> A foolish thing was but a toy,
> For the rain it raineth every day.
>
> But when I came to man's estate,
> With hey, ho, the wind and the rain,
> 'Gainst knaves and thieves men shut their gate,
> For the rain it raineth every day.
>
> But when I came, alas, to wive,
> With hey, ho, the wind and the rain,
> By swaggering could I never thrive,
> For the rain it raineth every day.

In this play the charmed circle of Shakespeare's 'happy'

comedy, that golden realm of marriage and the *discordia concors* seems to have admitted too much that is oppugnant to its nature for its joys to be either unforced or unmixed. Twelfth Night, we recall, marks the end of the festive season.

NOTES

1. References are to the Arden *Twelfth Night*, ed. J. M. Lothian and T. W. Craik (Methuen, 1975).
2. On the motif of enclosure in the play see Alexander Leggatt, *Shakespeare's Comedies of Love* (Methuen, 1974), pp. 221–54.
3. On this see also Philip Edwards, *Shakespeare and the Confines of Art* (Methuen, 1968), pp. 63–8.

3

Hamlet, Troilus and Cressida, Measure for Measure

The plays considered here are grouped together because they all show in particularly marked form a division between mind and body which is recurrent in Shakespeare's work. This similarity may be part of the fact that they are akin on other grounds (and to this we may add *All's Well That Ends Well*). All of them present a situation in which rule has gone wrong, resulting in national sickness or loss of control and licence: in *Hamlet* the true king has been murdered and Denmark spiritually blighted, in *Troilus and Cressida* Agamemnon's authority is being disregarded, in *Measure for Measure* the Duke has let the laws of Vienna slide into wanton disrespect, and in *All's Well* the king is at first sick, and though cured by Helena, is disobeyed by Bertram. The plays all, implicitly or explicitly, contain debates on large issues—Hamlet's discussions of life and death, the nature of value and worth in *Troilus and Cressida*, the issues of justice and mercy, restraint and freedom in *Measure for Measure*, and the marriage of social unequals in *All's Well*. In each of them action is for long frustrated, but is then driven forward in a rush. In *Hamlet* the slaying of Claudius is delayed until the sudden nexus of opportunity at the end; in *Troilus and Cressida* action is stagnant till the outburst of rage on both sides in the fifth act; in *Measure for Measure* Angelo's purpose cannot be altered until the access of good fortune which helps the plots of the disguised Duke; and in *All's Well* frustration is seen in Bertram's long refusal to accept his marriage to Helena. All the plays also contain a sense of the blighting influence of lechery on love and a strain of revulsion against the physical world, whether it be Hamlet's loathing of the flesh, Thersites' picture of the world in terms of disease and lechery in *Troilus and Cressida*, the hatred of sex by Isabella and Angelo in *Measure for Measure*, or the way in which Helena has to disguise herself as a whore to secure the affections of Bertram in *All's Well*. Separation of loves or of husbands and wives is a constant motif: Hamlet rejects Ophelia, Helen is false to Menelaus and Cressida to Troilus, Claudio in *Measure for Measure* is parted from Juliet by being imprisoned, and Angelo has cast off Mariana. These features can also many of them be seen in another, earlier, play in which the theme of disjoined mind and body is central—*Richard II*.

Hamlet

The division between mind and body in *Hamlet* is portrayed mainly through the motif of communication. This concerns not only communication through language, but the breakdown of relations between appearance and reality, words and deeds, thoughts and acts, and indeed the very organs and limbs of the human body itself. Our particular interest here will be with the way the lack of an absolute moral code and the divorce of mind from act in the world of *Hamlet* leads to inaccuracy and the inability to think clearly.

First we must give what will frequently be a familiar account of the broad theme. The breakdowns in *Hamlet* are brought about, as analogous breakdowns in *Troilus and Cressida*, *Measure for Measure*, *Lear* and *Macbeth* are brought about, by the spread of evil from one particular sin of commission or omission—a communication which destroys communication. In the case of *Hamlet*, of course, this sin involved the poisoning of Hamlet's father by his uncle Claudius—a poisoning carried out through the receptors of communication, the ears,[1] thereafter spreading through the whole body—and the subsequent seizing of the throne and the haste of Hamlet's mother's marriage to Claudius. The spread of evil that results is expressed in certain key passages, such as the following (it is Rosencrantz speaking to Claudius of the danger to the kingdom should he, Claudius, be harmed):

> The cease of majesty
> Dies not alone; but like a gulf doth draw
> What's near with it. It is a massy wheel,
> Fix'd on the summit of the highest mount,
> To whose huge spokes ten thousand lesser things
> Are mortis'd and adjoin'd, which when it falls,
> Each small annexment, petty consequence,
> Attends the boist'rous ruin. Never alone
> Did the king sigh, but with a general groan.
>
> (III, iii, 15–23; see also I, iv, 23–38)[2]

Hence the disease, poison and 'blight' imagery that runs throughout the play. Hence too the breakdown of healthy intercommunication of parts of the body or the state, or of word and deed.[3] 'Something is rotten in the state of Denmark' (I, iv, 90). Many characters are unable to speak accurately. Polonius is verbose, Osric elaborately courtly, the clown in the grave-digging scene pedantically over-exact, Laertes melodramatic and ranting, and Hamlet makes a whole range of raids on the inarticulate. There is much imagery concerned with what should be the proper relation of tongues, hands and hearts, and with speech generally.[4] No-one can see clearly. In *Macbeth*, where there is also regicide, the imagery is of darkness and smothering: here it is of people forced underground to work towards one another (even the ghost works underground in the 'cellarage' scene (I, v, 149–81); and Hamlet speaks of out-witting Rosencrantz and Guildenstern in language drawn from military mining, 'I will delve one yard below their mines/ And blow them at the moon' (III, iv, 208–9)). The idea of missing one's aim or avoiding another's also recurs in the play: as the Player King puts it, 'Our wills and fates do so contrary run/ That our devices still are overthrown;/ Our thoughts are ours, their ends none of our own' (III, ii, 206–8; see also IV, i, 42–4; IV, vii, 21–4; V, ii, 235–36). People's true motives and selves are concealed from one another: there is a gap between the external behaviour and the inner mental reality of most of the characters. Everyone is trying to find out about other people. The play, as Maynard Mack has pointed out, is full of questions—Is Claudius guilty? Is the ghost honest? Is Hamlet mad?—questions to which the characters are continually trying to find the answers.[5] All are confused, uncertain in direction: the most generous description of their searches is, as Polonius puts it, that they 'by indirections find directions out' (II, i, 66). In the end none of their indirections leads in the directions they would have wished: Polonius is accidentally killed, Claudius dies, Hamlet fulfils his pledge to the ghost only through chance and loses his own life in the process.

There is also a failure of communication between motive and act in the play. Hamlet is continually searching for a proper relation in himself between the two. He praises Horatio for his balance:

> As one, in suff'ring all, that suffers nothing;
> A man that Fortune's buffets and rewards
> Hast ta'en with equal thanks; and blest are those
> Whose blood and judgement are so well comeddled
> That they are not a pipe for Fortune's finger
> To sound what stop she please.
>
> (III, ii, 64–9)

Yet, while he can thus praise Horatio, he can as readily praise those who, like the players or Fortinbras, express passion, or act for little or no cause. Of a player who has just impersonated Hecuba's passion at the murder of her husband Priam, he asks, 'What's Hecuba to him or he to Hecuba,/ That he should weep for her? what would he do,/ Had he the motive and the cue for passion/ That I have?' (II, ii, 552–55); and, looking on Fortinbras leading his army to fight over a tiny patch of worthless land, he declares, 'I do not know/ Why yet I live to say "This thing's to do,"/ Sith I have cause, and will, and strength, and means,/ To do't. Examples gross as earth exhort me' (IV, iv, 43–6). When in the Mouse-trap play, 'The Murder of Gonzago', Lucianus, nephew to the player King and a figure of Claudius, enters to murder his uncle, he paints the conditions as

> Thoughts black, hands apt, drugs fit, and time agreeing,
> Confederate season, else no creature seeing.
>
> (III, ii, 249–50)

Such conditions are removed by the act they once furthered: in Denmark thoughts are no longer fit, hands are no longer apt and (the vision is here like Hardy's) even if one is ready to do the deed the conditions go wrong (the murder of Polonius).

Hamlet is at the centre of the play not by being in any final way an exception.[6] It is simply that his nature, being more sensitive and intelligent—indeed more fully cultivated, nearer to the Renaissance ideal of the perfect gentleman—than that of any other figure in the play, may the more amply show the corruption and confusion that pervade Denmark. With Hamlet it is, as Ophelia puts it,

> O, what a noble mind is here o'erthrown!
> The courtier's, soldier's, scholar's, eye, tongue, sword;
> Th' expectancy and rose of the fair state,
> The glass of fashion and the mould of form,
> Th' observ'd of all observers, quite quite down!
> (III, i, 150–54)

The best thing has gone bad, with all the harrowing force such a spectacle has, and with all the revelation of the power and ramification of evil. It is in Hamlet that we see the landscape of division and uncertainty that came from Claudius' act most fully and strikingly illustrated.

One of the consequences of that act is the disappearance of objective standards of value and conduct. We often speak of the 'revenge code' in connection with *Hamlet*, but the prince himself scarcely mentions it, save perhaps when he once berates himself as 'the son of a dear father murder'd,/ Prompted to my revenge by heaven and hell' (II, ii, 579–80). When the ghost first bids him revenge his murder, Hamlet vows to do so with a rambling verbosity which belies his determination, and then even proceeds to write the ghost's injunction down in his pocket book as a reminder (I, v, 95–111). Of course, the ghost's exact nature may be ambiguous, but there is more to the absence of codes of conduct throughout the play than this. In one of his soliloquies Hamlet wishes 'that the Everlasting had not fix'd/ His canon 'gainst self-slaughter' (I, ii, 131–32). In another he cannot decide whether it would be 'nobler' to suffer in silence or to make away with himself; and then though tempted by the idea of suicide, he backs off from it not because of any divine injunction against it but because of the thought 'in that sleep of

41

death what dreams may come,/ When we have shuffled off this mortal coil,/ Must give us pause' (III, i, 66–8). As if in summary of how in the medium that is Claudian Denmark all values have become shifting and relative, Hamlet says at one point to Rosencrantz and Guildenstern (he has been calling Denmark 'a prison'), 'there is nothing either good or bad, but thinking makes it so' (II, ii, 249–50). This moral predicament, and its consequences, makes the landscape of *Hamlet* close to that of *Troilus and Cressida*: in both plays Shakespeare seems to be exploring what happens when the context of the play wholly or largely remains that which the evil act has infected; in *Lear* and *Macbeth* there are alternative worlds, whether on the heath or from France in *Lear*, or in England in *Macbeth*.

For this reason Hamlet can never have an unthinking and stable motive for killing Claudius, even when he knows for certain that he is the murderer of his father. Or, to put it another way, he goes through the play on the assumption that if he can build up enough motive for killing Claudius, then he will be able to act. The very fact that he so divides motive from deed shows the medium of spiritual schism in which he is doomed to move.

Thus it is that we often find him comparing himself to other people to whip himself up by a sort of cult of personality. He rebukes himself in comparison to the actors who can produce tempests of passion on behalf of fictional characters while he can produce none on behalf of a real and much more closely related one. Then, in the same soliloquy (II, ii, 543 ff.) he proceeds to try to manufacture rage by contemplating and reviling Claudius: 'Bloody, bawdy villain!/ Remorseless, treacherous, lecherous, kindless villain!/ O vengeance!' (575–77); slumps back from such excess language and violence, 'Why, what an ass am I! This is most brave,/ That I . . ./ . . ./ Must, like a whore, unpack my heart with words,/ And fall a-cursing like a very drab,/ A scullion! Fie upon't! foh!' (578–83); and then turns to devising a scheme (the play) not to kill Claudius but to prove whether or not he is guilty, a question which has not evidently troubled him till this point. We see a similar attempt to spur himself into action later when Hamlet compares his inactivity to the motiveless activity of Fortinbras. There is no way of breaking the circle: Hamlet

ends this latter soliloquy with 'O, from this time forth,/ My
thoughts be bloody, or be nothing worth!' (IV, iv, 65–6)—
'thoughts', not deeds. The Player King's diagnosis seems
apposite both here and in relation to the whole play:

> I do believe you think what now you speak,
> But what we do determine, oft we break.
> Purpose is but the slave to memory,
> Of violent birth but poor validity.
>
> . . . .
>
> What to ourselves in passion we propose,
> The passion ending, doth the purpose lose.
> (III, ii, 181–84, 189–90)

So it is too with Hamlet's excessively violent language to his
mother in the closet scene, or with his ranting to Laertes over
the grave of Ophelia.

It is Hamlet's soliloquies which most fully and subtly exhibit
the breakdown of communication in Denmark: here in the
microcosm of a mind which is the glass of state, we see that
glass quite shivered to fragments. It is significant in this play
that there should be so many more or less philosophical
soliloquies, thoughts isolated from action and often from
context. 'To be, or not to be' (III, i, 56)—what a marvellous
question: marvellous because it could apply to almost anything, and yet has the simplicity to make this very vagueness
of reference pungent. It arises in relation to nothing specific in
the text, and one is not sure—nor does Hamlet seem sure—
what it means: it has the generality of a soul lost in a treeless
spiritual waste (one recalls 'How weary, stale, flat, and
unprofitable,/ Seem to me all the uses of this world!' (I, ii,
133–34)). It could refer to whether or not to carry out revenge
on his uncle, whether to be as one feels or to conceal it, whether
to live or die: *that* is the question only in the sense that all
questions come down to it. Now Hamlet tries to turn the
generality he senses in the question towards the more specific:

> Whether 'tis nobler in the mind to suffer
> The slings and arrows of outrageous fortune,
> Or to take arms against a sea of troubles,
> And by opposing end them?
> (57–60)

43

We would not accept that 'to suffer/ The slings and arrows of outrageous fortune' was 'To be', and that 'to take arms against a sea of troubles,/ And by opposing end them' was 'not to be', unless we were told so: the latter implies acting *against* circumstances, and, specifically, wreaking destruction on the corrupt Danish court; when we are told that it refers to death we feel a considerable jolt. And surely Shakespeare meant us to: for the jerk makes us feel that Hamlet himself was not very clear on what he wanted to say. It would seem that the image of taking arms against a sea of troubles was meant as his picture of putting things right in Denmark: but such is the context in which he lives and has his being that this action is described as impossible even as it is conceived (it is futile to take arms against a sea of troubles, whether or not the sea is considered metaphorically). It is then that Hamlet begins to shift towards death as the answer: 'And by opposing end them' suggests that there need be no actual struggle, but that one need only declare oneself in opposition for all troubles to cease; this could refer to declaring himself in the court, whereupon he might be destroyed, but at any rate there is hint here that his own death has become more of an answer to him. But why at the same time the question of which it is more noble to do?— the question of nobility seems strangely irrelevant, a stray code of conduct dragged in to do service as an arbitrary and soon-neglected standard.

The soliloquy now leaves all contact with the business of the play and enters the realm of pure speculation. We have to ask ourselves how seriously Hamlet is thinking, and under what pressure. True, there is profound world-weariness:

> To die, to sleep—
> No more; and by a sleep to say we end
> The heart-ache and the thousand natural shocks
> That flesh is heir to. 'Tis a consummation
> Devoutly to be wish'd.

But then the whole drift of the thought swivels back on itself, as Hamlet's speculation rambles out of this soporific consummation and happens upon another possibility. He thinks of dying, and sleeping, and then of dreaming; and then of the possibility of there being bad dreams in death; and then talks of

44

this new apprehension as though it had been at the forefront of
his mind all the time:

> To die, to sleep;
> To sleep, perchance to dream. Ay, there's the rub;
> For in that sleep of death what dreams may come,
> When we have shuffled off this mortal coil,
> Must give us pause. There's the respect
> That makes calamity of so long life.

This speech shows a mind and feelings dislocated from reality
and accuracy: here is a man who is supposed to be at least
planning to kill another but who instead spends his time
uttering large and weighty generalizations which trail off into
intellectual dilettantism.

Having moved from the view of death as a welcome 'No
more' to one of it as potentially a dream-filled horror, Hamlet
cannot manage either some resolution of the two apprehensions, or the choice of one of them. He oscillates between
longing and fear. As he continues, he at first veers back more
and more to his vision of outrageous fortune and death's
attractiveness, and forgets the fears of death to which he has
just given utterance:

> For who would bear the whips and scorns of time,
> Th'oppressor's wrong, the proud man's contumely,
> The pangs of despis'd love, the law's delay,
> The insolence of office, and the spurns
> That patient merit of th'unworthy takes,
> When he himself might his quietus make
> With a bare bodkin?

Many of these miseries, we may observe, are miseries which
Hamlet does not himself seem largely to have experienced: this
suggests how far the speech has moved from reality. But now
he realizes that with all this expression of the miseries of life
he has begun to go back on his point about the fearfulness of
death, and has to switch again:

> Who would these fardels bear,
> To grunt and sweat under a weary life,
> But that the dread of something after death—
> The undiscover'd country, from whose bourn
> No traveller returns—puzzles the will,

And makes us rather bear those ills we have,
Than fly to others that we know not of?

'Puzzles the will' is a fine description of what happens to
Hamlet. He is puzzled by his own behaviour, and this speech is
an attempt to rationalize and to make sense to himself of what
and why he is: but equally the speech shows how irrational and
discordant are his thinking and his psyche; indeed this
soliloquy is a portrait of a diseased sensibility, even of a kind of
madness, a madness that is far from being an *antic* disposition.
  Now Hamlet concludes of his reluctance to die that

> Thus conscience does make cowards of us all;
> And thus the native hue of resolution
> Is sicklied o'er with the pale cast of thought,
> And enterprises of great pitch and moment,
> With this regard, their currents turn awry
> And lose the name of action.

As throughout the soliloquy, Hamlet tries to give his thoughts
the force of general truths by subsuming himself in 'us'; yet
'their currents turn awry' is again an unconsciously apt
description of the flow of his thought here (as indeed equally of
the entire course of the actions in the play). Here he is suddenly
turning against his own insights in revulsion, sensing that the
course of his thought in the soliloquy is a type of the course of
all his thoughts. That this is his primary emphasis seems
further pointed in the way that 'enterprises of great pitch and
moment' could hardly refer so much to dying only as to any
enterprise, and particularly the enterprise to which Hamlet
has been enjoined by the ghost of his father.
  The question of thought and its status is of course one which
continually preoccupies Hamlet: should one think before
acting, or should one act unthinkingly? As with most issues he
is pulled both ways. A striking instance of this is the soliloquy
he utters while contemplating the army of Fortinbras.

> How all occasions do inform against me,
> And spur my dull revenge! What is a man,
> If his chief good and market of his time
> Be but to sleep and feed? a beast, no more!
> Sure he that made us with such large discourse,
> Looking before and after, gave us not

46

> That capability and godlike reason
> To fust in us unus'd.
>
> (IV, iv, 32–9)

One must surely be puzzled when what seemed to begin as an attack on his own inactivity as bestial leads to a self-enjoinder not to act but to *think*; presumably Hamlet only happened on this theme through the distinction between beasts and men— that is, what was used as an image becomes the prompter of discourse: first it is bestial not to act and then, thinking of the difference between beasts and men, it is bestial not to think. Now he moves on to try to find reasons for his failure to act— even when later in this speech (as in his earlier comment on the actors) he praises action born of little or no motive, reason or thought; that is, he tries to find reasons for having failed to be irrational:

> Now, whether it be
> Bestial oblivion, or some craven scruple
> Of thinking too precisely on th'event—
> A thought which, quarter'd, hath but one part wisdom,
> And ever three parts coward—I do not know
> Why yet I live to say 'This thing's to do,'
> Sith I have cause, and will, and strength, and means,
> To do't. . . .

But it *was* bestial oblivion that was made the cause of his inactivity a few lines previously: and since he there said that the spur to activity was thought, he cannot then proceed to claim that thought might be responsible for his delay. The ultimate cause of this uncertainty is Hamlet's desire not to abandon his rational self when he acts—to make his every move reasonable (hence the play-scene, designed to establish reasonable proof against Claudius—'I'll have grounds/ More relative than this' (II, ii, 599–600)). But Hamlet's experience is here that of all intellectuals: thinking may seem to make life's complexities less, and may provide causes for behaviour, but ultimately it stultifies performance, since all action has an element of the irrational and of risk in it: thus, without opportunity for thought, Hamlet slays Polonius, and with it, refuses to kill Claudius while he is praying lest his soul go to heaven rather than to hell. Nevertheless the larger fact that

Hamlet *is* an intellectual who, though also capable of action cannot of himself be both, is a function of the spiritual disease that pervades this particular play. Later in this soliloquy, having considered how Fortinbras and his army are 'Exposing what is mortal and unsure/ To all that fortune, death, and danger, dare,/ Even for an egg-shell', Hamlet decides,

> Rightly to be great
> Is not to stir without great argument,
> But greatly to find quarrel in a straw,
> When honour's at the stake.
>
> (IV, iv, 51–6)

(Here again thinking is contradictorily dismissed.) This is to take the position of Laertes, who could reply to Claudius' plea that he be calm in his desire for revenge on his father's murderer, 'That drop of blood that's calm proclaims me bastard' (IV, v, 114); or who could say of any moral obstacles to his revenge,

> To hell, allegiance! Vows to the blackest devil!
> Conscience and grace, to the profoundest pit!
> I dare damnation. To this point I stand,
> That both the worlds I give to negligence,
> Let come what comes; only I'll be reveng'd
> Most throughly for my father.
>
> (ibid., 128–33)

But Hamlet has really little kinship with this type of behaviour: he may wish for it, but he would not like to have it—like intellectuals who may enjoy mental pictures of violence but would eschew the fact. He asked the players to keep proportion and decorum between words and matter, and to 'o'erstep not the modesty of nature' (III, ii, 19–20). And it cannot be denied that Hamlet falls away from his own assertion in this soliloquy: for he speaks of what Fortinbras and his army risk all for as an 'egg-shell' and a 'straw', words which must undercut the seriousness with which he is committed to the points he is making. This process goes further in his next words:

> How stand I, then,
> That have a father kill'd, a mother stain'd,
> Excitements of my reason and my blood,
> And let all sleep, while to my shame I see

The imminent death of twenty thousand men
That, for a fantasy and trick of fame,
Go to their graves like beds, fight for a plot
Whereon the numbers cannot try the cause,
Which is not tomb enough and continent
To hide the slain?

Now he has shifted to consider that his praise of greatly finding quarrel in a straw does not apply to his case since he has more than sufficient cause to set him on a course of action. Now Fortinbras and his army become absurd in their motivation compared to that which should drive Hamlet. All the switching that has gone on throughout the soliloquy can leave Hamlet only, as we have seen, still trapped in his head: he ends, 'O, from this time forth,/ My thoughts be bloody, or be nothing worth!'

The resolution of the impasse is found only by chance. For when Hamlet has certain proof of Claudius' guilt in the plot against his life while at sea, he no longer actively seeks revenge: though he poses to Horatio that with the knowledge he now has 'is't not perfect conscience/ To quit him [Claudius] with this arm?' (V, ii, 67–8), the very asking reminds us of the old Hamlet who could not bring himself to act. But if it would be mistaken to see a new decisiveness in the Hamlet of the fifth act, there is certainly a new resignation, a recognition that 'the readiness is all' (V, ii, 215–16). He has realized that in the world of this play man alone cannot plan or act successfully: it is, so far as he is concerned, the action itself that must do the acting. So it is that a poisoned sword has found its way to his hand as a poisoned chalice intended for him by his uncle finds its way to his mother's lips. Yet these events themselves are the products of a human plan, the last scheme of Claudius to kill Hamlet. It is a scheme (clumsy enough in itself) which like all the other human schemes in this play goes amiss for its projectors. For, if this time Hamlet actually manages to slay a Claudius instead of a Polonius, and Claudius Hamlet, it also happens that in the process Gertrude is slain by the poisoned drink, Laertes unintentionally killed by Hamlet and Claudius himself despatched by the very instruments he planned for Hamlet's murder—a culminating instance, as Horatio is later to put it, of 'accidental judgments' and 'purposes mistook/

Fall'n on th' inventors' heads' (V, ii, 374, 376–77). To the last, mind and forethought are out of joint with body and action. Hamlet does not even know that what he thinks is a scratch is mortal, until he is told so.

Troilus and Cressida

Troilus and Cressida is even more directly philosophical than *Hamlet*, with frequent debates on the nature of such impersonal topics as value, time and order; as a part of this the portrayal of the opposition of mind and body is more overtly conceptual.[7] It is of a piece with this greater impersonality that the issues in the play are rarely moral, and there is little sense of conscience, even from Cressida. There is more stress, too, on the causes of human behavioural difficulties than concern with the unfolding of those difficulties in action; we follow not one but a number of central figures and societies, and have to trace the features common to them. The process is more analytic than dramatic: the object of the analysis is, first, the discovery of how the split between mind and body is the efficient cause of every condition—Greek, Trojan, martial, amorous—in the play, and then the search for a final cause.

So far as the lovers Troilus and Cressida themselves are concerned, Troilus has an idealist's view of Cressida, she a cynical realist's view of him: the two are disjoined as mind and body before they even come together. In the first scene we see how Troilus has made Cressida into his image of her, and watch him lose touch with accuracy in a series of amorous hyperboles so extreme that they collapse on themselves without the need of help from the picture we are then given (I, ii) of Cressida as a perfectly ordinary *jeune femme moyenne sensuelle* with a not inconsiderable streak of vulgarity. Because Troilus has a primarily mental picture of Cressida and loves her with, in his own words, 'so strained a purity', he finds it almost categorically impossible to assimilate his own witness of her eventual faithlessness: 'This is, and is not, Cressid!' (V, ii, 146).[8] Cressida, on the other hand, sees people for what they are: to Pandarus' attempts to make Troilus shine in her eyes by setting him beside Hector, she answers, 'O Jupiter! there's no comparison' (I, ii, 61); for her, Troilus 'is himself'

50

(ibid., 70). She intuits her own nature when she warns Troilus to beware of her, 'I have a kind of self resides with you,/ But an unkind self that itself will leave/ To be another's fool' (III, ii, 147–49). He is to be ' "As true as Troilus" ', largely fixed in his mental view of her; she ' "As false as Cressid" ', an extension of the shifting empirical world.

The split between mind and body is also to be seen in the Greek and Trojan council scenes (I, iii and II, ii), which lay bare the natures of both armies and the behaviour of their warriors. The Greek scene is far too long and fails to resolve anything. Agamemnon, who has the reason right before him in his own camp, takes thirty lines over misunderstanding why his generals are looking depressed; he thinks they are tired by the war and argues that adversity is the true test of worth. He also comes near saying that the object of war is more to display one's value than to win: the idealism of martial virtue seems preferred to the pragmatism of martial success. Nestor fills twenty-five lines of confused analogies[9] agreeing with Agamemnon. Ulysses gives fifteen lines worth of compliments to prepare the way for his degree speech, which, when it comes, takes sixty lines of discussion on the whole ordered nature of the universe and the effects of its overthrow to say that what is wrong is not the Trojans but the Greeks themselves, who are not obeying their leader. In another forty lines he gives an irrelevantly specific description of how Achilles lies in his tent all day with Patroclus, mocking Agamemnon and the other generals. Nestor goes on, at first briefly, to mention how others including Ajax have become infected by Achilles' behaviour, but then drifts off into outraged attack on Thersites, whom Ajax is employing to insult the Greek leaders for his own amusement. Finally Ulysses points out how Achilles and the others have nothing but contempt for the thought that must go into organizing the prosecution of war:

> They tax our policy and call it cowardice,
> Count wisdom as no member of the war,
> Forestall prescience, and esteem no act
> But that of hand; the still and mental parts
> That do contrive how many hands shall strike
> When fitness calls them on, and know by measure
> Of their observant toil the enemy's weight—

Why, this hath not a finger's dignity:
They call this bed-work, mappery, closet-war;
So that the ram that batters down the wall,
For the great swing and rudeness of his poise,
They place before his hand that made the engine
Or those that with the fineness of their souls
By reason guide his execution.

(I, iii, 197–210)

What Ulysses is portraying is a breakdown between mind and body in the Greek camp: but we ourselves see the split going further than he. For on the evidence of what we have just seen in the council scene, the 'still and mental parts' are more still than mental. It has taken a huge number of words for Ulysses to tell Agamemnon the obvious fact that what is wrong with the army is that many of its best warriors are refusing to fight. Close analysis of the scene will show numerous repetitions, orotundities,[10] vague generalizations and inconsistencies[11] which show a basic failure to think clearly, a failure brought about by the fact that the thinking is quite largely isolated from the simple empirical data of the situation and is therefore bound to lose accuracy. Even after all this discussion it has still not been decided what is to be done. Later, in a further windy discourse Ulysses eventually comes out with a device to make Achilles jealous and therefore the more ready to fight again, by having Ajax challenge and fight the great Hector, whom Achilles regards as his especial opponent; and in the event the scheme fails. Most strikingly of all, the entire council scene has not put the blame where it seems most immediately to belong—not on Achilles' or others' rebelliousness, but on Agamemnon's failure to assert his own authority.[12] (And that he lacks authority is underlined by the interruption of Aeneas, who cannot tell who is in charge in the Greek camp (I, iii, 215–56). The real facts are evaded.

In the parallel Trojan council scene (II, ii) the arguments are on the whole far tighter and more coherent, but in the end, just as in the Greek scene, the whole discussion goes for nothing. Where the Greek generals might be seen as all 'mind', the debate between Troilus and Hector is, like that different dialogue between Troilus and Cressida, one between 'mind' and 'body', extreme idealism and pragmatism. The Trojans

52

are discussing whether to prolong the war by keeping Helen any longer. Troilus argues that they should stay true to their original valuation of Helen and their decision to go to war on her behalf; Hector, that her value has been reduced in proportion to the number of good lives spent on her. Thus Troilus maintains, 'What's aught, but as 'tis valued?'; Hector, that 'value dwells not in particular will:/ It holds his estimate and dignity/ As well wherein 'tis precious of itself/ As in the prizer' (II, ii, 52–6). Troilus so forsakes reality that he can use as analogy for the rape of Helen from her husband 'I take today a wife. . . .' (61 ff.): keeping to the theft of another person's wife is made equivalent to remaining faithful to one's own.[13] But in the end, in a sudden *volte-face*, Hector throws away his position and embraces that of Troilus. The reason is not that he has come to agree with Troilus' idealism but that he has seen how Helen is a stimulus to noble deeds and hence fame in time to come. She is 'a cause that hath no mean dependence/ Upon our joint and several dignities' (192–93). In other words, egotism wins, and the part, the self, is put before society, the whole. As Hector puts his 'particular will' first here, so he is to do later when he goes to his death despite entreaty and warning; or when he founds principle on whim in his 'I am to-day i' th' vein of chivalry' (V, iii, 32); or when he is now merciful to his opponents, now savage and rapacious in hunting down a man to slay him and strip him of his armour: he loses touch with outer reality. And the promised increase of fame proves unfounded: as a direct result of their prosecution of the conflict, Troilus loses Cressida and Hector his life, both in ignominious circumstances.

The final move in the divorce of mind from body in the play is made in Ulysses' speech on fame to Achilles, where he argues that no-one is of value in his own right, but only insofar as he makes others praise him:

> no man is the lord of anything,
> Though in and of him there be much consisting,
> Till he communicate his parts to others;
> Nor doth he of himself know them for aught
> Till he behold them formed in th'applause
> Where they're extended. . . .
>
> (III, iii, 115–20)

This is Troilus' 'What's aught, but as 'tis valued?' with a
vengeance: where Troilus' solipsism founded itself on a fixed
and unchanging valuation of a person made at one time, that of
Ulysses makes all value mutable, subject to changes in the
perceiving mind to which Troilus did not admit. Here mind
has lost touch with body or external reality to the extent that
everything is mental, or, like Berkeley's tree, exists only when
perceived. And, more bitter still, more destructive of value, the
perceiving mind can often be taken in by false representations
of value, as with Ajax, 'most dear in the esteem/ And poor in
worth' (129–30), so that applause is no index to merit, and all
one can do is seek praise for its own often empty sake; now
valour's show and valour's worth are irretrievably divided.
The vision is one of external reality, here in the form of heroic
deeds, trying to be granted objectivity by the subjective
medium of mind, straining to establish itself by being constantly on the move, hoping to become permanent by subject-
ing itself to transience, struggling to be valued by that which
has no lasting notion of value. The world becomes a fragmented mass of subjective apparitions:

> let not virtue seek
> Remuneration for the thing it was;
> For beauty, wit,
> High birth, vigour of bone, desert in service,
> Love, friendship, charity, are subject all
> To envious and calumniating Time.
>
> (169–74)

Directly expressing the divorce of mind and body, the play is
full of images of division. There is the war, and the severed love
of Troilus and Cressida. There is the divided blood of Ajax that
prevents Hector from fighting with him. There are local
remarks such as that of Ulysses on Achilles, ' 'twixt his mental
and his active parts/ Kingdomed Achilles in commotion rages'
(II, iii, 172–73), or of Troilus on Cressida's witnessed
faithlessness, 'If there be rule in unity itself,/ This is not she'
(V, ii, 141–42; see also 146–52); and many incidental mentions
such as Agamemnon's certainty that nonsense will never
'divide' Ulysses' lips (I, iii, 72), or Troilus' declaration
concerning Trojans and Greeks, 'No space of earth shall

sunder our two hates' (V, x, 27).[14] Without mind being in control of physical reality, that reality fragments: the play is full too of mention of parts of the body and of limbs; of the sense of disintegration into fractions, orts, fragments, scraps, bits and greasy relics; and of disease imagery (emanating particularly from Thersites).[15] More largely the dualism of mind and body is mirrored in the plot of the play.[16] For most of it, while what passes for thought prevails, there is no action: the scheme to rouse Achilles fails, and the contest between Ajax and Hector is abortive. At the end, however, inaction suddenly gives way to a frenzy of activity, now in a context of total loss of control by mind: Hector is crazed with egotism, Achilles with the lust for brutish revenge, Troilus with jealous rage.

For the original cause of the dualism in this play, the act which explains why the characters and the medium are what they are, we must look back beyond the personages we see and their common egoism[17] to the deed that brought about warfare in every sense of the word in the beginning. That deed was the rape of Helen. Ulysses' 'degree' speech, and particularly his statement that 'Take but degree away, untune that string,/ And hark what discord follows!' (I, iii, 109–10), is applicable not finally to Agamemnon but to the origin of the war in the fact that degree was shaked when a Greek wife Helen left her husband Menelaus for the Trojan Paris. This not only caused the war, but was an initial act of chaos, an overthrow of degree which has infected every enterprise associated with it. The sin repeats itself: Menelaus' failure as a husband and master recurs in Agamemnon as leader of the Greek army; Helen's faithlessness spreads to other women and her selfish egotism to all the characters in the play; and the divorce of husband from wife is mirrored in the opposed armies themselves, in the disjoining of Troilus and Cressida, and most deeply in the split between mind and body that pervades the whole play. And it is in the end because no character is aware of this final cause that neither thought nor the action from which it is so continually disjoined in this play can be either accurate or effective.

Measure for Measure

Where in *Hamlet* and *Troilus and Cressida* the protagonists are

55

often engaged in trying to join mind and body, thought and action, in *Measure for Measure* the efforts of the characters are frequently directed at keeping these opposites apart. Isabella and Angelo are both ascetic rejecters of the body who yet find themselves surprised by its continued and destructive presence. Angelo the apparently cold justice is amazed to find himself lusting after the pure Isabella as she pleads for the life of her brother Claudio, but it is his own and her puritanism that causes the desires of the flesh to return by the back door,[18]

> Never could the strumpet
> With all her double vigour, art and nature,
> Once stir my temper: but this virtuous maid
> Subdues me quite. Ever till now
> When men were fond, I smil'd, and wonder'd how.
> (II, ii, 183–87)[19]

As for Isabella, she shows in herself how the body and the senses overturn their rejection as she describes with masochistic relish the pains that she would endure to avoid saving Claudio by prostituting herself, 'Th' impression of keen whips I'd wear as rubies,/ And strip myself to death as to a bed/ That longing had been sick for. . . .' (II, iv, 101–3).[20] And she too is astonished when Angelo shows awareness of her as a physical being. The central irony of Isabella's plea is that she is a nun pleading for forgiveness of the very kind of physicality that she herself abhors.

The split between mind and body is also seen in the imposition by Angelo of the grid of law and punishment on the free expression of sex outside the legality of marriage. Certainly too much freedom has led to licence: but too much restraint is tyranny, and may backfire on itself. The emphasis in the play on the particularly 'fleshly' sin of fornication heightens the split. In Isabella the division is seen in the way that her plea for her brother is made not so much for him personally as because she becomes excited by an intellectual and spiritual argument for its own sake, rather in the manner of a fervent bluestocking. At first, despite Lucio's promptings, she is reluctant to plead for Claudio because of her repugnance at his act, and a few perfunctory refusals by Angelo are enough to make her ready to give up, 'O just but severe law!/ I had a brother, then. . . .'

(II, ii, 41–2). It is only when she makes the issue one of a contrast between earthly justice and heavenly mercy that she begins to catch fire:

> Well, believe this:
> No ceremony that to great ones longs,
> Not the king's crown, nor the deputed sword,
> The marshal's truncheon, nor the judge's robe,
> Become them with one half so good a grace
> As mercy does.
>
> (58–63)

Warming to her theme, she replies to Angelo's 'Your brother is a forfeit of the law,/ And you but waste your words,' with 'Alas, alas!/ Why, all the souls that were, were forfeit once,/ And He that might the vantage best have took/ Found out the remedy' (71–5). What moves Isabella is not Claudio's cause so much as an impersonal zest for debate and moral earnestness;[21] in a sense she has only the mask of compassion, as Angelo has only the mask of justice. And this impersonal, intellectual argument can lead her to become so cut off from outer reality that she contradicts her own stated revulsion: where at the outset she declared Claudio's sin to be heinous, she later reduces it to a peccadillo for the sake of the argument, 'Who is it that hath died for this offence?/ There's many have committed it' (89–90; see also II, iv, 42–50). When Angelo picks her up on this inconsistency she argues that she was led into it out of love for her brother (II, iv, 114–20): but this explanation is not the evident one. With their strained and passionate purity she and Angelo are remarkably alike; the play should have married them.

Angelo demands her body as ransom for Claudio's; she will not accede lest she corrupt her soul. She goes to Claudio and asks that he lay down his body to save her spirit. We are back once more with the puritanical prig, shocked by the wicked ways of the world. The oppugnancy of mind and body is highlighted in the scene where the disguised Duke counsels Claudio to 'Be absolute for death,' and suggests a whole series of mental means by which he may become ready for it: 'Reason thus with life:/ If I do lose thee, I do lose a thing/ That none but fools would keep. . . .' (III, i, 5 ff.). This is reminiscent of

57

Gaunt's advice to Bolingbroke in *Richard II* to reduce the weight of his banishment by the use of his imagination: here too mind is to be imposed on experience. Claudio, however, later responds to similar counsel from Isabella with the intractable physicality of death:

> Ay, but to die, and go we know not where;
> To lie in cold obstruction, and to rot;
> This sensible warm motion to become
> A kneaded clod; and the delighted spirit
> To bath in fiery floods, or to reside
> In thrilling region of thick-ribbed ice;
> To be imprison'd in the viewless winds. . . .
> (III, i, 117–23)

(Here, echoing a major polarity of the play which parallels that between mind and body, death is seen as a confinement, a prison, as against the freedom of life.)

In the middle section of the play we are literally concerned with 'body'. One body is substituted for another in the night, so that Angelo can enjoy his lust and Isabella retain her innocence. Similar exchange is carried out in the prison in relation to death. When Angelo continues to insist on the execution of Claudio and asks for his head, the disguised Duke struggles to find a condemned criminal whose head resembles Claudio's: and when his choice, Barnardine, proves recalcitrant, the body of a dead prisoner Ragozine is found an adequate substitute. Throughout we are strongly aware in all the plotting of mind trying to circumvent the problems of body.

Such attempted circumvention is of course the preoccupation of the play as a whole, which concerns the imposition of mind, or civilization, on body, or desire. Mind is seen as restraint (imaged in prisons[22] and death), the body as freedom; each in isolation goes to an extreme and is abused. Isabella wishes too great a restriction upon herself in entering a convent (I, iv, 1–5), Lucio is too unrestrained. The Duke leaves Vienna because he has been too liberal; but the deputy he leaves is too restrictive. The first two acts 'liberate' questions about the nature of law and of the characters themselves which are suppressed by the next three until a happy ending is manu-

factured. The Duke schemes to frustrate the evil that Angelo
lets loose by purely mechanical means; Isabella's character is
submerged until she suddenly appears as a marriageable
woman at the end of the play; above all, the sense of action as
emerging dangerously from character is cancelled by tricks
and legerdemain.[23] And all of this can be seen as deriving from
the basic severance of mind from body in the play. There can
be no marriage of these opposites in the spiritual landscape of
this drama; the human marriages, actual or projected, with
which the play ends are all unions into which the characters
have been manipulated (Isabella, Claudio, Mariana), or
forced (Angelo, Lucio). The medium of *Measure for Measure*
is as in many of Shakespeare's plays too polarized and extreme
to make the resolution of duality more than a willed hope.

The theme of the split between mind and body particularly
interested Shakespeare in the period *c*. 1595–1604. We saw it
in *Richard II*; it is present too in the *Henry IV* plays, in the
emphasis on Falstaff's flesh and its attempt to capture Hal's
mind. A central preoccupation of *A Midsummer Night's Dream*
is how far love sees with the eyes or with the mind. In *The
Merchant of Venice* an actual lump of flesh is the bond demanded
by Shylock, and Portia uses the skill of her legal mind to
oppose it. In *Twelfth Night*, Orsino, Olivia and Malvolio are all
mentally disjoined from the world by self-indulgence or
egotism. In most of the comedies the oppositions are eventually
re-integrated in a Renaissance *discordia concors*; but such
marriage does not appear possible where the issues are seen in
more serious light. We find a form of mind-body division in
Othello also, where Desdemona sees Othello's 'visage in his
mind', Iago uses his mind and no real physical evidence to
persuade Othello that his wife has betrayed him in body, and
Othello is continually shaken in his resolve by the actual
physical presence of Desdemona. Beyond this period, as we
shall see later, there is a form of division of mind from body in
Macbeth, and in the difference between the 'political' plays
Timon of Athens, *Antony and Cleopatra* and *Coriolanus*, and the
late romances. A recent critic has also found the dualism
markedly present in *Love's Labour's Lost*, *The Taming of the
Shrew* and *King Lear*.[24] What in Shakespeare particularly drew

59

him to this theme we shall never know: but certainly it is more recurrent and its diverse effects more exhaustively explored in his work than in that of any other writer of his day. Its repeated use suggests a Shakespeare who had experienced something of such division in himself.

NOTES

1. See also Terence Hawkes, *Shakespeare's Talking Animals: Language and Drama in Society* (Edward Arnold, 1973), p. 115.
2. References are to *William Shakespeare: The Complete Works*, ed. Peter Alexander (Collins, 1951). For previous accounts of the spread of evil in *Hamlet*, see e.g. Wolfgang H. Clemen, *The Development of Shakespeare's Imagery* (Methuen, 1951), pp. 112–18; H. D. F. Kitto, *Form and Meaning in Drama* (Methuen, 1956), ch. 9, esp. pp. 328–37; John Holloway, *The Story of the Night: Studies in Shakespeare's Major Tragedies* (Routledge and Kegan Paul, 1961), pp. 29–32.
3. See for example John Paterson, 'The Word in *Hamlet*', *SQ*, 2 (1951), 47–55; Maynard Mack, 'The World of *Hamlet*', *Yale Review*, 41 (1952), 502–23; Hawkes, op. cit., pp. 105–26; Maynard Mack, Jr., *Killing the King: Three Studies in Shakespeare's Tragic Structure* (New Haven and London, Yale University Press, 1973), pp. 95–121 *passim*; Inga-Stina Ewbank, 'Hamlet and the Power of Words', *SS*, 30 (1977), 85–102.
4. See e.g. I, iii, 59–60; III, ii, 17–18, 400; III, iii, 97–8; III, iv, 78–9; IV, v, 7–10; IV, vii, 120; V, ii, 356.
5. Mack, 'The World of *Hamlet*', pp. 504–6.
6. See Kitto, pp. 260–62.
7. My view of this play owes much to D. A. Traversi, *An Approach to Shakespeare*, 2nd ed. (Sands, 1957), pp. 75–81.
8. References are to the New Cambridge *Troilus and Cressida*, ed. Alice Walker (Cambridge, Cambridge University Press, 1957).
9. His remarks on flies versus tigers seem rather off the point; and his bovine analogy suggests that cows are put on their mettle by thunderstorms. His uncertainty at this seems mirrored in his vague 'the thing of courage'.
10. On the repetitions and orotundities, see T. McAlindon, 'Language, Style and Meaning in *Troilus and Cressida*', *PMLA*, 84 (1969), 35–6; Rosalie L. Colie, *Shakespeare's Living Art* (Princeton, N.J., Princeton University Press, 1974), pp. 320–21.
11. For instance, Ulysses in his 'degree' speech pictures the perfect hierarchy in terms of the sun controlling the planets, but when he comes to describe cosmic chaos he speaks of it as arising not, as would be consistent, when the sun is lax, but 'when the planets/ In evil mixture to disorder wander' (94–5): that is, instead of blaming the general, whom his analogy previously portrayed as preventing rebellion, he blames his subordinates.

12. See also Johannes Kleinstück, 'Ulysses' Speech on Degree as Related to the Play of *Troilus and Cressida*', *Neophilologus*, 43 (1959), 59.
13. See also Walker, p. 169.
14. See also I, iii, 316; II, iii, 242–43; III, ii, 147–49; IV, iv, 33–48, 94–7; IV, v, 83–6; V, ii, 107–8.
15. On disease imagery, see also R. J. Kaufmann, 'Ceremonies for Chaos: The Status of *Troilus and Cressida*' *ELH*, 32 (1965), 149–53.
16. On discontinuity of action and form in the play as an imitation of its fragmented vision, see Richard D. Fly, ' "Suited in Like Conditions as Our Argument": Imitative Form in Shakespeare's *Troilus and Cressida*', *SEL*, 15 (1975), 273–92.
17. On this see also R. A. Foakes, *Shakespeare: The Dark Comedies to the Last Plays, From Satire to Celebration* (Routledge and Kegan Paul, 1971), pp. 47–51.
18. See also Darryl J. Gless, *'Measure for Measure', the Law, and the Convent* (Princeton, N.J., Princeton University Press, 1979), pp. 96–8, 131–32, 216–17.
19. References are to the Arden *Measure for Measure*, ed. J. W. Lever (Methuen, 1965).
20. See also Harriet Hawkins, ' "The Devil's Party": Virtues and Vices in *Measure for Measure*', *SS*, 31 (1978), 107.
21. Claudio says of her, 'she hath prosperous art/ When she will play with reason and discourse,/ And well she can persuade' (I, ii, 174–76); the word 'play' is telling. See also David L. Stevenson, 'Design and Structure in *Measure for Measure*: A New Appraisal', *ELH*, 23 (1956), 275.
22. On images of prison and of confinement in the play, and their symbolic significance, see also Gless, pp. 94–6.
23. See also A. P. Rossiter, *Angel with Horns and Other Shakespeare Lectures* (Longmans, 1961), p. 164; Harriet Hawkins, *Likenesses of Truth in Elizabethan and Restoration Drama* (Oxford, The Clarendon Press, 1972), pp. 68–76, and ' "The Devil's Party" ', pp. 110–13.
24. Stanley Wells, '*The Taming of the Shrew* and *King Lear*: A Structural Comparison', *SS*, 33 (1980), 55–66.

4

Othello, Anthony and Cleopatra

Commentators on *Othello* may on the whole be divided into
those who agree with the protagonist's picture of himself as
being 'not easily jealous' and those who do not. Here it will be
argued that both views, however diametrically opposed, are
valid, and that there is an explanation for this in Shakespeare
himself.

First, on the side of Othello's *not* being easily jealous, there is
the jealousy of Iago.[1] True, there is a perfunctory element in
Iago's statement of some of his jealousies, but this might as
much be a function of his thorough domicilement with them as
an index to motiveless malignity. To one jealousy he does
recur, and on the second occasion with a fervour of fury: his
suspicion that Othello has been to bed with his wife Emilia. In
the opening scene of the play he tells Roderigo that his hatred
of Othello comes from the appointment of Cassio over his
head: but he could hardly tell Roderigo, who is himself in love
with Desdemona, of his desire to be 'even with [Othello], wife,
for wife' (II, i, 294).[2] The expression of his supposed professional jealousy has an argumentative and mocking ring
which removes weight from it (the only exception to this being
the revealing aside on Cassio, 'A fellow almost damn'd in a fair
wife'):

> But there's no remedy, 'tis the curse of service,
> Preferment goes by letter and affection,
> Not by the old gradation, where each second
> Stood heir to the first: now sir, be judge yourself,
> Whether I in any just term am affin'd
> To love the Moor.
> (I, i, 35–40)

He simultaneously accepts Cassio's promotion as the way of the world and offers it as a motive for revenge. (It is interesting that while he sees himself as the unrewarded loyal retainer, it is just such a picture of himself that he goes on to reject in his contempt for the 'duteous and knee-crooking knave,/ . . . doting on his own obsequious bondage' (45–6).) We leave Iago's rather flippant account here feeling that his hatred of Othello far exceeds its announced cause.

In soliloquy we are more ready to accept personal revelations as true ones. We are given two soliloquies by Iago, in both of which he states his motive to be sexual jealousy. The first occurs after reassurance of the unsteady Roderigo in Venice:

> I hate the Moor,
> And it is thought abroad, that 'twixt my sheets
> He's done my office; I know not if't be true . . .
> Yet I, for mere suspicion in that kind,
> Will do, as if for surety.
>
> (I, iii, 384–88)

and the second after a setting-on of Roderigo in Cyprus:

> I do suspect the lusty Moor
> Hath leap'd into my seat, the thought whereof
> Doth like a poisonous mineral gnaw my inwards,
> And nothing can, nor shall content my soul,
> Till I am even with him, wife, for wife.
>
> (II, i, 290–94)

In a few lines he adds, 'I fear Cassio with my night-cap too' (302).

Now the way in which these motives occur, placed in the middle of soliloquies, happened on almost in passing, has suggested to several commentators that they are not the whole truth concerning what drives Iago. But the issue here surely turns on how one reads these revelations. If one takes them naturalistically, then it does seem odd that Iago should have to remind himself of his own motivation.[3] If, however, one takes Iago in both cases as a mouthpiece for information which could not be conveyed by any other character in the play, or in any context other than soliloquy, then we must see him speaking here not as Iago would, but as Shakespeare must through him if the information is to be put over at all. As such it is a clumsy job,[4] and it is significant that it requires two attempts to put it over: but short of bardolatry, there is absolutely no reason why Iago's words should not be seen in the light of reportage.[5]

But whether less or more, the motive of sexual jealousy is clearly and repeatedly there. We hear it again from Emilia at the end when she speaks to Iago of the man who has poisoned Othello's affections:

> Some such squire he was,
> That turn'd your wit, the seamy side without,
> And made you to suspect me with the Moor.
> (IV, ii, 147–49)

In fact there was not evidently any 'such squire': Iago's suspicion and jealousy appear to have been as near self-begotten as they could be. It is true that Iago has a cynical view of life, and thus could be said to be more pre-disposed to jealousy than Othello, who has not: but the evidence is that the Moor, portrayed by Iago as credulous and prone to jealousy, is on the face of it far less so than himself. The man who is most easily jealous in *Othello* is Iago.

One could draw an analogy—and since Iago is frequently referred to as a demi-devil it might well be more than an analogy—between Iago and Othello on the one hand and Satan and Adam on the other: just as Satan falls self-tempted and self-deceived, so does Iago; just as man can only be perverted by external temptation, so also with Othello. We will not take the comparison further here, except in respect of *Paradise Lost*. We accept, in reading that poem, that Eve can be perverted by just one major speech of temptation from Satan (a speech which in brief rehearses several of the points made by Iago to Othello); whereas many playgoers and readers are outraged that Othello should fall after what they feel is also a brief battery. One explanation for these different responses must be that we know that man has fallen, whereas Othello's fall is contingent. This of course does not *justify* the difference in our response. One could only do something to remove that difference by making the analogy between Othello and Adam a closer one.[6] But it can be said that it is the very contingency in Othello's story which makes the reader feel him the more a gull than in fact he may be. The story is inherently such as to exasperate.

Also giving the impression that Othello is not easily jealous is the fact that throughout the play, and particularly in its later stages, Othello has not merely Iago but his own creator working against him.[7] Let us rehearse some of the familiar instances of this first. The source of the play, Cinthio's story in his *Hecatommithi* (the third tale of the seventh decade), makes little of Othello's colour or of any sense of his alienation from sophisticated Venetian manners as factors to be played on in arousing his jealousy and suspicion: apart from a mention by Desdemona of the Moor's hot nature, there is nothing said that might make his case untypical. Shakespeare makes the blackness, the simplicity and the barbarity all factors in the awakening of Othello's anger by Iago: his Othello has the scales of his own human predicament weighted against him. One consequence of this is that Othello's condition is a highly unrepresentative and special one. The idiosyncrasies of his intense love for Desdemona are begotten by this: coming from such different cultures, the two could not be expected save through long intercourse to arrive at an understanding of the peculiarities of each other's personalities and backgrounds; what has drawn them together at first is an intense but unlocalized bond. This is certainly a position which can be preyed upon. That there is a Iago to prey upon it only compounds the unfairness in such a context. Truly, in the light of this, one can only be tempted to agree with Rymer's derisory moral for the play, that 'This may be a caution to all Maidens of Quality how, without their Parents consent, they run away with Blackamoors'; or, as he also puts it, 'What instruction can we make out of this Catastrophe? Or whither must our reflection lead us?'[8]

It was Rymer also who first remarked the most unfortunate importunity of Desdemona: 'tho' she perceives the *Moor* Jealous of Cassio [actually, she does not], yet will she not forbear, but still rings *Cassio, Cassio* in both his Ears.'[9] Thus she agrees to sponsor Cassio's suit to be restored to Othello's favour,

> my lord shall never rest,
> I'll watch him tame, and talk him out of patience;

His bed shall seem a school, his board a shrift,
I'll intermingle every thing he does
With Cassio's suit.

(III, iii, 22–6)

Out of patience she talks him indeed. She will not cease
pestering him about Cassio just when Iago has opened his case
(ibid., 43–85); or again at the moment when Othello is asking
for the missing handkerchief (III, iv, 46–94). Fine theatre,
perhaps, but a rather melodramatic portrait of causality.

But there are many more manipulations by Shakespeare
than this.[10] For example, when the newly-dismissed Cassio,
who has been gaining the promise of Desdemona to sue with
Othello on his behalf, sees Othello and Iago approach, he
decides to leave her; Desdemona tries to dissuade him, 'Why,
stay and hear me speak,' but he insists, 'Madam, not now, I am
very ill at ease,/ Unfit for mine own purpose' (III, iii, 31–3). Of
course, he is ashamed, but he has been told that Othello is
already well-disposed towards him (III, i, 45–51). His
behaviour is therefore contingent. But out of this contingency
Iago makes the first moves of his practice against Othello:

Iago. Ha, I like not that.
Oth. What dost thou say?
Iago. Nothing, my lord, or if—I know not what.
Oth. Was not that Cassio parted from my wife?
Iago. Cassio, my lord? . . . no, sure, I cannot think it,
    That he would sneak away so guilty-like,
    Seeing you coming.
Oth.   I do believe 'twas he.

(III, iii, 35–41)

When Desdemona comes forward to them, she tells Othello
only that 'I have been talking with a suitor here,/ A man that
languishes in your displeasure,' and Othello has to ask first, his
name, and later, 'Went he hence now?', all of which puts him in
the position of finding out things which by that necessity may
appear to have been deliberately held back from him. After
this, Desdemona begins such a litany on behalf of Cassio as to
reverse the impression of concealment while increasing that of
her potential involvement with Cassio. No wonder Othello
eventually asks her to 'leave me but a little to myself' (86). Now

all of this stems from four contingencies, together with Iago's slight muddying of the water: working backwards, these are the violence of Desdemona's importunity on Cassio's behalf, the obliqueness with which she introduces Cassio, Cassio's departure from her and, lastly, the fact that Othello and Iago first enter at a distance, so that it is possible for Othello to be uncertain of Cassio's identity.[11] The last is quite a significant fact. It means that Othello is trying to establish the physical truth of what is before him while Iago can begin his solicitation without being fully attended to, but with his words still having an unconscious affect. Othello, looking before him, does not consciously hear Iago's 'Ha, I like not that'; and again he does not take immediate notice of his 'Cassio my lord? . . . no, sure, I cannot think it,/ That he would steal away so guilty-like,/ Seeing you coming'—had he done so he would surely have drawn a conclusion favourable to Cassio by replying, 'Nonsense! It's obvious that the poor fellow can't face me yet.'[12] Othello's admission of Iago's insinuation here is directly caused by the simple fact of the physical distance Shakespeare has placed between the two groups.

These lines are crucial because they are the *données* on which Iago builds: after this he has Othello to himself for a long time. Whenever the external world presents itself in the play hereafter, the innocent is made by Shakespeare to take on what could be construed as the lineaments of the corrupt. Othello is not like Leontes, who dirties the world by himself. Furthermore, Shakespeare often twists or ignores facts to make the plot work. Cassio, Othello tells Iago, not only knew of his love for Desdemona 'from first to last', but also 'went between us very often' (III, iii, 95–101; see also Desdemona at 71–4).[13] The wondrous handkerchief was Othello's first gift to Desdemona (III, iii, 443). Desdemona, Emilia tells us, is so careful of the handkerchief which Othello has 'conjured' her to keep, 'That she reserves it evermore about her,/ To kiss, and talk to' (III, iii, 299–300). We have just seen Desdemona attempt to bind Othello's painful brow with it. Clearly the handkerchief is frequently in evidence—and then strikingly, since it is 'Spotted with strawberries' (III, iii, 442)—and Cassio would probably have seen it; nor can we say that he would have paid it only passing attention, since when he finds it in his chamber he is

67

sufficiently admiring of it to ask Bianca to copy the design on it for him because 'I like the work well' (III, iv, 177–78, 187). We are asked, so that the plot may work, to accept that Cassio has no prior knowledge of the handkerchief, when his past doings have been such as to give him strong likelihood of having seen it often. And, in a different connection, we are asked to accept that Iago, having heard all he has of Cassio's role in the wooing of Desdemona by Othello, can be sure that Cassio will not know to whom the handkerchief belongs when he finds it in his chamber (III, iii, 326–29).

There is a further problem with the handkerchief. After Iago's first long interview with Othello, Desdemona and Emilia enter while Othello is alone, and when Othello speaks to his wife bitterly of the pain on his forehead, she offers to bind it with the handkerchief. Upon which,

> *Oth.*   Your napkin is too little:
> [*She drops her handkerchief.*
> Let it alone, come, I'll go in with you.
>   (III, iii, 291–92)

This leaves the handkerchief for Emilia (uncharacteristically) to pick up and give to Iago. (In Cinthio's account there is no such accident: the ensign has it stolen.) Clearly Othello sees the handkerchief here, and he will certainly know that he pushed it away. Whether he sees it fall, and whether the 'it' of 'Let it alone' refers to the handkerchief or to his forehead, it is impossible to determine. But that he should subsequently attribute its loss by Desdemona to her having given it to Cassio is simply to forget his own sight of it.[14] Again, when Iago shortly after this scene tells Othello that he has just seen Cassio wiping his beard with the handkerchief, Othello does not for a moment recall that he has just seen it in his wife's hand. Of course, Othello is being reduced to Iago to the point where he is partly incapable of rational recall, but even so the juxtaposition of scenes is too much to take here.

In the scene where Othello is placed by Iago to hear, without being seen, a conversation between him and Cassio ostensibly on the subject of Cassio's illicit dealings with Desdemona, but in fact (unknown to Othello) about his relations with his mistress Bianca, Shakespeare works another piece of sleight-of-hand. It is hard enough to accept that the upright Cassio, the man of such true grace, politeness and understanding of the nature and value of the love of Othello and Desdemona, should have a whore at all (he was married in the source, and Othello did not overhear the subject of the mirth between him and Iago); hard enough too to take Cassio's ready laughter (not certainly present in the source) when he is so miserable at his loss of status and reputation. But worst of all is the way in which the name 'Bianca' never recurs after Iago has mentioned it to Cassio before beckoning Othello forward to overhear the conversation—particularly when, to Iago's shock, Bianca herself enters:

> *Cas.* She was here even now, she haunts me in every place. I was t'other day talking on the sea-bank, with certain Venetians, and thither comes this bauble; by this hand, she falls thus about my neck:—
> *Oth.* Crying 'O dear Cassio!' as it were: his gesture imports it.
> *Cas.* So hangs, and lolls, and weeps upon me; so hales, and pulls me, ha, ha, ha!
> *Oth.* Now he tells how she pluck'd him to my chamber. I see that nose of yours, but not that dog I shall throw't to.
> *Cas.* Well, I must leave her company.
> *Enter* BIANCA.
> *Iago.* Before me! look where she comes.
> *Cas.* 'Tis such another fitchew; marry, a perfum'd one. What do you mean by this haunting of me?
> (IV, i, 131–45)

Obviously the phrase ' 'Tis such another fitchew' makes it possible for Othello to believe that there is another fitchew, and that that is his wife. The language is twisted in order to sustain Iago's deception. Furthermore, of course, the sheer luck for Iago's scheme in Bianca's entry with the handkerchief before Othello's eyes, is a cruel twist of fate: in the source Iago took Othello to see the Captain's wife working on the handkerchief at her window.

There is another instance of such unfortunate language in the scene where Othello is trying to bring himself to murder Desdemona. He faces her with the accusations Iago has manufactured, and she steadfastly denies them. When she says that Cassio will testify that the imputation that she has given him the handkerchief is false, Othello tells her that 'his mouth is stopp'd,/ Honest Iago hath ta'en order for't.' Desdemona says, 'My fear interprets then, . . ./ What, is he dead?' The question cuts short the inquiry she might otherwise have been able to make into Iago's behaviour, and Othello answers, in growing rage, 'Had all his hairs been lives,/ My great revenge had stomach for 'em all.' At this Desdemona cries out in language which, though in fact that of innocence, is made to sound the phraseology of unmasked guilt and of revealed whoredom:

> Alas, he is betray'd, and I undone.
>
> (V, ii, 77)

This language is for Othello a confirmation of the deed: 'O strumpet, . . . weep'st thou for him to my face?'; and he proceeds at once to murder her. While it cannot be said that these words alone precipitate Desdemona's death, their absence might well have given her larger scope in which to try to convince Othello.

The factors so far outlined must considerably reduce our ability either to feel that Othello is easily jealous, or that his tragedy is one which may in part reasonably be ascribed to his personal responsibility.[15] It is so very striking how Shakespeare at almost every point alters what in Cinthio is reasonable, or a part of Iago's plan, to the unreasonable and the unlucky, that the critical mind is tempted to try to see some deep point in it. No such point, however, easily presents itself. For instance, the 'method' goes clean against the notion often advanced, that Othello ceases to take notice of facts when Iago has awakened his jealousy: this would be demonstrated only by having the data of the external world run *counter* to Iago's insinuations, not with them, while Othello held to the deception practised on him. We have no direct evidence that 'Iago serves and is in turn assisted by the powers of evil, in the disturbing and consistent run of luck that he is made to enjoy in carrying out his plans':[16] demi-devil Iago may be, but the play lacks the supernatural dimension.

There is throughout *Othello* a recurrent play on the words 'bound' and 'free' and their cognates.[17] Of course this motif can be seen as commenting on the way in which Othello's

70

freedom is bounded by Iago's mesh of insinuation; but one need not relate the insistence of the motif simply to the *coherent* content of the play: it may well be that, sensing that Othello was rather more a victim than an agent, Shakespeare began unconsciously to portray this in his language.

Another factor working against Othello is the sheer skill and potency of Iago's solicitation: the deployment of such skill further suggests that Othello is not easily jealous. Of course, with our privileged insight into Iago's schemes, we are given the scope to mock Othello (like the famous member of the audience who felt impelled to stand up and shout, 'Oh, you great black fool, can't you see?'): matters are so arranged by Shakespeare that we stand in a superior position to him. But the facts, from his point of view, are that he is faced with a man whom he trusts and who finds it a burden to impart to him information concerning his wife which will cause harm. He is also, with his open nature, desirous that things should be brought into the open, and therefore runs ahead of Iago at certain points. Iago's method is one of indirection, and of continually removing certainty from what he is saying (the stylistic expression of his removal of certainty regarding Desdemona's nature):

> *Iago.* Did Michael Cassio, when you woo'd my lady,
>   Know of your love?
> *Oth.* He did, from first to last: . . . why dost thou ask?
> *Iago.* But for a satisfaction of my thought.
>   No further harm.
>
> (III, iii, 95–9)

Iago states that his question was innocent and simultaneously that he meant 'No further *harm*' by it, thus drawing on further investigation. He similarly cuts beneath certainty when, having gained Othello's assent to his assertion that men should be what they seem, he declares, 'Why then I think Cassio's an honest man' (ibid., 133)—thus leaving out the undermining conditional for Othello to intuit, '*If* men are in fact what they should be, namely, what they seem, *then* we may suppose Cassio an honest man.'

Having teased Othello to a pitch, Iago replies to the demand that he 'give the worst of thought/ The worst of word', thus:

71

> Good my lord, pardon me;
> Though I am bound to every act of duty,
> I am not bound to all that slaves are free to;
> Utter my thoughts? Why, say they are vile and false:
> As where's that palace, whereinto foul things
> Sometimes intrude not? who has a breast so pure,
> But some uncleanly apprehensions
> Keep leets and law-days, and in sessions sit
> With meditations lawful?
>
> (143–45)

The first lines are meant to confuse: slaves are not free to anything, including the utterance of their worst of thoughts. Only if 'slaves' here meant 'villains', which reading the use of 'bound' and 'free' here prevents, could the line make sense. In any case there is little of substance in what Iago says, and Othello is left to untangle its vapidity as best he may. Then Iago implies that his keeping of his thoughts to himself is with the objects both of sparing Othello pain and of preventing a possible falsehood. In this way he confounds the one with the other, 'vile and false', and can then drop the matter of their possible falsity (which has been used by him as the reason for not being positively accusatory), and go on in such a way that the sole reason for the thoughts' concealment will seem the desire to spare Othello pain—which will prompt the latter to further question and leave him with less thought of possible falsity. Yet even all this is done glancingly, for no sooner has Iago implied it in 'Why, say they are vile and false,' than he moves away from answering it to expatiate irrelevantly, via two different images, on the way vile thoughts can intrude on the mind. But in the process he moves from the foulness of the thoughts to their being 'uncleanly apprehensions'—suggesting in the latter phrase a greater degree of objective truth in them, which is heightened by the legal context in which they are placed.

On Othello's further request Iago can push this point again, while once more insisting that Othello would be well advised not to gain this knowledge:

> I do beseech you,
> Though I perchance am vicious in my guess,
> (As I confess it is my nature's plague

To spy into abuses, and oft my jealousy
Shapes faults that are not) I entreat you then,
From one that so imperfectly conjects,
You'ld take no notice, nor build yourself a trouble
Out of my scattering and unsure observance;
It were not for your quiet, nor your good,
Nor for my manhood, honesty, or wisdom,
To let you know my thoughts.

(148–58)

The syntax is long enough to lose the hearer, and Iago's shift
from first to third person is also confusing. First he says he may
be wrong; then he says it is in his character to notice wrongs
that do exist; then he says he is inclined to see ills that are not
present. He leaves Othello no certainty as to what he is saying.
The process is repeated more largely in the rest of the speech.
Iago does not recur to his earlier point concerning his possibly
biased point of view: vaguely at first, he says that he 'imperfectly conjects', and then that his observation is 'scattering and
unsure', which puts the uncertainty more to the account of
inevitably frail human perception in the midst of a puzzling
and multiplex world; this is a different point from his earlier
'admission' that his personal nature made him see evil where
in fact there might be none. As for Othello himself, he is bidden
first not to take notice of Iago's clouded judgments, and then
not to build himself a trouble by doing so—by which is meant
both a trouble over nothing and a trouble over something
possibly real. At the same time, the notion of perception has
shifted from one where Iago's mind makes what it sees to one
whereby it is a poor because helpless receptor, 'unsure
observance'. Now Iago can move on to the more definite
statement which is still covered by those previous to it, 'It were
not for your quiet, nor your good'—meaning both 'You would
only cause yourself unnecessary suffering by getting suspicious' and 'You are better off ignorant of the facts.' Again
'Nor for my manhood, honesty, or wisdom' can be interpreted
as 'It would be a cad's trick to tell you', 'What I think may be
false and therefore I would risk my honesty in divulging it' and
'It would be unwise in me to let you know what I think.' It is all
very general as well as confusing. And Iago throws in the
syntactically-heightened word 'jealousy' to further the work. It

73

is thus that he continues, always hinting in generals, leaving Othello the more ready to leap to particular conclusions the more he is held in hand, until, on the basis of the whole vague solicitation, out of which Othello has learnt nothing more positive than some unexplained interest of Iago's in Cassio's dealings with Desdemona, and of his having some obscure suspicions concerning Cassio, the Moor begins to fill in the blanks:

> 'tis not to make me jealous,
> To say my wife is fair, feeds well, loves company,
> Is free of speech, sings, plays, and dances well;
> Where virtue is, these are more virtuous. . . .
> (187–90)

Once this process has begun, a little blowing will keep Othello burning till he is like 'the mines of sulphur'.

While it is true that Iago says earlier of Othello that he has 'a free and open nature . . . That thinks men honest that but seems to be so:/ And will as tenderly be led by the nose . . ./ As Asses are' (I, iii, 397–400), it is also Iago who later describes Othello as 'of a constant, noble, loving nature' (II, i, 284); and in any case Othello's trust is seen not as a vice, but as growing out of his virtue. Certainly Othello is led, but in this area of reading it is far less *as* an ass than *by* a fox. Thus, if we consider only the skill used to topple Othello, he again will not look very easily jealous. In other contexts involving jealousy, no such elaborate machinery is necessary to make a Iago, a Claudio or a Leontes instinctively and instantly jealous of their ladies, who are quite innocent. And if we say that Othello turns from Desdemona on the basis of mere innuendo from Iago, we have also to remember that subtle innuendo is the prime technique employed in arousing his jealousy.

So far we have considered the ways in which Othello might be seen to be not easily jealous. But at the same time throughout the play he is portrayed as singularly prone to jealousy. The most striking way this is seen is in the discrepancy between the apparent purity of his love for Desdemona and the speed of his distrust of her on Iago's suggestion. Our first impression of the love relation between himself and Desdemona—unless we have a rooted dislike of

74

romantic language or a highly suspicious cast of mind—is surely favourable.[18] We are told only that Brabantio invited Othello to his household because he delighted to hear Othello's tales of his travels and martial exploits, and that Desdemona would also come and listen when she could. These tales were thus not unsolicited egoistic outpourings: they were a traveller's tales by a traveller whose experiences had been particularly striking. Then, observing Desdemona's fascination, Othello

> Took once a pliant hour, and found good means
> To draw from her a prayer of earnest heart,
> That I would all my pilgrimage dilate,
> Whereof by parcel she had something heard,
> But not intentively: I did consent. . . .
>
> (I, iii, 151–55)

Othello can be quite as devious as Iago when he wishes! Listening to the tale, which arouses her wonder and sympathy, Desdemona 'wish'd/ That heaven had made her such a man' (162–63). She hints to Othello that she has begun to fall in love with him, and, as he puts it, 'Upon this hint I spake' (166). Brabantio, happy to listen to Othello's stories, reveals his racial prejudice when Iago tells him of Othello's involvement with his daughter. Iago, with his jealous hatred of Othello and his reduction of all love to lust; Roderigo, with his frustrated desire for Desdemona; and Brabantio with his ignorant outrage: all these act in effect as foils, making us inclined to think even better of Othello's and Desdemona's love. The Venetian Duke sets the seal on this attitude with his 'I think this tale would win my daughter too,' or to Brabantio, 'Your son-in-law is far more fair than black' (171, 290).

With this in mind it comes as a real shock to find Othello ready to trust Iago before his wife, and becoming potentially uncertain after only a few vague words by Iago and some solicitation on Cassio's behalf by Desdemona,

> Excellent wretch, perdition catch my soul,
> But I do love thee, and when I love thee not,
> Chaos is come again.
>
> (III, iii, 92–4)

Even after a further one hundred and fifty lines with Iago it is jolting to hear Othello, as Iago leaves, musing, 'Why did I marry?' (ibid., 246); and then, left to himself, pushing the point to the limit—first, 'if I do prove her haggard,/ Though that her jesses were my dear heart-strings [as if they are not],/ I'ld whistle her off, and let her down the wind,/ To prey at fortune,' and then, going further, 'She's gone, I am abus'd, and my relief/ Must be to loathe her' (264–67, 271–72).

Thus on the one hand we have the setting for a portrayal of a man not easily jealous: that is, we have another man in the play who is jealous *without* external prompting, we have a highly subtle solicitation designed to make the Moor jealous, and we have a series of remarkable contingencies and twists in the plot to further Iago's designs. And yet the man who is thereby implicitly nearly impervious to jealousy is in fact, when it comes to his actual behaviour, jealous with a velocity which is initially beyond belief.

Initially—but then of course we look back and inspect his relationship with Desdemona much more narrowly than we did at first. When we do so we look at Desdemona's desire to be one with Othello's nature or identity in a more critical light. She says,

> my heart's subdued
> Even to the utmost pleasure of my lord:
> I saw Othello's visage in his mind,
> And to his honours, and his valiant parts
> Did I my soul and fortunes consecrate.
>
> (I, iii, 250–54)

She even uses Othello's energetic language to describe her own feelings, 'That I did love the Moor, to live with him,/ My downright violence, and scorn of fortunes,/ May trumpet to the world' (248–50); and she insists on going to the wars with him. Equally, Othello declares to the Venetian senate that marriage to Desdemona will in no way alter his commitment to military business: 'The tyrant custom . . ./ Hath made the flinty and steel couch of war/ My thrice-driven bed of down' (ibid., 229–31); and—

> no, when light-wing'd toys,
> And feather'd Cupid, foils with wanton dullness
> My speculative and active instruments,

That my disports corrupt and taint my business,
Let housewives make a skillet of my helm,
And all indign and base adversities
Make head against my reputation!

(268–74)

Seen in this light the love of Othello and Desdemona becomes potentially weak—and Othello capable of being easily jealous —in that Desdemona wants to be Othello and he does not want in any way to be Desdemona (his remarks on the bed of war imply that he is naturally a bachelor). Or, to put it another way, what they share is Othello only: her subduing her identity to his means that she leaves him no Desdemona to know. Submission is essential to her nature, in the way that she later takes Othello's cruel treatment and accusations of her, without questioning them or attempting to justify herself (her importunity on behalf of Cassio is a self-assertion imposed upon her by the exigencies of the plot). The fact that both the lovers have so thoroughly refused the claims of the woman against the man, of the public against the private life, business against domesticity, might arguably make Othello peculiarly open to an evil solicitation which has reference to an area of life of which in a sense he has been allowed to remain ignorant. Certainly in this connection it would be significant that when he has become irreversibly jealous he should take particular leave of his professional life: *in his farewell speech.*

Farewell the plumed troop, and the big wars,
That make ambition virtue: O farewell,
Farewell the neighing steed, and the shrill trump,
The spirit-stirring drum, the ear-piercing fife;
The royal banner, and all quality,
Pride, pomp, and circumstance of glorious war!
And, O ye mortal engines, whose wide throats
The immortal Jove's great clamour counterfeit;
Farewell, Othello's occupation's gone!

(III, iii, 355–63)

From this point on Othello becomes increasingly immersed in the private and domestic world, until, like Cassio, he is in his turn cashiered. At the end of the play, with the struggle over and the plot revealed, he declares how 'I have done the state some service, and they know't' (V, ii, 340), and tries in his last act, his own self-murder, to recapitulate the deed he once did on 'a malignant and a turban'd Turk' in the service of the state of Venice.

The larger dimension of this is Othello's absolutism (apart from that of other people in the play). There seems in retrospect something unstable because extreme in his love. Thus his reply to Brabantio's warning, 'She has deceiv'd her father, may do thee'—'My life upon her faith' (I, iii, 293–94)— seems too great a readiness to go to the limit. Similarly we now feel that his declaration to Desdemona when he has come ashore in Cyprus and finds her there before him,

> It gives me wonder great as my content
> To see you here before me: O my soul's joy,
> If after every tempest come such calmness,
> May the winds blow, till they have waken'd death,
> And let the labouring bank climb hills of seas,
> Olympus-high, and duck again as low
> As hell's from heaven. If it were now to die,
> 'Twere now to be most happy, for I fear
> My soul hath her content so absolute,
> That not another comfort, like to this
> Succeeds in unknown fate
>
> (II, i, 183–93; see also 196–97),

is too violent a rapture, however justified his joyful relief. We also feel that Othello sees love not so much as a relationship in time but as a condition founded on moments of intense joy (in both his quoted declarations, even as he asserts his assurance and joy, he thinks of his death): and this seems to be underlined in Desdemona's temporal corrective, 'The heavens forbid/ But that our loves and comforts should increase,/ Even as our days do grow' (193–95).

The obverse of this is Othello's readiness to doubt Desdemona as extremely as he trusted her (though his continuing and largely unacknowledged love for her is at war with this impulse). 'My relief/ Must be to loathe her': of course the jealous person wants certainty, but there is an extraordinary preparedness in Othello to go the whole negative distance; what is important to him is not faith in the other person but self-protection, personal peace of mind. His 'to be once in doubt,/ Is once to be resolv'd' (III, iii, 183–84) intended as an assertion of faith in Desdemona, is ironically the reverse statement. Thus 'I had rather be a toad,/ And live upon the vapour in a dungeon,/ Than keep a corner in a thing I love,/ For others' uses' (ibid., 274–77). Again, when he returns to Iago after meeting Desdemona it is 'Ha, ha, false to me, to me?' and 'I swear, 'tis better to be much abus'd/ Than but to know't a little' (339, 342–43). The same absolutism is behind 'I had been happy if the general camp,/ Pioners, and all, had tasted her sweet body,/ So I had nothing known' (351–53), or his demand, in reverse mode, that Iago prove Desdemona faithless beyond any shadow of question, 'so prove it,/ That the probation bear no hinge, nor loop,/ To hang a doubt on: or woe upon thy life!' (370–72). Even the terms in which he sees Iago's evil, should he be lying about Desdemona, 'Never pray more, abandon all remorse./ On horror's head horrors accumulate:/ Do deeds to make heaven weep, all earth amaz'd,/ For nothing canst thou to damnation add/ Greater than that' (375–79), seems more immediately a product of Othello's extremism than an accurate valuation of sin. The very absoluteness with which he committed himself to faith in Desdemona now pushes him to the opposite: he sees it himself in stark terms of a transformation from white to black:

> By the world,
> I think my wife be honest, and think she is not,
> I think that thou art just, and think thou art not;
> I'll have some proof: my name, that was as fresh
> As Dian's visage, is now begrim'd, and black
> As mine own face: if there be cords, or knives,
> Poison, or fire, or suffocating streams,
> I'll not endure it: would I were satisfied!
>
> (389–96)

It is not that Othello is wholly convinced of his wife's infidelity at once, but that he *wants* to be. It is for this reason that he keeps repeating his absolute renunciations of her: thus when Iago has told him the tale of Cassio's lascivious dream and of Desdemona's handkerchief being in Cassio's possession, he goes again to the limit,

> Now I do see 'tis true; look here, Iago,
> All my fond love thus do I blow to heaven, . . .

79

'Tis gone.
Arise, black vengeance, from thy hollow cell,
Yield up, O love, thy crown, and hearted throne,
To tyrannous hate.

(451–56)

Ironically, having said love has gone, he then asks it to yield up. Othello's psychological condition is one whereby his desperate need for certainty is at odds with his continuing love for Desdemona and is continually surprised and frustrated by it. Iago now goads Othello with calls for patience and moderation, so alien to him—'Patience I say, your mind perhaps may change' (459)—at which Othello falls back on an analogy of revengeful thought as a natural flood which will destroy love.

Never, Iago. Like to the Pontic sea,
Whose icy current, and compulsive course,
Ne'er feels retiring ebb, but keeps due on
To the Propontic, and the Hellespont:
Even so my bloody thoughts, with violent pace
Shall ne'er look back, ne'er ebb to humble love,
Till that a capable and wide revenge
Swallow them up.

(460–67)

The mention of looking back, or of ebbing to humble love rather defeats the object; and Othello goes on to see this as happening when his bloody thoughts have been swallowed up. Sensing the *voulu* element here, he pushes on to a vow which has nothing to do with the mutability of water, 'Now by yond marble heaven,/ In the due reverence of a sacred vow,/ I here engage my words.'

But the point remains Othello's constant desire to be absolute and monochromatic in his responses. By the end of the play his absolutism has reached a point where, rather than moving from tiny evidence to extreme conclusion, the extreme conclusion is used to refute contrary proof. His questioning of Emilia (IV, ii), as soon as the answers exculpate Desdemona, speedily turns to attempted condemnation of the witness, 'She says enough, yet she's a simple bawd/ That cannot say as much: this is a subtle whore,/ A closet, lock and key, of villainous secrets' (20–2; here again there is the unregistered doubt of 'And yet she'll kneel and pray, I ha' seen her do't'

80

(23)). In his subsequent questioning of Desdemona, he does not listen to her answers on her innocence, 'What, not a whore? . . ./ . . . I cry you mercy,/ I took you for that cunning whore of Venice,/ That married with Othello' (88, 90–2). In order to slay Desdemona he has to get into a rage which will permit his extremism to crush all thought of love or pity dragging it back. Even the nature of Desdemona's death seems to sum up Othello's absolutism: he has to wring the life out of her as he thinks he has the love from himself; and just as his feelings cannot wholly be crushed, so he fails to kill her at once and she has speech enough left to expose him should she wish.

Clearly therefore Othello can be seen as easily jealous, whether from the point of view of our being initially shocked at the promptness with which he responds to Iago, or from the retrospective view which finds explanation in the natures of Othello, Desdemona and their love relation for the speed of his submission. Thus the play contrives to give us two impressions, both that Othello is not easily jealous, and that he is. Why is this?

In order to answer this we should look at the precise moral status of the flaws in Othello's relationship with Desdemona, and then consider whether those flaws are confined to them. The first point to make concerning these defects is that no prescription is offered, only description. Desdemona was like this, Othello like that, and that is all. Their limitations, such as they are, do not emerge from any clear moral weakness which would offer us a 'lesson'. In short, they are highly particular. If one asks what made Desdemona want to subdue herself to Othello, no moral or philosophical answer is offered, only, 'Because that was what she was like'; and similarly with Othello, if one asks what made him such an absolutist. This play is full of particular personalities and contingent events. Iago weaves the whole of his plot round the nature of Othello's character as he conceives it—'The Moor [has] a free and open nature . . ./ That thinks men honest that but seems to be so:/ And will as tenderly be led by the nose . . ./ As asses are' (I, iii, 397–400); 'The Moor . . ./ Is of a constant, noble, loving nature' (II, i, 283–84). (The stress on personality here can be contrasted with the attempt in *Macbeth* by Lady Macbeth to obliterate it, in the form both of her own femininity and of her

81

husband's scruples.) Othello, in short, has no clear fault, though he may be unstable. And everything in the play— Othello's blackness, his role in relation to sophisticated Venice, his having a right-hand man like Iago, his going to Cyprus, events there falling out as they (with frequent manipulation) do, Desdemona's persistent importunity over Cassio—is wholly contingent and particular. *Othello* is, indeed, Shakespeare's most 'particular' play, a play without 'significance'.

To put it another way: Othello's absolutism is not to be made over to his jealousy, to which it is anterior. It may be true that, as Iago says (though not specifically of jealousy), 'Dangerous conceits are in their natures poisons,/ Which at the first are scarce found to distaste,/ But with a little act upon the blood/ Burn like the mines of sulphur' (III, iii, 331–34). But the Othello we have seen before he is jealous is absolutist by nature. He is the opposite of Shakespeare's Antony in refusing love any power save a co-operative one over his romantic world and his role as warrior; and Desdemona is the opposite of Cleopatra in accepting this. Othello and Desdemona married are two persons become one in a dangerous sense, for the one that they have become is not a new composite but involves one of the partners engulfing the other (swallowing and engulfing imagery is recurrent in the play). Othello cannot compromise, nor entertain divided loyalties—it is perhaps significant in this connection that when Desdemona publicly commits herself to him she describes her own subjection to such split sympathies, 'My noble father,/ I do perceive here a divided duty. . . .' (I, iii, 180–89): it is certainly a contrast with Othello. Later Desdemona sees that she owes help to Cassio as well as love to Othello; the latter however, becomes wholly committed to Iago and his suspicions. The absolutism which contributes to Othello's becoming suspicious of his wife is not the product of jealousy itself, but is part of Othello's nature. In this sense it emerges only from his particular personality: it is simply a quirk that Othello happened to have. And to this extent it is in no way significant: Othello's extremism is not symbolic of anything but is merely a special personality trait bestowed upon him by his creator; and therefore it must seem wholly arbitrary.

This point concerning arbitrary imposition is sharpened when we consider that Othello's absolutism is not confined to him, but exists throughout the play. Where Othello (at first) and Desdemona see nothing but good in all things (Desdemona is, later in the play, pushed to a point of apparent gullibility in a direction opposite to Othello's, so that she can seem a fool), Iago sees only evil and cynicism: 'Virtue? a fig! 'tis in ourselves, that we are thus, or thus'; love is 'merely a lust of the blood, and a permission of the will' (I, iii, 319–20, 335–36). Similarly, if Othello moves from trifles to absolute doubt of Desdemona, so does Iago in his suspicion of his wife's adultery with Othello, 'I know not if 't be true . . ./ Yet I, for mere suspicion in that kind,/ Will do, as if for surety' (ibid., 386–88)—and this despite his apprehension of Othello as 'of a constant, noble, loving nature' (however subsequently overwhelmed in his 'the lustful Moor' (II, i, 284, 290)). Brabantio speaks as absolutely as Othello of how his 'particular grief' over the loss of his daughter to the Moor 'Is of so flood-gate and o'erbearing nature,/ That it engluts and swallows other sorrows,/ And it is still itself' (I, iii, 55–8). When Roderigo hears of Desdemona's marriage to Othello he vows to Iago, 'I will incontinently drown myself', at which Iago tells him not to make so much fuss over nothing (ibid., 305 ff.). Iago performs a similar function when, on his dismissal as lieutenant by Othello for being drunk on guard, Cassio portrays his loss in apocalyptic terms:

> *Cas.* Reputation, reputation, I ha' lost my reputation! I ha' lost the immortal part, sir, of myself, and what remains is bestial; my reputation Iago, my reputation!
>
> *Iago.* As I am an honest man, I thought you had receiv'd some bodily wound, there is more offence in that than in reputation.
>
> (II, iii, 254–60)

If Iago a little undercuts his own position here, Cassio is absurdly shrill, 'O thou invisible spirit of wine, if thou hast no name to be known by, let us call thee devil!' (273–75), and Iago is right at least in saying 'Come, you are too severe a moraler' (290). But the question that obviously remains is what such extremists are doing in this play in the first place.

The imagery itself of the play is in part founded on absolute contrasts. The central image here is of black and white[19]—

the black Othello and the white Desdemona, and this extends to the pervasive imagery of light and darkness: it expresses total ethical polarity, the tendency to see things in terms of absolute good or bad, which comes to a head in the scene where Othello murders Desdemona—'whiter skin of hers than snow', 'Put out the light' (meaning in one way 'Have done with goodness altogether'). Desdemona who, falling in love with Othello, went beneath the physical appearance, ignored colour, to find 'Othello's visage in his mind', contrasts with Othello, who begins to equate his blackness and the evil he feels done to him, 'my name, that was as fresh/ As Dian's visage, is now begrim'd, and black/ As mine own face' (III, iii, 392–94). The play is also saturated with references to hell and heaven, far more even than the play to which one would think they were more obviously applicable—*Macbeth*. For instance, Iago warns Brabantio to look to his daughter, 'Or else the devil will make a grandsire of you' (I, i, 91); tells Roderigo that he hates Othello 'as I do hell's pains' (ibid. 154); says of his plot, 'Hell and night/ Must bring this monstrous birth to the world's light' (I, iii, 401–2), and 'Divinity of hell!/ When devils will their blackest sins put on,/ They do suggest at first with heavenly shows,/ As I do now' (II, iii, 341–44); or speaks of women as 'Saints in your injuries; devils being offended' (II, i, 111). Brabantio at first thinks Othello used 'practices of cunning hell' to win Desdemona (I, iii, 102). Cassio speaks of Desdemona as 'divine', and invokes 'the grace of heaven' upon her (II, i, 73, 85); he calls the drink that ruins him 'devil' (II, iii, 275, 287, 299). From Othello we hear, 'duck again as low/ As hell's from heaven' (II, i, 188–89), 'If she be false, O, then heaven mocks itself' (III, iii, 282), 'All my fond love thus do I blow to heaven' (ibid. 452), 'Now by yond marble heaven' (ibid. 467), 'the fair devil' (ibid. 485), 'The devil their virtue tempts, and they tempt heaven' (IV, i, 8), 'Devil!' (ibid. 235), 'Had it pleas'd heaven/ To try me with affliction. . . .' (IV, ii, 48–9), 'Patience, thy young and rose lipp'd cherubin,/ I here look grim as hell!' (ibid. 64–5), 'this sorrow's heavenly' (V, ii, 21), or, 'when we shall meet at count,/ This look of thine will hurl my soul from heaven,/ And fiends will snatch at it' (ibid. 274–76). All the characters swear continually by 'hell' and 'heaven'.

In sum, inordinate difficulty and equally inordinate ease characterize Othello's loss of trust in his wife: it seems on the one hand that his love is so perfect as to be violable only by the most extreme and arbitrary means, and on the other that it is so unsteady as to begin to collapse at the least touch. If we put Othello's readiness to doubt down to his absolutism, little of moral significance can be made out of such a trait, and absolutism goes far beyond Othello himself, to pervade the play. It would seem therefore that these features in the play must be referred to divisions in Shakespeare himself, divisions associated with an inability to portray a love relationship in a state of change from healthy to unhealthy. Add to this the fact that Othello and Desdemona are rarely presented together in the play save in the context of imminent separation; that even their courtship is reported, and their public avowals of love before the Venetian Senate are conducted in isolation: and the impression begins to come over that Shakespeare has less sense of love as a relationship lasting and developing over time, than as a series of isolated ecstatic moments; and furthermore that in the end he is not interested so much in love as a *relationship* at all as in the individual in or out of love. Since *Othello* is the only play in which he has to make a changing love relationship central (*Antony and Cleopatra* is a special category), his mode of presentation becomes divided: unable to manage the transition he portrays the love as on the one hand so perfect as to be brought down only by external trickery, and on the other so weak that a straw makes it crumble; he has no way of showing love go bad except by force or by suggesting retrospectively that it always was bad.

These points must now be substantiated from consideration of Shakespeare's treatment of love relationships throughout his work.

Shakespeare and Relationship

First, to put the case again: Shakespeare, it will be argued here, rarely presents a heterosexual relationship in a process of development: his tendency is to portray people as being either wholly in or out of love. Again, while he can give some scope to changing relationships between man and man—as between

Othello and Iago, Brutus and Cassius, or Coriolanus and Aufidius—or among members of the same family, as in *Hamlet, Measure for Measure, Lear* and *The Tempest*, the idea of relationship is not finally of central concern in his plays. Shakespeare's emphasis is primarily on the individual. In the Sonnets, too, even the relationship with the Friend is conducted at a distance, and the far fewer sonnets to the Mistress show the writer as either passionately involved with or wholly repelled by her. To take a contrast, in his *Edward II* Marlowe portrays the king's homosexual liaisons and the consequent disintegration of his marriage; in *Richard II*, with a similar situation, Shakespeare goes no further with Bushy, Bagot and Green than to describe them as favourites and depict only the disastrous effect on the kingdom of the powers to which they are given access; nor is there any hint of jealousy from Richard's wife, from whom in any case he is kept largely separate throughout. Nothing in the nature of drama as a genre inhibits the portrayal of changing relationships—one could cite also the work of Webster, Middleton, Chekhov, Ibsen or Pinter, for example. We may say that there is an element of dramatic convention behind it—it is useful for the sake of intrigue, misunderstanding, or suspense to have one lover separate from another (as can frequently be seen in the works of Beaumont and Fletcher, Massinger, or Ford): but actually Shakespeare is rather non-'conventional' in the more realistic expectations regarding the portrayal of love-relations that his plays awaken, and yet in awakening frustrate. He brings his men and women together on the stage and yet they do not truly interact; he starts by depicting them as married or as lovers and yet has them rarely meet. Certainly, over forty plays of widely differing characters, the recurrence of such situations is remarkable.

In Shakespeare's love-comedies what is portrayed is not the development but the establishment of relationships—and these relationships are often only the end point of a condition of the characters being cut off from or *out* of relation with one another. *A Midsummer Night's Dream* depicts the purging of bad relations between Hermia and Lysander, Helena and Demetrius, Hippolyta and Theseus and Titania and Oberon. At first Demetrius spurns Helena and vies in love with

Lysander for the hand of Hermia, who does not love him. At the same time these lovers 'dote' on the object of their regard: that is, their love is fanciful rather than rational, and in this sense excessive and corruptible. Theseus, in aligning himself with Hermia's father Egeus' demand that his daughter bow to his reason and judgment, shows himself excessive on the other side. The point of the play becomes the removal of 'wrong' love in each lover, and the sorting of lovers into proper couples. 'Dotage' and 'fancy' are changed into true love not by the interactions of the partners of each couple but by magic: Puck (accidentally) uses the flower Love-in-Idleness to make both men fall in love with the rejected Helena, and in the end leaves Demetrius so, but turns Lysander back to love of Hermia. The process of magical change itself, and the suffering it causes before all is put right, represents and accomplishes education in love, whereby fancy and judgment, hitherto at variance, are conjoined. This change works on each character in isolation: it is not the product of a relationship. The relation of Oberon and Titania is treated similarly: Oberon uses magical punishment to bring Titania out of her 'dotage', while he is humbled by his proxy blunders in controlling human fates; when the magical monstrosity that is Bottom transformed to an ass has driven out the monstrosity of excessive cupidity then all things come right—Puck can use the flower correctly, and Oberon and Titania be reunited. But spiritual change is the product neither of growth nor of the impact of one psyche upon another, but the effect of magic. We are to suppose, also, that these alterations and the change from dotage to true love which they imply, accomplish also a similar transformation in the love of Theseus and Hippolyta. With the relationships established, the interest shifts to Bottom's play and the mixture of fun and conceptual statement which it represents. We hear nothing more of the feelings of Demetrius and Helena, or of Lysander and Hermia for one another; their marriages, and that of Theseus and Hippolyta are briefly reported (IV, ii, 15–17); and Theseus, after his reflection to Hippolyta on the nature of love, and his welcome of the lovers, 'Joy and fresh days of love/ Accompany your hearts!', changes the subject, 'Come now, what dances shall we have?' (V, i, 29–30, 32).

In *The Taming of the Shrew* Katherina is tamed by a trick, not by the effect of a relationship: Petruchio acts in isolation against her; and, at the end, the 'relationship' so established simply replaces female with male dominance. In *The Merchant of Venice* a single choice (that of the right casket) does the office of wooing. In *Much Ado About Nothing* Beatrice and Benedick are brought to realize their love for one another by a device (for most of the play they are cut off from one another by their supposed mutual loathing); and Claudio has so little relationship with Hero that he can distrust her instantly upon the accusation of her involvement with Borachio. In *As You Like It* there is no clear relationship between the lovers Rosalind and Orlando, for although in the forest of Arden Rosalind knows who he is while she educates him in the proper method of wooing, she herself is disguised as a man, Ganymede, so that Orlando does not know her. When at last she appears as her true self and Orlando recognizes her, they are married and the play ends. In *Twelfth Night* one of the central themes is that solipsistic vision which ignores the reality of the loved person. Duke Orsino loves in isolation, having no relationship with Olivia and ultimately needing none; and she does not love him. She has cut herself off from the world in excessive devotion to the memory of a dead brother—that is to a relationship which cannot change. Olivia falls in love with Viola disguised as Caesario: there is no relationship here, both because only one partner is doing the loving and because of the hidden sexual incompatibility. The marriages at the end between Orsino and Viola undisguised, and Olivia and Sebastian (Viola's identical twin brother) are founded on no prior psychological development between each couple.

Shakespeare's idea of love is not one of gradual enamourment, as, for example, Sidney's Astrophel describes it, 'Not at first sight, nor with a dribbed shot,/ Love gave the wound which, while I breathe, will bleed,' and, 'I saw, and liked: I liked, but loved not;/ I loved, but straight did not what Love decreed' (*Astrophel and Stella*, ii). This is not to deny that Shakespeare's lovers often have to win their ladies' favour by proving their own love, as Beatrice makes Benedick challenge Claudio for his treatment of wronged Hero, or as the ladies enforce year-long trials on their lovers at the end of *Love's*

Labour's Lost. But such cases are only suspensions of judgments already reached: or, as Phebe in *As You Like It* quotes, ' "Who ever lov'd that lov'd not at first sight?" '

Frequently in Shakespeare's plays a love- or marriage-relationship is no sooner presented or established than it is destroyed or disintegrates. In *Romeo and Juliet* the lovers are enamoured at first sight and soon declare themselves to one another (I, v; II, ii). This love and their feeling for one another remain constant and unchanging from beginning to end: what does change them is the increasing force of external obstacles to their union—first the fact that they are from opposed families, and then Romeo's banishment on his slaying of Tybalt for killing Mercutio. The poignancy of the play lies in the fixed intensity of the love and the destructive power of circumstance and accident. Much of the play is concerned with the struggle for a relationship: the lovers never meet save in dangerous contexts or at a distance; the absence of such relationship seems here summed up in the fact that like Pyramus and Thisbe they do not die together and at the same time, but each in isolation, and one in delusion that the other is dead—exactly as happens again in *Antony and Cleopatra.*

In the 'problem' plays we seem continually to be concerned with divorce. In *Hamlet* we see only the break in the relation of the prince with Ophelia, and nothing of their prior encounters; Hamlet's excessive assertion of his love for her at the end of the play shows how in the context of the evil pervading Denmark he really could not get into 'accurate' relation with anyone. In *Troilus and Cressida* the fact that Helen has left her husband Menelaus creates the spiritual context in which Cressida will be false to Troilus. Troilus is in a sense divorced from Cressida from the outset, since he pays small attention to what she is really like but only to his picture of her. He does not conceive of his relation with her as being a relationship at all, in the sense of its being bounded by time and change; when he sees her deserting him he refuses in part to acknowledge the truth of his senses—'This is, and is not, Cressid': for him she is what he made of her, once for all. Cressida sees herself as falling out of love with Troilus even at the moment she falls into it (III, ii, 147–49); and no sooner have she and Troilus come together than they are sundered by the war. In *All's Well* the central theme is the disjunction between the 'noble' Bertram and his 'meaner' wife Helena. For most of the play Bertram is separated, whether in fact or knowledge, from Helena, and she is able to ensure his marital fidelity only by a trick; and as for his final repentance and love these are drawn out of him in a perfunctory manner which partly undercuts the supposed reconciliation. *Measure for Measure* starts with the separation of Claudio from Juliet by his imprisonment for getting her with child. Angelo wants Isabella only for sexual gratification, not for a relationship, and she does not want him at all; at the end he is made to marry Mariana, for whom he has evinced no affection, and the Duke, who has previously shown no interest in her, nor she in him, marries Isabella.

The motif of divorce is continued in the tragedies and late comedies. Othello's attitude to Desdemona changes while he is in almost total isolation from her. Lady Macbeth is as we shall see in effect no more than a catalyst for her husband's murderous thoughts, after which she and he become steadily more isolated from one another. In *Cymbeline* Posthumus is for most of the play away from Britain and his wife Imogen; the only contact he has with her is in the form of a trick executed by Iachimo to test her fidelity to him—which, so tested, implies his own infidelity and lack of true relationship to her (though he is not ultimately to be seen as personally responsible in this). In *The Winter's Tale* Shakespeare goes further with this theme of suspicion. No sooner have we had the long, happy and unchanging relation of Leontes and Hermione, and of them both to Polixenes, set before us in the opening talk of the courtiers, than like goodness grown to a pleurisy we see Leontes forming suspicions of his wife's behaviour with Polixenes, suspicions which grow in isolation from her until he casts her out, decrees the death of their new-born child and finally hales Hermione to trial. When, faced by the expression of the anger of the oracle in the death of his son Mamillius, Leontes as suddenly repents as before he grew jealous, he is told that his wife has died, and until the end of the play he is not reunited with her. The young lovers in both *The Winter's Tale* and *The Tempest* are, meanwhile, shown as falling in love at once and then remaining in that state of first enamourment throughout, in a steady and undeveloping relationship.[20]

In the histories and Roman plays apart from *Antony and Cleopatra* love does not play a great part. Richard III sums it up in announcing himself 'not made for sportive tricks'. In *1 Henry IV* we see Hotspur either patronizing or leaving his wife; and Hal's wooing of the French princess at the close of *Henry V* is a mere awkward game surrounded by political necessities. Coriolanus' wife Virgilia is only his 'gracious silence'; and though the bond between Coriolanus and his mother gives her power to change his actions, she does not alter his character, to which he constantly reverts. Caesar in *Julius Caesar* ignores the pleas of his wife Calphurnia on the Ides of March, and goes to his death. In this play, however, there is a strong, if briefly-presented, relationship between Brutus and Portia: even here, though, Portia is second fiddle to Brutus' plans, and he sees little of her before she takes her own life.

Relationship in 'Antony and Cleopatra'

Antony and Cleopatra presents one of the most striking portraits of the lack of relationship and development in love in Shakespeare's plays: here a love-bond would seem to be central to the play, and yet in fact, as a bond, it is not. The play is full of actual or possible betrayals—Antony leaving Fulvia for Cleopatra, Cleopatra for Octavia, and Octavia for Cleopatra again; and Cleopatra—possibly—betraying Antony to Thidias, fleeing from Actium, packing cards with Octavius in the second sea-battle, trying to make terms with him after Antony's death. Yet curiously the reactions of the injured parties never strike the note of real pain, never quite sound as though the betrayals really matter.

Take for instance Cleopatra's reaction to the news of Antony's marriage with Octavia. She may want to be angry, but her language and behaviour become comic. The messenger is threatened with absurd torments:

> Hence,
> [*Strikes him.*
> Horrible villain, or I'll spurn thine eyes

91

Like balls before me; I'll unhair thy head,
> [*She hales him up and down.*
Thou shalt be whipped with wire and stew'd in brine,
Smarting in lingering pickle.

(II, v, 62–6)[21]

Shakespeare could easily have made the scene more serious and heart-rending than this: there is nothing inherently funny about feminine jealousy, as the case of Clytemnestra can witness. The same comic effect is present in the later interview with the messenger, where Cleopatra asks him to describe Octavia in detail, and for fear of her temper, he paints Octavia unattractively; after which Cleopatra purrs, 'The fellow has good judgment' (III, iii, 25). This treatment has two effects. First, it tends to reduce Antony's performance in our eyes to the level of an amorous peccadillo. Secondly it suggests either that fidelity is not important to the love relation, or else that Cleopatra cannot hit the right tone or vocabulary to match what Antony has done to her. But then we feel that these may in fact be aspects of one thing: because the love does not exist in simple terms of constancy, it is impossible for either partner to feel true pain at inconstancy; yet, because neither is consciously aware of this fact, they still go through the motions of behaving as though fidelity were essential.[22]

The same is true of the scene (III, xiii) where Thidias comes from Caesar to win over Cleopatra after Actium. He tells her that Octavius knows 'that you embrac'd not Antony/ As you did love, but as you fear'd him,' and after a momentary 'O!' Cleopatra is prepared to fit in with this picture,

> He is a god, and knows
> What is most right. Mine honour was not yielded,
> But conquer'd merely.

(56–62)

She goes on to offer complete submission to Caesar, 'Tell him, from his all-obeying breath I hear/ The doom of Egypt.' Giving Thidias her hand, she remarks that 'Caesar's father oft,/ When he hath mus'd of taking kingdoms in,/ Bestow'd his lips on that unworthy place,/ As it rained kisses.' If all this were simply mockery of Caesar, Enobarbus would not say, as if to Antony, 'Sir, sir, thou art so leaky/ That we must leave thee to thy sinking, for/ Thy dearest quit thee.'

Previously informed by Enobarbus that Cleopatra is betraying him, Antony now enters: 'Favours? By Jove that thunders!' The saurian Thidias retorts bluntly, and Antony flies even further into a rage. But in this rage there is a falsity of tone which prevents us from taking it completely seriously, and from believing that Antony is, himself, finally in earnest. 'Ah, you kite!', 'Take hence this Jack, and whip him,' 'Moon and stars,/ Whip him,' 'Whip him, fellows,/ Till like a boy you see him cringe his face,/ And whine aloud for mercy,' 'Tug him away: being whipp'd/ Bring him again.' Somehow he keeps missing the true accent of anger: the insistence on whipping makes his words ineffectual. Compare Lear when 'shut out' by Goneril, or even Troilus witnessing Cressida's betrayal: there is a harshness, a reality to the pain felt— 'Detested kite . . .!', 'Let it not be believed for womanhood!', 'O false Cressid! false, false, false!' Antony's rage, as rage, does not come over with the weight of an emotion accurately felt—that is, as one in which words match feelings. To say in illustration of one's loss of authority,

> of late, when I cried 'Ho!'
> Like boys unto a muss, kings would start forth,
> And cry, 'Your will?'

is nothing other than to make that authority comical.

When Antony turns on Cleopatra, the air of absurdity thickens,

> Have I my pillow left unpress'd in Rome,
> Forborne the getting of a lawful race,
> And by a gem of women, to be abus'd
> By one that looks on feeders?

This is no more than to say, 'Have I thrown over Octavia— to marry whom I was false to you—in order to be thrown over by *you*?' Whatever Antony says after this it must be preposterous. What he in fact does is turn Cleopatra into a comic *summa* of indiscriminate sexual appetite,

93

> I found you as a morsel, cold upon
> Dead Caesar's trencher: nay, you were a fragment
> Of Gnaeus Pompey's, besides what hotter hours,
> Unregister'd in vulgar fame, you have
> Luxuriously pick'd out. For I am sure,
> Though you can guess what temperance should be,
> You know not what it is.

The excessive *meiosis* makes us laugh, and indeed Antony seems almost to enjoy pursuing it from Caesar to Pompey. How far this is from Othello's 'Was this fair paper, this most goodly book,/ Made to write "whore" on?'! Even more comic are the last three lines from Antony as he is now: and indeed he goes on to announce this explicitly,

> O, that I were
> Upon the hill of Basan, to outroar
> The horned herd, for I have savage cause,
> And to proclaim it civilly, were like
> A halter'd neck, which does the hangman thank
> For being yare about him.

The final proof of his instability here comes when Cleopatra, catching him at a point of temporary exhaustion, dislodges him from his position with an assertion which sounds more certain than he does. When he asks, 'Cold-hearted toward me?', she declares,

> Ah, dear, if I be so,
> From my cold heart let heaven engender hail,
> And poison it in the source, and the first stone
> Drop in my neck: as it determines, so
> Dissolve my life; the next Cæsarion smite
> Till by degrees the memory of my womb,
> Together with my brave Egyptians all,
> By the discandying of this pelleted storm,
> Lie graveless, till the flies and gnats of Nile
> Have buried them for prey!

After this Antony can only reply, 'I am satisfied,' and change the subject.

Something of the idiom of the Thidias scene recurs even after the final sea-battle, when Antony comes in roaring that Cleopatra has betrayed him to Caesar (IV, xii). His speech misses full seriousness, 'This foul Egyptian hath betrayed me,' 'Triple-turn'd whore', 'this grave charm', 'right gypsy', 'The witch shall die,/ To the young Roman boy she hath sold me.' When Cleopatra enters, he tells her to 'Vanish, or I shall give thee thy deserving,/ And blemish Caesar's triumph'; and bids her, 'let patient Octavia plough thy visage up/ With her prepared nails,' which, with its suggestion of the whetstone and its alliterative slaver of anticipation, seems as far from harsh as it is from Lear's confident threat to the inhospitable Goneril, that when Regan hears of her performance, 'with her nails/ She'll flay thy wolvish visage.' The inaccuracy of Antony's feelings is demonstrated in his immediate *volte-face* (similar to that in the Thidias scene) when he is told that Cleopatra is dead, 'I will o'ertake thee, Cleopatra, and/ Weep for my pardon' (IV, xiv, 44–5).

Clearly with all these 'betrayals', actual enough as they are to the injured party, the reception of the news is comic enough to make us question the real seriousness of the offence to the sufferer. The tone in the language of both lovers is frequently not only far from tragic, but also false to the emotion ostensibly felt. And the reason for this may be stated as that for much of the play the love of Antony and Cleopatra has considerably less to do with fidelity or with a relationship existing through time than they think—and thus they are continually behaving on the assumption that it is founded on a bond demanding trust where, in the end, it is not.

We may say that the essence of the love of Antony and Cleopatra rests in moments of ecstasy, flashes of light, when, as Cleopatra puts it, 'Eternity was in our lips, and eyes,/ Bliss in our brows' bent' (I, iii, 35–6—it is typical of the love that its eternity should be described as finding itself only in the transient). Cydnus is one such moment: and, significantly, at her death Cleopatra relives it, 'I am again for Cydnus,/ To meet Mark Antony.' 'That time? O times!—' she says, looking back while Antony is away: the phrase catches moments of pleasure come randomly to white heat. But only at random: to try self-consciously to *make* such moments is always to fail—just as the love itself cannot be fixed in a relationship. When Antony returns from his temporary victory against Octavius, Cleopatra greets him, 'Lord of lords,/ O infinite virtue, com'st thou smiling from/ The world's great snare

95

uncaught?'; and he replies,

> My nightingale,
> We have beat them to their beds. What, girl, though grey
> Do something mingle with our younger brown, yet ha' we
> A brain that nourishes our nerves, and can
> Get goal for goal of youth. Behold this man,
> Commend unto his lips thy favouring hand:
> Kiss it, my warrior.
>
> (IV, viii, 16–24)

We feel here an element of romanticizing not far removed from the idiom of Tennyson's Ulysses. Both Antony and Cleopatra are consciously playing the parts of the Old but not Contemptible and the Male-Worshipping Lover-Queen in order to manufacture a poignant moment out of their love. (A director could point up the falsity of this when Cleopatra extends her regal hand to Scarus, by having the soldier uncertain quite what he is to do—which could explain Antony's prompting 'Kiss it, my warrior.')

Just as the love of Antony and Cleopatra does not make up a relationship, so it cannot be said to develop. It simply oscillates between trust and distrust until the end. The oscillation produces no development: the change described in Caesar's image of the changing loyalties of the populace,

> This common body,
> Like to a vagabond flag upon the stream,
> Goes to, and back, lackeying the varying tide,
> To rot itself with motion
>
> (I, iv, 44–7),

which is sometimes adduced to symbolize supposed changes in the love of Antony and Cleopatra, is cancelled out by an Antonine image whereby such oscillation is seen as producing not decay but fruitfulness:

> The higher Nilus swells,
> The more it promises: as it ebbs, the seedsman
> Upon the slime and ooze scatters his grain,
> And shortly comes to harvest.
>
> (II, vii, 20–3)

Till the very end there is no spiritual development in the protagonists; we do not often see them together. There is little inner life in the play, and hardly any soliloquy. The distance between the first scene, in which Antony rejects the world for love, and the deaths of the lovers is a purely narrative one, whereby their love is reduced to having no place on earth to exist.

It has often been pointed out that Egypt, unlike Rome, is a context in which it is impossible to measure or to be precise, and that it is this that determines the special lack of fixity in the love of Antony and Cleopatra. Even acknowledgment of this lack of measure is itself undermined in Egypt: Antony's first words, 'There's beggary in the love that can be reckon'd' are at once countered by Cleopatra's 'I'll set a bourn how far to be belov'd'; and it is she at the end who sees Antony in gigantic terms.[23] She does not for much of the play know whether Antony is to her the third in line of her Roman admirers or her 'man of men' (I, v, 66–75); and Antony is in similar case with her. To live in Egypt is to be beset with ambiguity and uncertainty: the play is full of incidents in which we cannot be quite certain of what is happening—whether Cleopatra was prepared to treat with Thidias, whether she meant to betray Antony with her fleet, whether she had any idea of temporizing with Caesar after Antony's death.[24] The oft-remarked imagery of melting and 'discandying' that runs through the play can be seen as in part an expression of the indefinite, ungraspable character of the love, as indeed may the play's very formlessness, with one act running into another and no clear structure or definite finale (the two separate and slow deaths of the central figures). Perhaps the most striking image in this connection is that in which Antony speaks of his fixed identity as fading like a cloud or water in water under the influence of his experience (IV, xiv, 1–14).

It is true that at the end of the play something like constancy enters the love of Antony and Cleopatra. Before his suicide Antony speaks for the first time of himself as a bridegroom; his death is in one way a contract of loyalty to Cleopatra, a way of 'fixing' his love for ever (IV, xiv, 99–101). Similarly Cleopatra speaks of Antony as a 'husband' (V, ii, 286–87), and also, with all her deviousness, shows a loyalty to the dead Antony which she did not *certainly* exhibit to him alive.[25] She declares herself no longer changeable but 'marble-constant' (V, ii, 239). As Ernest Schanzer has pointed out,[26] the imagery and phraseology used by Antony become increasingly mirrored by those of Cleopatra towards the end of the play: the two are to some extent 'married' by it. Nevertheless the relationship cannot be said to have altered, since except in the realms of hope, there is no more relationship; and further, each of these changes in attitude takes place independent of the other partner, and when that partner is or is felt to be 'fixed' in death.

Although what we may now designate as the absence of a developing relationship between Antony and Cleopatra could be explained in terms of the particular spiritual environment of this play, it is clear that seen against the absence of developing amorous relationships throughout Shakespearean drama, this explanation is not only local but question-begging: why did Shakespeare choose to create a context in which the lovers would be incapable of having a relationship? And this returns us to our contention, namely, that Shakespeare, for whatever reason, is simply incapable of portraying a love-relation that lasts through time and develops under its pressure. His lovers are people of the either/or—either wholly for or against the beloved; Antony, significantly, is described as an extremist in all things.

The rest, of course, is surmise. We know that, apart from occasional visits to Stratford, Shakespeare was absent from his wife Ann Hathaway for most of their marriage. It can readily be supposed therefore both that *that* relationship did not change very much, and that there really can have been little of what one would term 'relationship' in it. What Shakespeare felt about his wife we cannot know for certain, but we can risk the guess, from the tendency in his plays and in his sonnets to portray heterosexual love in polarized terms of good or bad, that he continually oscillated between feelings whose extremity was exacerbated by his distance from her.

NOTES

1. For a previous account of this, see Kenneth Muir, *Shakespeare's Tragic Sequence* (Liverpool, Liverpool University Press, 1979), pp. 106–14.

2. References are to the Arden *Othello*, ed. M. R. Ridley (Methuen, 1958). For the range of opinions on Iago's jealousy see e.g. A. C. Bradley, *Shakespearean Tragedy*, 2nd ed. (Macmillan, 1905), pp. 222–37; R. B. Heilman, *Magic in the Web: Action and Language in 'Othello'* (Lexington, Kentucky, University of Kentucky Press, 1956), pp. 30–4, 95–6; Bernard McElroy, *Shakespeare's Mature Tragedies* (Princeton, N.J., Princeton University Press, 1973), pp. 103–6, 109; and their references.
3. And the fact that Iago does not refer directly to these motives again would also be telling (Bradley, pp. 222–26) had the play been *about* him after the first two acts, but in fact Iago becomes simply functional in the production of jealousy, and is not again considered for himself until the end.
4. But no more clumsy than, for example, Prospero's recapitulation to Miranda and to Ariel of their past history in *The Tempest*, I, ii.
5. See also Muir, pp. 75–6.
6. For a critical survey of Christian readings of *Othello*, see Robert H. West, 'The Christianness of *Othello*', *SQ*, 15 (1964), pp. 333–43.
7. Cf. E. E. Stoll, *'Othello': An Historical and Comparative Study* (Minneapolis, University of Minnesota Press, 1915), who says that Iago's plan depends on luck and that he succeeds only because *'ainsi le veut l'auteur'* (pp. 29, 41).
8. Thomas Rymer, *A Short View of Tragedy* (1693), repr. in J. E. Spingarn, ed., *Critical Essays of the Seventeenth Century* (Oxford University Press, 1908), II, pp. 221, 252.
9. Ibid., p. 224; see also pp. 242, 244, 246. For later accounts see e.g. Margaret L. Ranald, 'The Indiscretions of Desdemona', *SQ*, 14 (1963), 127–39; A. L. French, *Shakespeare and the Critics* (Cambridge, Cambridge University Press, 1972), pp. 95–101.
10. The time-scheme of the play, whereby it would have been impossible for Cassio to have committed adultery with Desdemona after her actual marriage to Othello, is less of a problem since Arthur McGee's 'Othello's Motive for Murder', *SQ*, 15 (1964), 45–54, which shows that in Shakespeare's day a betrothal or engagement before marriage (often the gift of a handkerchief) was frequently taken as a true contract, or *sponsalia de praesenti*. Betrayal before the legal ceremony would in this case be felt as adultery.
11. This part of the scene is not in the source, but Shakespeare perhaps took the notion of uncertain identity from the scene where the Captain flees, partially glimpsed, from the Moor's house.
12. Stoll, p. 21, sees this as pure convention.
13. In Cinthio's account Cassio has not been a go-between, but nonetheless recognizes the handkerchief and attempts to return it.
14. Further, as Stoll points out (pp. 40, 42), Desdemona herself does not recall the episode when questioned about the handkerchief by Othello, and Emilia does not speak up about the handkerchief when she has cause and opportunity.
15. It need hardly be added that while there is an element of 'unfairness' in most tragedy, what we are concerned with here is an unfairness

which has no connection with a pattern of fate, providence or sin and retribution, and which in no way answers to the conceivable vicissitudes of life.

16. D. R. Godfrey, 'Shakespeare and the Green-Eyed Monster', *Neophilologus*, 56 (1972), 219.
17. E.g. I, ii, 25–8, 65, 98–9; I, iii, 182, 195–98, 265, 397; II, ii, 8–10; II, iii, 328, 332–33, 336; III, i, 39, 56; III, iii, 7, 117–19, 138–39, 189, 199, 203–4, 214, 217, 259, 290, 346, 422, 471, 477; III, iv, 34, 36, 42, 118, 126; V, ii, 54, 221, 303. And, incidentally, the death of Desdemona, unlike that in the source, is by smothering.
18. See the fine account in John Holloway, *The Story of the Night*, pp. 42–5, 158–65.
19. See also Doris Adler, 'The Rhetoric of Black and White in *Othello*', *SQ*, 25 (1974), 248–57.
20. However, it should be said that the accounts of Albany and Goneril in *Lear* and of Cleon and Dionyza in *Pericles* do concern developing marital relationships. Albany sees Goneril's evil and says so, but yet remains on her side with the forces of Regan and Edmund until the end; and Dionyza, who has treacherously plotted against the life of Marina, brings her husband into collusion despite his outrage at her. Here Shakespeare has described relationships in which there is psychological interaction and development, if both play minor and brief parts in their plays.
21. References are to the Arden *Antony and Cleopatra*, ed. M. R. Ridley (Methuen, 1954).
22. Contrast Brents Stirling, *Unity in Shakespearian Tragedy: The Interplay of Theme and Character* (New York, Columbia University Press, 1956), pp. 157–92, who explains the comic element only in terms of Shakespeare seeking to make the lovers look partially absurd—that is, as a comment by the author rather than an expression of the nature of the characters.
23. On this and the theme of measure in the play see Janet Adelman, *The Common Liar: An Essay on 'Antony and Cleopatra'* (New Haven, Yale University Press, 1973), pp. 102–57.
24. See also Adelman, pp. 14–24.
25. However both also speak of themselves as lovers in the afterworld (IV, xiv, 50–4; V, ii, 294–302): this is a marriage of hearts, not a legal (and 'measurable') contract.
26. Schanzer, *The Problem Plays of Shakespeare* (Routledge and Kegan Paul, 1963), pp. 134–38.

5

King Lear

Lear is perhaps the finest product of Shakespeare's preoccupation with dividedness. Throughout the play there are frequent gaps between what we would expect and what we find performed, whether it be by the characters or by the universe in general. Our demand for pattern is continually refused, at progressively deeper levels; seeming chaos covers order, and that order a further chaos. By being forced into moving from one level of comprehension to another (like the characters, who are continually on the move) we are brought to experience the vision of the play directly.

Much is said, not only by critics, but by the characters themselves within this play concerning its meaning, and the pattern of spiritual development it portrays: yet it is on the surface one of the most chaotic plays Shakespeare wrote. The characters act absurdly or without clear motive; the plot seems extremely clumsy; the central figure is for much of the time mad and often incomprehensible, and there seems no coherent or established line of psychic development on his part;[1] and, seemingly near to a misanthropic vision, what would seem peccadilloes are treated as ultimately heinous crimes, so that the reverse of Lear's 'None does offend' seems equally strongly maintained.

To take the last point first. The original sin of Gloucester lay in begetting a bastard, Edmund, who like that sin is to rise up against him and wreak vengeance. The Gloucester we see at the beginning of the play is certainly rather seedy, a somewhat ignorant old hearty enjoying his mannish joke with Kent: 'though this knave [Edmund] came something saucily to the world before he was sent for, yet was his mother fair; there was good sport at his making, and the whoreson must be acknowledged.'² But no more than this, and indeed any fault in his lechery is at least socially excused. Gloucester is at first lewdly indirect: to which,

> *Kent.* I cannot conceive you.
>
> *Glou.* Sir, this young fellow's mother could; whereupon she grew round-womb'd, and had, indeed, Sir, a son for her cradle ere she had a husband for her bed. Do you smell a fault?
>
> *Kent.* I cannot wish the fault undone, the issue of it being so proper.
>
> (I, i, 12–18)

This is certainly insensitive and vulgar, but we do not feel it to be more.

When Lear enters (and before) no one questions the sense of dividing the kingdom as he proposes, though we may. At this stage it can appear that he is bringing into being an explosive political situation. Yet in one way it is hard to see how the situation could be otherwise. He is old, and his daughters will soon have the kingdom anyway. Without a male heir the problem of political instability is inevitable. By the rule of primogeniture the kingdom should go to whichever is the older of Regan and Goneril, since we know that Cordelia is the youngest daughter: yet it is clear from what we see later in the play (and from the hinted rivalry of the Dukes of Albany and Cornwall in the first scene) that should only one daughter be given the kingdom, another would not be slow in the attempt to unseat her: it is specifically to this end that Lear has divided his kingdom relatively equally among all three, 'that future strife/ May be prevented now' (I, i, 44–5). It is beyond this point that we sense personal folly in Lear, however. He proposes to abdicate and not to abdicate: he will remain king without the burdens of his office; he wishes to renounce his cares while retaining his ceremonious pride. Our sense of his folly moves towards an intuition of his ignorance not only of his own children but of himself when he announces that he will divide the land according to public protestations of love for him to be uttered by each daughter in turn, 'Which of you shall we say doth love us most?' (I, i, 51). This 'love-test' has often been seen to be absurd, an un-

realistic folk-tale device calling for a rather strained sus-
pension of disbelief on our part, but it is arguable that its very
absurdity, the gap in comprehension we experience in coming
upon it, mirrors the gap in Lear's comprehension of the true
natures of his own children.

By this point Lear's folly is certainly more evident and
greater than Gloucester's, and it involves moral ignorance
both of self and others close to him, but one does not yet feel it
a positive evil: it is only when Cordelia in effect refuses the
outrage of the test that we are made aware of the deeper
implications and origins of what Lear is doing, and this is now
exemplified in his apparently unwarranted and over-violent
outburst against her, in which he casts her off:

>   by the sacred radiance of the sun,
> The mysteries of Hecate and the night,
> By all the operation of the orbs
> From whom we do exist and cease to be,
> Here I disclaim all my paternal care,
> Propinquity and property of blood,
> And as a stranger to my heart and me
> Hold thee from this for ever. The barbarous Scythian,
> Or he that makes his generation messes
> To gorge his appetite, shall to my bosom
> Be as well neighbour'd, pitied, and reliev'd,
> As thou my sometime daughter.
>
> (109–20)[3]

This goes far beyond the frustrated rage of a doting parent: it
exhibits the evil from which such folly issues, and does so to
added effect through the sudden sheer break with the manner
which has preceded it. The steady authority and control with
which Lear stated his intentions ('Give me the map there.
Know that we have divided. . . .', 'We have this hour a
constant will to publish. . . .', even the lines opening the above
speech, 'Let it be so; thy truth then be thy dower') now
change to a picture of a man at the mercy of himself, his own
passion's slave, dethroned from reason. We suddenly see that
his giving up rule expresses the rule he has given up over
himself; and that it is self-slavery on his part which is
projecting itself into making others his masters. In short, we
perceive that the entire abdication scene has ultimately no

political cause behind it, nor even mere folly: it symbolizes
abdication from control over not only the passions but evil
itself. But the point is the *seeing*: at first we do not, now we do;
at first we are easy-going with and blind to sin, now we are
rigorous and wide-eyed. Seeing and insight are of course
central themes in *Lear*. What counts though is our involvement. We perceive that we judged shallowly, and in this way
we are educated. We are made to follow lines of spiritual
development parallel to those which the characters are to
undergo. And the means by which this is brought about is by
a technique of disjunction, of apparent incongruity in motives
and acts or a seeming lack of pattern which forces us to look
beneath the surface to find the deeper connections; as Kent
puts it, 'See better' (I, i, 158).[4]

This method of using what seem at a psychological level to
be discontinuities to drive us to a deeper reading is also to be
seen in the abdication scene when Cordelia gives her apparently rather bleak and unloving reply to Lear's demand that
she tell him how much she loves him. Her immediate
response is 'Nothing'; then 'I cannot heave/ My heart into my
mouth'; then 'I love your Majesty/ According to my bond; no
more nor less'; then

> Good my Lord,
> You have begot me, bred me, lov'd me: I
> Return those duties back again as are right fit,
> Obey you, love you, and most honour you.
> Why have my sisters husbands, if they say
> They love you all? Happily, when I shall wed,
> That lord whose hand must take my plight shall carry
> Half my love with him, half my care and duty:
> Sure I shall never marry like my sisters,
> To love my father all.
>
> (I, i, 87–104)

It is, as Bradley said, an 'unhappy speech'. The limp list of
returned duties, the bleak measurement and division of love
(which is part of what is detestable in Lear's attitude) and the
handholds offered for those who wish to see her as a jealous
prig, seem to banish goodness even at the moment where we
are asked to feel that it is in operation. Surely, it is sometimes
posed, if she really loved her father she might have humoured

him here, seen his emotional needs more than his moral ones? This, however, is in part to endorse Lear's self-pitying view of himself. Some critics are prepared without further ado to see Cordelia as less than perfect here: one, A. L. French, even argues that the 'fact' that Cordelia is not a saint means that saintliness, and hence spiritual perfectibility, are never a real issue in Lear;[5] and certainly, if one does accept that Cordelia here is 'bitterly angry—absolutely furious at the way her father has put her in a false position',[6] then this picture is hard to reconcile with the later portrait of her as perfection or as 'queen/ Over her passion' (IV, iii, 14–15).

But it is mistaken to stop short at psychology:[7] the gap in expected behaviour (mirroring the frustration of Lear's own expectations) invites a different type of reading. Cordelia, Regan and Goneril are alike Lear's children, and as children extensions of himself. That side of Lear's spirit which is of a piece with the natures of Regan and Goneril is dominant at the beginning of the play. Cordelia cannot speak because he cannot hear her—cannot hear her as she is, but only false-hoods of the kind that come easily to Goneril and Regan. (The way that Lear listens only to his evil daughters here is ironically extended later when he can hear nothing *but* them, in the sense that he blames everything in the universe on them—III, ii, 9, 14–24; III, iv, 14–20, 63–4, 69–75; III, vi, 15–79; IV, vi, 97–133.) In order for Cordelia to speak at all, she has to use Lear language, has to have her love filtered through the evil medium that chokes the beginning of the play. Or, in other terms, fair must appear foul where foul appears fair. This symbolic or 'spiritual' level of reading is forced on us by the jerk we feel; and is, incidentally, encour-aged by the unreal, folk-tale mode of the love-test itself. And it extends throughout the play. Lear's banishment of Cordelia symbolizes his spiritual ignorance, and his eventual tem-porary re-discovery of her marks the presence of some goodness and understanding in him. His folly in dividing the kingdom gives evil scope; his departure from Regan and Goneril is in terms of the spiritual narrative their final separation from humanity and the beginning of his journey from inhumanity; and his loss of reason is matched in their descent from control to naked cruelty. In a sense Lear dies at the end of the play because all his children are dead. Similarly, the fact that he begot one pure and two evil children expresses the random character of the universe, whereby good and evil spring together, or, as Cordelia puts it 'idle weeds . . . grow/ In our sustaining corn' (IV, iv, 5–6). This spiritual narrative also explains the disguising of themselves by Kent and Edgar. Since Lear and Gloucester cannot recognize goodness, or give a place to it in themselves, it must go disguised until they can. Lear and Gloucester are for the time disguised from themselves.

Why later does the disguised Kent behave as he does to Oswald, steward to Goneril? When Kent returns to Lear's service disguised as Caius, Goneril has lost patience at a lengthy sojourn in her castle of her father and one hundred of his knights, who, according to her, are behaving in an unendurably riotous and abusive manner; she has bid Oswald treat them all more coldly, so that matters may 'come to question' (I, iii). Kent is present when Lear tries to force renewed subservience out of Oswald:

> *Lear.* O! you sir, you, come you hither, sir. Who am I, sir?
> *Osw.* My Lady's father.
> *Lear.* 'My Lady's father!' my Lord's knave: you whoreson dog! you slave! you cur!
> *Osw.* I am none of these, my Lord; I beseech your pardon.
> *Lear.* Do you bandy looks with me, you rascal?
> > [*Striking him.*
> *Osw.* I'll not be strucken, my Lord.
> *Kent.* Nor tripp'd neither, you base foot-ball player.
> > [*Tripping up his heels.*
> *Lear.* I thank thee, fellow; thou serv'st me, and I'll love thee.
> *Kent.* Come, sir, arise, away! I'll teach you differences: away, away! If you will measure your lubber's length again, tarry; but away! Go to; have you wisdom? [*Exit Oswald.*] So.
> *Lear.* Now, my friendly knave, I thank thee: there's earnest of thy service. [*Gives Kent money.*
> > (I, iv, 82–99)

Obviously there is scope for an actor to make Oswald appear unpleasant by giving his words a sarcastic or mocking tone, but there is no certain warrant for doing this, and his language and behaviour seem most immediately those of a

106

polite servant doing the duty required of him by his mistress. And while his refusal to recognize Lear as King is effectively a deadly insult to his pride, it is so far as the facts are concerned no less than just. Our first feelings are more likely to be that the behaviour of Lear somewhat bears out Goneril's complaint, and that Kent's performance is that of a retainer seeking to earn favour by imitating the behaviour of his master. Nevertheless we are also, contradictorily, aware that Kent can gain little from serving Lear, and that his reason for entering Lear's service was, as he told him, that 'you have that in your countenance which I would fain call master'— 'that' being 'Authority' (I, iv, 29–32); and immediately after this passage with Oswald the Fool offers Kent his coxcomb 'for taking one's part that's out of favour' (104). Kent sees the regality that is native to Lear, not the trappings, and serves it when he cannot gain by it. Yet this scene is so presented that he appears the time-pleasing lackey he is not: again we are asked to push beyond the surface appearance and make the deeper connections.

When Lear finally breaks with Goneril, he decides to go to Regan, sending Kent ahead to her with a letter describing his experience at Goneril's hands. Meanwhile Goneril has despatched Oswald to her sister to ensure that Regan's treatment of Lear does not differ from her own. Kent meets Oswald before Gloucester's castle by moonlight. To Oswald's request as to where his group may set their horses, Kent tells him, 'I' th' mire' (II, ii, 4). Oswald says he does not recognize Kent, but Kent does him, and proceeds at length to describe him as a time-serving knave. Oswald is astounded. 'Why, what a monstrous fellow art thou, thus to rail on one that is neither known of thee nor knows thee!'; but Kent retorts, 'What a brazen-fac'd varlet art thou, to deny thou knowest me!' He then bids Oswald draw, accusing him of coming to Regan from Goneril with letters against the king (not *on the surface* true, since Goneril's letter seemed designed only to preserve a common front to Lear's 'abuses'); Oswald calls for help and Kent starts to beat him. At the noise, enter Edmund, Cornwall, Regan, Gloucester and servants. Oswald, who has in fact been worsted, insists that the struggle had come to a point where only Kent's age made him spare his life. Kent maintains a constant flow of detraction of Oswald, ending in a warning to the assembled company against slaves of his ilk, who 'turn their halcyon beaks/ With every gale and vary of their masters,/ Knowing nought, like dogs, but following' (79–81)—which is in fact on the face of it what we have seen rather more of from himself in the preceding scene with Lear (though looking back further we recall that it was precisely Kent's refusal to turn his halcyon beak for Lear, his open defiance of his master, which had him turned away and reduced to the disguised condition of an apparent toady in the first place). When Gloucester asks what caused the quarrel, Kent replies, 'No contraries hold more antipathy/ Than I and such a knave' (88–9); and when Cornwall asks him why he calls him knave, 'His countenance likes me not' (91). Cornwall, with apparent justification in the midst of so seemingly unjustified a motive, replies, 'No more, perchance, does mine, nor his, nor hers'; to which Kent has this to say:

> Sir, 'tis my occupation to be plain:
> I have seen better faces in my time
> Than stands on any shoulder that I see
> Before me at this instant.

This it is that eventually lands Kent in the stocks.

We are meant at first to feel that Kent's behaviour is unwarranted so that at a deeper level we may see its justification. Later on (II, iv, 27–45), he offers more 'concrete' reasons for his dislike of Oswald, but these are withheld here so that we should feel that his behaviour has no simple cause or reason. Oswald, who has had two previous meetings with Kent, on one of which the latter made his character strongly felt, says he does not know him. He can have no reason not to recognize him, for he has nothing to lose: we must therefore explain his anomalous behaviour at a spiritual rather than a merely psychological level of causation—he cannot know or recognize Kent because he is falsehood and Kent plain-spoken truth; and his ignorance of such truth shows his ignorance of himself. What is also suggested is that the Oswalds of this world have no sense of human individuality or identity: on the evil side in this play there are two sisters, interchangeable in nature one with the other; and part of

Lear's evil in the opening scene was the attempt to reduce the personalities of his daughters to the level of rubber stamps of his own desires. We are constantly pushed beyond the merely psychological level of reading. What is shown here and elsewhere in the play is that to judge by the criteria of normal and reasonable behaviour is totally inadequate where good and evil are so starkly opposed. Here, as Christ put it, 'He that is not with me is against me';[8] the polarity of 'all' and 'nothing' is a *leitmotif* of the play. If Oswald has any of our sympathy, we are placed with those who punish Kent, with the evil—there is no compromise. No *reason* is needed for hating Oswald: 'His countenance likes me not.' It is at such a primal and instinctive response, whether of unreasoning and unmotivated virtue or vice, that the action of much of the play is conducted.[9] If Lear says 'reason not,' so does the play. In this sense, to judge by the mere superficies may be to make the reverse of a superficial judgment. (Equally, as is characteristic of this play, it may not be: it is Kent also who, presumably not merely polite, says to Gloucester of his illegitimate fathering of Edmund, 'I cannot wish the fault undone, the issue of it being so proper' (I, i, 17–18).) Kent is, like us watching this play, helpless to do much with his insight. But he has at least become more comprehending; and so, the play suggests, if we will see, may we. Thus by such apparent breaks in motive or justification or reason we are invited to come out of our normal, morally careless selves, to sympathize at a deeper level and to see the ultimate implications of being unable to do so.

The case is similar in the portrayal of the growth of evil in the drama. It has recently been argued that Goneril and Regan are fairly reasonable people for the first half of the play, and that, operating by a desire to simplify the moral issues, Shakespeare then proceeded to degrade and blacken them, starting with the episode of blinding Gloucester.[10] But the very violence of Gloucester's blinding is meant to jerk us away from any lax complicity and sympathy we have felt with them thitherto, as we were jerked with the savagery of Lear's outburst to Cordelia. Lear and his knights may have been a provocation to Goneril, but if she were true and loved him to the extent she protested, she would also exercise the key virtues of this play,

109

love and patience, in dealing with her father, rather than seek to provoke matters further on her own side. But she is, in a key word of the play, nothing: she has, like the speaker in Blake's 'Poison Tree' nothing to put against her anger, 'I told it not, my wrath did grow.' In some ways too she is like Macbeth: she feels no bond for her father, no motion of virtue towards him, and therefore vice may enter unopposed; her own and her sister's hollow protestations of love for Lear indeed directly parallel those of loyalty for Duncan expressed by Macbeth; unlike them, however, Macbeth is at least encumbered with something of a guilty imagination.

We can see how the evil, finding no barrier, grows in Goneril during her first conversation with Oswald. At first she says, 'If you come slack of former services,/ You shall do well; the fault of it I'll answer'; but then she makes it an order from herself, and there is no more talk of faults, 'Put on what weary negligence you please,/ You and your fellows; I'd have it come to question' (I, iii, 10–11, 13–14). But the 'question' is not really 'open discussion' but 'contentious debate': what she wants is an open breach—

> If he distaste it, let him to my sister,
> Whose mind and mine, I know, in that are one,
> Not to be over-rul'd. Idle old man,
> That still would manage those authorities
> That he hath given away!
>
> (15–19)

She does not know surely that Regan's mind is at one with hers, or she would not feel an immediate need to write her a letter to make it so (26–7): distrust opens even as trust is asserted. She rebukes Lear for being as obdurate as she says she and her sister are; and though Lear may have yielded one authority in giving up kingship, he still deserves from his daughters the dues of a father. Goneril's complaint, super-ficially reasonable as it may appear, is in fact morally blind and corrupt. She now moves to even more deliberate purpose, and darker hints, 'I would breed from hence occasions, and I shall,/ That I may speak' (25–6): here she is beginning to think not so much of a local but of a more final solution to the Lear question. As yet her moves are done behind her servants;

but she is preparing to turn Lear off in person. She engineers things so that Lear will seem to provoke the quarrels, and she can wash her hands of blame. As she says, 'If he distaste it, let him to my sister': it is in precisely the same way that she, Edmund, Cornwall and Regan later bring Lear to the point where he can do nothing but leave Gloucester's castle for the heath, where it can appear that he went of his own free will rather than that he was largely brought to it by their provocation of his rage.[11]

Any suggestion that Lear should have been reasonable and accepted hospitality on his daughters' terms, with his followers dismissed, seems mistaken.[12] What is going on between Lear and his daughters is in part a battle of authorities: Goneril and Regan are seeking in fact if not immediately in overt purpose to strip Lear of the effects of majesty with which he still surrounds himself. At a common-sense level they may have some right: so far as we can tell from Lear's own character, his followers, who must to some extent express (indeed symbolize) it, are probably riotous and unmannerly as Goneril claims—and we have some illustration in Kent's behaviour. Further, as Regan says, it is difficult to see how two households could co-exist happily under one roof (II, iv, 242–44). It is clear too that at the level of actual wrongs done to him, Lear's outbursts against Regan and Goneril, like those against Cordelia, are grossly in excess of the apparent provocation, and that they are in part a picture of Lear's own diseased spirit. But they point us to the level which does matter in the play, the level not so much of deeds but of the moral nature from which they issue. The central fact is that Goneril and Regan said they loved their father more than anything else in the world. At the level of practical politics they may have been wise to be hypocrites, but this play is concerned with the deeper stratum of the horror that they *are* hypocrites, that though they may have some surface worldly cause for their behaviour to Lear,[13] they could not find in themselves any of that true love for him which, as Cordelia says, has nothing to do with 'causes' and 'reasons':[14]

Lear. If you have poison for me, I will drink it.
 I know you do not love me; for your sisters

111

> Have, as I do remember, done me wrong:
> You have some cause, they have not.
> *Cor.*   No cause, no cause.
>
> (IV, vii, 72–5)

We are reminded of Lear's earlier, unanswered, question, 'Is there any cause in nature that make these hard hearts?' (III, vi, 78–9). Goodness is finally as unmotivated and as spontaneous as evil.

Regan and Goneril have come to the point of asking Lear why he needs even one follower when, having uttered his 'O! reason not the need' speech, he rushes out into the storm (II, iv, 266 ff.). In that speech he states the claims of common humanity, claims to which his daughters are deaf:

> Allow not nature more than nature needs,
> Man's life is cheap as beast's. Thou art a lady;
> If only to go warm were gorgeous,
> Why, nature needs not what thou gorgeous wear'st,
> Which scarcely keeps thee warm.
>
> (268–72)

To give up his train is to give up his pride—some of which is proper pride, his own identity. (Again, at a merely politic level, to stay is certainly to render himself powerless and at the mercy of his daughters.) Lear's desire to keep the name and the addition to a king is largely folly as the Fool points out, and illusion, as does Poor Tom, but it comes from a wish to preserve what kingship symbolizes, even while he gives it away—control over himself, and a self over which to have control. And, at a symbolic level, as we shall see, the degree to which he can preserve his distance from Goneril and Regan measures his own dissociation from evil. To go on the heath is a positive and heroic, even while also a self-pitying one: Lear is moving away from evil in the only direction left to him—that which leads to mental and physical suffering.

Meanwhile, the reasonable people he leaves behind still feel reasonable. Why should Lear need followers? They are a perpetual menace to public quiet and personal safety, a drain on the household economy, and too many for adequate entertainment:

Reg. This house is little: the old man and 's people
   Cannot be well bestow'd.
Gon. 'Tis his own blame; hath put himself from rest,
   And must needs taste his folly.
Reg. For his particular, I'll receive him gladly,
   But not one follower.
Gon.   So am I purpos'd.
                                        (II, iv, 290–95)

All of which is true, and much more that they have left out:
Lear, we notice, is no longer their father but 'the old man';
they have cut themselves off from him, and this is symbolized
in their closing the gates of the castle against him. Shakespeare does not care for castles: they symbolize for him
severance of the ego from the world, and from the true self.
When Lear goes, and Regan and Goneril let him, they bid
farewell to human ties as surely as Macbeth or Lady Macbeth
in cutting themselves off from human kindness and com-
punction. Being nothing as they are, they now have nothing
to stop them sinking into nothingness. If we are ready to
respond at the level of awareness the play asks, it cannot
come as more than a surface surprise, bidding us once more to
that level, to hear that the sisters have turned to active
hostility against Lear and his friends (III, iii, 1–15; III, iv,
152–55, 167; III, vi, 92). As Lear has gone mad so, in
parallel, has their reasonable mask dropped away for the
passions beneath; and as Lear sees men reduced to the level
of beasts, they become them. We can see it happening in the
conversation after Lear's departure, 'to wilful men,/ The
injuries that they themselves procure/ Must be their school-
masters' (II, iv, 304–6): in the larger vision of the play this
is true, but it is a truth for no other man to endorse or help
into being.

Another apparent disjunction occurs in the account of
Edmund's success in securing Gloucester's hostility to Edgar
and the latter's flight. Gloucester has told Kent that he likes
his sons Edgar and Edmund equally, so that it seems strange
to find him believing at once the contents of a forged letter
describing treachery to his father on Edgar's part which
Edmund gives to Gloucester. But on the spiritual level to
which such discontinuities constantly invite us, Gloucester

113

has, in saying that he loves his sons equally, said that he loves the natural and the unnatural alike, or, that he cannot tell the difference between truth and falsehood. And his readiness to believe Edmund shows that he does not know Edgar, which ignorance of his own natural child is, as in the case of Lear, an expression of his ignorance of himself.

Edmund then tricks Edgar into believing that his father is in a rage with him and intent on doing him harm, and advises him to stay in his (Edmund's) lodging, and, when he ventures out, to go armed. Edgar, we may say, is ignorant of Edmund's true nature, but his ignorance comes in part from innocence: or as Edmund, the only evil character who can think well of people even while he intends them harm, puts it,

> A credulous father, and a brother noble,
> Whose nature is so far from doing harms
> That he suspects none; on whose foolish honesty
> My practices ride easy!
>
> (I, ii, 186–89)

More truly, however, Edgar's gullibility, like Cordelia's abruptness, also symbolizes the complete dominance of evil at this point in the play: ultimately mere character has little to do with what is happening. This is heightened further in the psychologically strange scene of Edgar's departure. Edmund, who has told Gloucester where Edgar is, comes to tell Edgar that his father has found out his place of concealment and is coming for him, and that Edgar must flee at once. (Gloucester is here aligned with Cornwall and Regan, who are also said to think Edgar has plans against them.) Then Edmund says,

> I hear my father coming; pardon me;
> In cunning I must draw my sword upon you;
> Draw; seem to defend yourself; now quit you well.
> Yield; come before my father. Light, ho! here!
> Fly, brother. Torches! torches! So, farewell. [*Exit Edgar.*
>
> (II, i, 29–33)

Then, by wounding himself, Edmund can pretend to Gloucester when he arrives that he was attacked by his brother. Even allowing for the haste of the scene, one would imagine that Edgar would question why it was necessary for him to fight with Edmund before his flight and why Edmund

114

could not mediate on his behalf. Here again the question is posed so that we may answer it at a deeper level: at this point in the play goodness is helpless to do other than let itself appear wickedness.

This is further enforced by the condition of Gloucester. Edmund is unlike Regan and Goneril in that he initiates the plot against his father: but Gloucester is, like Lear, the first cause, the progenitor of the evil in his family, and as with Lear the good child will be put aside for the bad until the father is clear-eyed and clear-souled enough to take truth. Here evil and good are confounded by him. Edmund, in a fiend's arch-mock, tempts Gloucester with the substantial truth, telling him that Edgar vowed, if brought before his father, to deny all knowledge of his supposed parricidal letter and to portray it as a plot got up against him by Edmund. That Gloucester is as resentful of Edgar's supposed readiness to outface his treacherous letter as he was before that he wrote it—'O strange and fast'ned villain!/ Would he deny his letter, said he?' (II, i, 77–8)—is intended to show how far evil has become his good, and good his evil here. Gloucester now says of Edgar, 'I never got him,' and terms Edmund 'Loyal and natural boy'—thus making the unnatural his 'nature' and cutting himself off from the natural, as surely as Lear in banishing Cordelia, or Regan and Goneril shutting the castle door on their father.

On the next occasion that we see Edgar, he is hiding in a wood. The country is up against him, and all the ports are watched. He resolves on disguise. He will go on a journey into vacancy, a *via negativa*, that he may find himself and others, since for the time he cannot exist—'Edgar I nothing am' (II, iii, 21). But why the particular disguise that he chooses?—

> the basest and most poorest shape
> That ever penury, in contempt of man,
> Brought near to beast; my face I'll grime with filth,
> Blanket my loins, elf all my hairs in knots,
> And with presented nakedness outface
> The winds and persecutions of the sky.
>
> (II, iii, 7–12)

There is no rational necessity for this as against another

disguise—except perhaps that no one is likely to ask questions of him because of it: it is once more at the level of the spiritual narrative that it most makes sense. Like Cordelia who, cast off by her father, was to the king of France 'most rich, being poor;/ Most choice, forsaken; and most lov'd, despis'd' (I, i, 250–1), goodness has been outcast as a beggar, forced to go unaccommodated, without dowry or identity, that in the end it may be most truly itself, 'Thou losest here, a better where to find' (ibid., 261). And, later, when the disguised Edgar encounters Lear, he does so when Lear is at the point where he can for the first time understand something of the phenomenon of beggary and the considerations it must provoke concerning man's nature generally—Edgar is, to say the least, thereby an aid to reflection.

Edgar remains concealed even from his father, to whom he pretends he is a yokel. Here too we have to move away from 'normal' expectations of human behaviour. At a psychological level we must be outraged at Edgar's taking upon himself the right to keep his father suffering for his moral good ('Why I do trifle thus with his despair/ Is done to cure it'— IV, vi, 33–4). We are faced by the prospect either of finding him repulsive (the course of several commentators, and, at one point (V, iii, 192), of himself), or else of feeling the motivation so unacceptable, however correct the moral diagnosis, that we look beyond the ego of Edgar, to consider that whatever Edgar may say about his own purposes, these are overridden by the larger spiritual movement in the play. On the latter reading we conclude that here it is not really a case of Edgar's refusing to remove his disguise but of his being in a real sense unable to do so, because Gloucester is not yet ready to see him properly and for what he is (this might account for the changes in Edgar's disguises around the cliff-scene). In the same way in the first scene we saw how Cordelia could not speak properly because her father could not hear her.

The play has something reminiscent of the structure of some comedies. Characters act outwith their natures, or there are motivational jerks, because they are part of a symbolic or conceptual narrative. And, as in comedy madness is often used to drive out madness, delusion delusion, so in

116

Lear the central figures are made mad that they may become sane, and blind that they may see. Further, comedy often ends with a restoration unlooked-for by the characters, a piece of good luck or providential aid; *Lear*, and in this it is alone among Shakespeare's tragedies (even in comparison to *Romeo and Juliet*), ends with a totally unexpected series of bad luck— the loss of the battle and the just-too-late attempt to save Cordelia from execution. What is one to say of such a comedy in reverse? It may be that it is nearer to true tragi-comedy than any other of Shakespeare's plays, in the idea that the most hideous suffering may be attended with or lead to the most searing joys. Certainly it is a play which deals with resolved paradoxes, of poverty fused with richness, of loss with gain, of the way down with the way up.

What touches us most about *Lear* is its sheer lack of compromise with everyday, reasonable standards: it goes to the bottom of human relationships, showing that the roots of social as much as of antisocial life are primal and instinctive.[15] The storm is in part a symbol of the destruction of the conscious self ('Singe my white head!' (III, ii, 6)). Thus, after the rational and politic standards by which the Fool exposes him, Lear encounters on the heath the unaccommodated madness of Poor Tom, which begins to reveal to him the deeper level of the disease in his conscience. This is also one reason for Tom's being a beggar, and why part of Lear's thinking during and after his time with him is directed at the corruptions and the superficiality of civilized life. Looking on Tom, he reflects,

> Thou wert better in a grave than to answer with thy uncover'd body this extremity of the skies. Is man no more than this? Consider him well. Thou ow'st the worm no silk, the beast no hide, the sheep no wool, the cat no perfume. Ha! here's three on's are sophisticated; thou art the thing itself; unaccommodated man is no more but such a poor, bare, forked animal as thou art. Off, off, you lendings! Come; unbutton here.
> [*Tearing off his clothes.*
> (III, iv, 103–12)

There is sentimentality and facile involvement here: Lear ignores his initial horror at Tom's nakedness to lurch into the absolutism of saying, 'Yes, man is no more than this'; he thinks Tom is more real without clothes than he with them, and therefore seeks to get down to spiritual bedrock by stripping himself. The removal of mere clothes, however, will not be enough; and that man *is* more than this, as Lear at first supposed, is ironically indicated in the fact that Poor Tom is the noble Edgar in disguise. Yet the movement is 'right' in the context of the whole play: one must go beneath the shell, one must search for the objective spiritual correlative, one must become nothing if one will hope to be anything. (The point is not of course stated anything so baldly as this; but, given the symbolic mode of the play, as 'point', it is central.)

Lear goes mad to be sane, Gloucester blind to see. But it is not just this: they become cut off from the world of reason or sense-impression that they may more truly be in touch with the real world. The mere egos of the characters are not finally important: their true selves are. The dislocated narrative of the play, in which many of the events occur scattered over a featureless heath, and the story is continually suspended by social and metaphysical reflections, furthers the sense of mental breakdown. The play enacts and demands sympathy and insight which go below reasons and rational structures: if society would be destroyed by the spiritual transformations that might be wrought by these seeings, then let society go:

> When usurers tell their gold i' th' field;
> And bawds and whores do churches build;
> Then shall the realm of Albion
> Come to great confusion.
>
> (III, ii, 89–92)

That is the invitation, the proffered vision: but in the play, Cordelia, who ultimately embodies these values, dies.

This penetration beyond merely reasonable standards of judgment is also asked of our reaction to Lear's experience of the storm. Reason might ask what was so bad in Lear's being out for one night in the wet, and why so much is made of it in the play. It is not only Lear who says, 'In such a night/ To shut me out?' (III, iv, 17–18), but also Kent, Gloucester and Cordelia who insist on it. Kent says,

118

                    things that love night
Love not such nights as these; the wrathful skies
Gallow the very wanderers of the dark,
And make them keep their caves. Since I was man
Such sheets of fire, such bursts of horrid thunder,
Such groans of roaring wind and rain, I never
Remember to have heard; man's nature cannot carry
Th'affliction nor the fear.

                                        (III, ii, 42–9)

To the commonsense mind this must sound like 'laying it on a bit thick'. Others are not slack in the same office. The Fool declares, 'This cold night will turn us all to fools and madmen' (III, iv, 78–9); the disguised Edgar reminds us that 'Poor Tom's a-cold' (ibid., 151); Gloucester speaks of 'this tyrannous night' and says, 'What a night's this' (ibid., 155, 174); Cordelia cries, 'What? i' th' storm! i' th' night?/ Let pity not be believ'd!' (IV, iii, 29–30), and 'Was this a face/ To be oppos'd against the warring winds?/ To stand against the deep dread-bolted thunder?/ In the most terrible and nimble stroke/ Of quick, cross lightning? to watch—poor *perdu!*—/ With this thin helm?' (IV, vii, 31–6). It seems strange to sense that a storm, of whatever violence, should be considered such a horror for Lear, who in the event proves not so old or weak as to be physically harmed by it; and at the time of his departure from Gloucester's castle we suppose that since he is still accompanied by some of his knights, they will be some help in sheltering him (it is not till III, i, 16–17 that we find that the 'desperate train' with which he was attended when he left (II, iv, 307–9) has shrunk to the Fool). At the level of commonsense comparisons Gloucester's physical suffering in having his eyes torn out and then himself being ejected on to the heath must seem far greater than Lear's. Lear himself says, to Kent, that the physical suffering caused by the storm, on which the other characters lay such emphasis, is not important to him:

    Thou think'st 'tis much that this contentious storm
    Invades us to the skin: so 'tis to thee;
    But where the greater malady is fix'd,
    The lesser is scarce felt. Thou'ldst shun a bear;
    But if thy flight lay toward the roaring sea,

Thou'ldst meet the bear i' th' mouth. When the mind's free
The body's delicate; this tempest in my mind
Doth from my senses take all feeling else
Save what beats there.

(III, iv, 6–14)

This of course does not alter the fact that even if Lear does not
pay attention to the weather he is still at a physical level
suffering it. And it might seem that Shakespeare has made it
so violent a storm because he wants to produce sympathy
for Lear which might not have been forthcoming had he only
been shut out on a drizzly evening. But this would be absurd:
it would have been more likely via the latter kind of evening
that we might have been led to the perception, asked by this
play, that degrees in physical pain are in a sense unimportant.
Shakespeare clearly has other reasons for giving this storm its
special extremity.

Here again we have to read further, if we are to read with
humanity at all. Lear's followers have gone: gone not only for
the psychological reason that, as the Fool puts it, 'That sir
which serves and seeks for gain,/ And follows but for form,/
Will pack when it begins to rain,/ And leave thee in the
storm' (II, iv, 78–81), but symbolically, in that Lear has lost
all control over the external world—as is further imaged in
his pathetic attempts, Canute-like, to control and direct the
storm (III, ii, 1 ff.). The storm, indeed, symbolizes loss of
control. (Its metaphysical nature is indicated in the Fool's
words, above.) It is not primarily physical.[16] Nor is it the
storm in Lear's head only: the emphasis of the whole play is
not merely personal—Lear and Gloucester are in the same
spiritual plight. It is a storm which expresses in elemental
disruption unnatural acts. To that storm those who may
benefit from it are exposed: its destructiveness is a symbol
of the breaking of spirit that is going on in them. Those
characters who see it purely in meteorological terms are
performing the office of 'straw-men': their insistence on mere
weather, in seeming excessive, invites us to look deeper, to see
that the physical largely expresses a metaphysical storm and
it is there that most pain lies.

Later, from the characters who meet Lear there are
repeated comments on his piteous mental torment when mad,

in what might again seem to be 'telling' rather than 'showing'. When Lear enters, *'fantastically dressed with wild flowers'*, Edgar comments, 'O thou side-piercing sight!' (IV, vi, 85); a gentleman finds Lear 'A sight most pitiful in the meanest wretch,/ Past speaking of in a King!' (ibid., 205–6); Gloucester, recently blinded, reflects, 'The King is mad: how stiff is my vile sense/ That I stand up, and have ingenious feeling/ Of my huge sorrows!' (ibid., 281–83). But here the gap to be exposed is any that exists between the audience and the play. Lear's pain is here none other than the madness itself, and the characters are 'right' to respond to it as they do. What Shakespeare is doing here is pointing out the sort of horrified sympathy to which he invites us—or, if we are incapable of it, showing us that we are so. Such comments are, seen thus, the measure of our engagement. If we remain outside, shut in the castles of our own egos, we in some degree save ourselves, if selves we can be said to have. If we, like his few followers, stay with Lear despite his self-pitying outbursts, his arrogance, and his finally distancing madness, then we will suffer.

Thus this play could be said to be *about* disjunction, the gap between common understanding and truth. Hence the symbols of division: the notion with which the play begins, of division of the kingdom, is founded on the idea that the play explodes—namely, that true love can be measured, and that the free expression of the spirit may be equated with parcels of land. After this we hear of different divisions—those between children and their parents, or between allies (III, i, 19–21), or within the self (III, iv, 14–16; IV, ii, 34–6); or, as Gloucester superstitiously registers it:

> Love cools, friendship falls off, brothers divide: in cities, mutinies; in countries, discord; in palaces, treason; and the bond crack'd 'twixt son and father. This villain of mine [Edgar] comes under the prediction; there's son against father: the King falls from bias of nature; there's father against child.
>
> (I, ii, 110–17)

Measurement of love is ironically exposed in Lear's pathetic attempts to assess the love of Regan and Goneril for him in terms of the relative fractions of his meinie to whom they will give house-room—he says to the latter, 'Thy fifty yet doth double five-and-twenty,/ And thou art twice her love' (II, iv, 261–62). Regan and Goneril are themselves to be ironically 'placed' in a second love-contest, for Edmund, at the end of the play, wherein, unlike Lear, he perceives their natures.

If love defies measurement, there is also disjunction between our attempts to measure evil or pain, and their realities. There is always a lower deep, a worse pain, a greater ill, than the one we are now saying is worst; a kind of spiritual Parkinson's Law operates here. In this sense all pain is relative, and the least slight as damnable as the worst. Thus Lear, turning back to Goneril from Regan, declares, 'Those wicked creatures yet do look well-favour'd/ When others are more wicked; not being the worst/ Stands in some rank of praise' (II, iv, 258–60). Edgar says, 'When we our betters see bearing our woes,/ We scarcely think our miseries our foes' (III, vi, 105–6). Later, having just accounted himself the worst in fortune, and gladly, because he imagines that this makes him immune to vicissitude ('The lamentable change is from the best;/ The worst returns to laughter' (IV, i, 5–6)), Edgar sees his blinded father for the first time and has to admit, 'O Gods! Who is 't can say "I am at the worst"?/ I am worse than e'er I was' (25–6). Similar is the sympathy awakened in Gloucester by his knowledge of Lear's condition, which makes his own pain seem much more trivial:

> The King is mad: how stiff is my vile sense
> That I stand up, and have ingenious feeling
> Of my huge sorrows! Better I were distract:
> So should my thoughts be sever'd from my griefs,
> And woes by wrong imaginations lose
> The knowledge of themselves.
>
> (IV, vi, 281–86)

The Dover Cliff scene is in part a symbol of this. The blind Gloucester, led by the disguised Edgar, and intent on suicide, is brought, he is told, to the lip of the cliff. The abyss is described in terms of gradations, which suggests stations on the descent into pain where one might continually say, and be wrong in so doing, that one was at the worst; further, the account insists on the immeasurable nature of the gulf. But the central point here is that Gloucester *thinks* he has thrown himself down when he has only fallen on the grass where he stood. Measurement is wholly subjective.

More generally, the Dover Cliff scene can be viewed as a symbol of the method of the entire play. Throughout the play we experience apparent disjunctions in motivation and causality, disjunctions which are not really there when perceived aright. So with 'Dover Cliff', which though presented to Gloucester as a vast precipice, is not really present at all, and would not have been so to him had he been able to see. At the same time, on the fictive plane, the cliff as a series of levels going down symbolizes the kind of descent into insight continually required of the reader of this play, the forsaking of the level of mere commonsense perception for that of true spiritual awareness.

The play is filled too with divisions between apparent desert and reward. More than any other tragedy of Shakespeare's, *Lear* insists on the gap, the disproportion of lack of 'measure', between seeming merit and suffering. The sheer violence of the scene in which Gloucester's eyes are torn out, the apparent gulf between what has gone before—semi-rational behaviour, conversation at a non-physical level—and this, where control goes and the brutally physical thrusts itself on us, is prodigious. Above all initially we are outraged at the cruel injustice with which Gloucester is being treated. A different kind of disjunction—and one rather less immediately abrupt—is present in Lear's going mad: it may be hard at first to see why he goes insane under the stimulus only of filial ingratitude. These 'disproportions' drive us to see the deeper connections which partly cancel them. We perceive that Gloucester, who has not distinguished truth from falsehood, natural from unnatural, in some degree deserves to be blind indeed; and we see too that in the same way Lear's past pride and irrationality deserve degradation, isolation and madness. But this does not remove the outrage, the monstrosity of pain and loss in the universe. We come to a position almost impossible to hold in one act of mind and yet most true to the opaque ambiguity of life because of that: that the suffering, whether in losing one's eyes, one's senses or one's all in one's daughter, is at once deserved and sheerly unjust. And that is a disjunction which we do not overcome.

In a sense, as Lear realizes, none—and all—do offend. The universe is found to be not very discriminating. Albany's assertion that 'All friends shall taste/ The wages of their virtue, and all foes/ The cup of their deservings' (V, iii, 302–4), fails before the deaths of Cordelia and of Lear. Albany's gods are not very just; but neither, since the play also encompasses the deaths of *all* the evil characters, can we call them, as Gloucester at one point does (IV, i, 36–7), wholly unjust. The play shows only the gap between expectation and act, the frailty of apparent merit. In this sense Edmund's (surprising) dying repentance is drawn out deliberately. Hearing Edgar's account of their father's death he feels a few twinges of pity, but says he needs time to come round, 'This speech of yours hath mov'd me,/ And shall perchance do good; but speak you on' (V, iii, 199–200); thus our sense of the hideous randomness of things is heightened when, on his eventual further repentance, he sends to the prison where Lear and Cordelia are lodged to stop their being executed on his instructions (there is even a further small delay while he remembers that he should send a token so that his message will be obeyed—ibid., 248–51). Fate will not fit in with moral schemes and spiritual changes: Edmund's repentance is in practical terms futile. Almost the last note of the play is one of acute question of the irrational, disproportionate character of life, which refuses all heed to worth:

> Why should a dog, a horse, a rat, have life,
> And thou no breath at all?
>
> (ibid., 306–7)

The play asks us to move like Lear beyond practical or rational considerations such as those offered to him by the Fool into the social and spiritual questioning that arises from his encounter with Poor Tom. But when we have descended this first level of the cliff, and found the underlying spiritual causes that remove such apparent discontinuities as Cordelia's refusal, Edgar's passivity, Kent's obtuseness or the sudden fullness of the evil of Goneril and Regan, we see below these patterns, these ordering factors in seemingly random experience, a deeper and less eradicable level of the random, a universe to which any kind of belief, code, or system of rationality, whether Kent's fatalism, Albany's optimism, Edmund's pragmatism or Gloucester's pessimism, is inadequate.

Nor even can we be complacent as to how much Lear himself comes to see through his sufferings. It would be mistaken to say that in any real sense he has *earned* Cordelia when he is reunited with her. He has been shown the wickedness of his other daughters. He went mad partly because at first he would see only their wrongdoing, not his own. He has become a little saner when he has begun to blame himself. But we should not exaggerate the worth or indeed the accuracy of his insights, nor any pattern in his spiritual development.[17] Thus when, outside the hovel on the heath, he declares,

> Poor naked wretches, whereso'er you are,
> That bide the pelting of this pitiless storm,
> How shall your houseless heads and unfed sides,
> Your loop'd and window'd raggedness, defend you
> From seasons such as these? O! I have ta'en
> Too little care of this. Take physic, Pomp;
> Expose thyself to feel what wretches feel,
> That thou mayst shake the superflux to them,
> And show the Heavens more just
> (III, iv, 28–36),

we feel that the sentiment may be right, but it has only been perceived, not fully absorbed. It is Lear's first sight of the wrongs he has been doing, and he speedily shifts from blame of himself to 'Pomp' in general; again, the way he loads on the adjectives of gushing sympathy, 'Poor naked', 'pelting . . . pitiless', 'houseless', 'unfed', 'loop'd and windowless', removes some conviction from what he is saying. Slightly facile too is the later attack on the rich (which comes after a particularly diseased attack on women wherein he does not reflect that he must be including Cordelia (IV, vi, 120–30): claiming 'A dog's obey'd in office' (161), he proceeds,

> Thou rascal beadle, hold thy bloody hand!
> Why dost thou lash that whore? Strip thine own back;
> Thou hotly lusts to use her in that kind
> For which thou whipp'st her. The usurer hangs the
>   cozener.
> Thorough tatter'd clothes small vices do appear;
> Robes and furr'd gowns hide all. Plate sin with gold,
> And the strong lance of justice hurtless breaks;

125

Arm it in rags, a pigmy's straw does pierce it.
None does offend, none, I say, none.

(162–70)

True in part, perhaps, but if wholly true, as A. L. French observes, 'no society so profoundly corrupt could last for six months.'[18] Further, while it may have some validity in relation to Lear's kingdom, there is the question of how far Lear is applying his insights to himself, or, as French puts it, 'Is he saying that *his* regime, before he abdicated, was totally corrupt?';[19] and this question recurs with every one of his supposed insights (the earlier 'O! I have ta'en/ Too little care of this' comes over more as an indictment of remissness than as a sense of sinful complicity, personal assent to evil). Here again there is a sense of intemperance in the contrition, a too violent and general heaping of dust and ashes on the world of authority. First there is the very specific vision of the beadle lashing the whore (an extension of the fascinated horror of Lear's revulsion against women just previously); then we move on to different sins and sinners as classes, '*The* usurer hangs *the* cozener', then more impersonal still, 'Robes and furr'd gowns', until we come to the total generality of 'sin' and 'justice'. Each sequent 'insight' comes in the form of a violent jet of mental movement, portraying a psyche lashing out at all things, without control or perspective. And this is typical of most of Lear's perceptions. We can say that he has begun to see some of the truth about himself and humanity, and that sometimes he utters what are general truths, but these are not fully earned or a part of himself. As French observes, Gloucester's insights go further and sound more real:[20]

> Let the superfluous and lust-dieted man,
> That slaves your ordinance, that will not see
> Because he does not feel, feel your power quickly;
> So distribution should undo excess,
> And each man have enough.

(IV, i, 67–71)

He half-knows that he is indicting himself here. Thus, while when Lear meets Cordelia again he does so recognizing his humanity and hers, that recognition is, as French says, 'precarious'.[21] Cordelia's forgiveness of him (though it is not

126

presented as anything like this) is not the consequence of his worth, but the expression of uncalculating love, which bridges the spiritual gap. It is perhaps as a symbol of the precariousness of Lear's development that he loses Cordelia: as he says at the end, 'I might have sav'd her' (V, iii, 270). In this sense her death is the fullest expression of his original rejection of her, a rejection the full moral meaning of which—as it applies to him—he has not fully comprehended and has therefore not fully rescinded. His life with her in the prison (V, iii, 8–19) was to be one of happy isolation from the world, which also meant isolation from himself. In a sense too, only by losing her, only by her dying, does he find her fully—comprehend her real value. With her death he is finally unaccommodated, and in a more terrible storm on a heath without friends or shelter, even a prison. It is not so much that Lear needed to repent: it is that he had to come to a certain level of being. He finds that ontological bedrock and dies on it only at the last.

The good are divided from the evil as being from doing. Lear, at first possessed by evil, 'does' or acts in his division of the kingdom: thereafter he is increasingly passive; the theme of 'patience' is continually iterated as the condition of worth. Cordelia's forces lose the battle and she and Lear are finally imprisoned as a symbolic terminus to the helplessness of good. (It is true that Edgar challenges and slays Edmund in combat, but the scene of the challenge is so poorly presented and badly written[22] as to suggest that Shakespeare was going against the spiritual grain of his play here.) When Edmund, dying, wishes to do good in stopping the execution of Cordelia, he is too late; this is another 'reason' for his strange delay. The evil have no being, because they build their lives on emptiness: they put value on material possessions instead of true need, and thereby demonstrate that the material is the least substantial of substances; increasingly all they can do, insatiably, is act. Lear, on the other hand, spends some part of the play trying to look further into the nature of mankind and, if to a far lesser extent, himself: he contemplates and begins to see; his journey, incomplete though it is, is founded on increasing fullness of identity towards the ultimate point where, as Edgar puts it, 'Ripeness is all' (V, ii, 11). Part of his search is for the fundamental *being* of man: he says (if sentimentally) of the 'unaccommodated man' he sees in Poor Tom, 'thou art the thing itself' (III, iv, 109). The play is full of images of seeing, and of the stripping away of coverings.[23] These govern the evil as well as the good: by the end the former are revealed for what they are, though apart from Edmund it is not they who learn about themselves. (At the beginning of the play the good, who know themselves, have to disguise or hide themselves from others while evil is dominant; the evil, on the other hand are disguised from the outset, both from others and from themselves, and the process of the play is to expose them for what they fully are.) Since perception is a good, and it opens up the evil fully, we may say that to a limited extent good is seen to be metaphysically the stronger.

The point of the play is the awareness it asks, not the sense to be made of the universe. Through Lear the universe blandly produced Cordelia on the one hand and Goneril and Regan on the other. How can there be either meaning or meaninglessness, pattern or certain lack of it? Kent's conclusion is as sensible or as absurd as any other:

> It is the stars,
> The stars above us, govern our conditions;
> Else one self mate and make could not beget
> Such different issues.
>
> (IV, iii, 33–6)

Lear's madness, mixed as it is with reason and leading to some sanity, is here ultimately a symbol of the fact that no clear sense can be made of the universe, not even clear nonsense. The cosmos is an indecipherable blend of meaning and no meaning, sanity and insanity, pattern and the lack of it.[24]

What is truly needed is sympathy, and more sympathy. The two 'objective correlatives' here are Gloucester's and Lear's deaths, both the result of over-charged hearts, both the result of final perception, not of meaning in life or even of their own natures, but of love for another person, a perception so deep that it tips over into the nothingness of death. That the one perception is experienced in joy—Gloucester's heart 'Burst smilingly'—and the other quite possibly in total agony, expresses the finally ambiguous nature of the universe. It is only at the end, as we have seen, when Lear comes on absolute 'somethingness', the full nature of human love, that the root of his own being is touched. And as soon as this happens, he experiences total nothingness in the midst of that something. All the paradoxes have come indifferently into being: one may only be clothed when one is naked, found when lost, king when beggar, sighted when blind, sane when mad, and have being only in nothingness. The theme of different kinds of nothing laces the play.[25] At first Lear is a nothing by being insubstantial, the shadow of a king (I, iv, 239). He says, 'Nothing will come of nothing' and 'nothing can be made out of nothing' (I, i, 90; I, iv, 138–39). His words are prophetic in one way in relation to his wicked daughters, but in another in relation to himself. From a shadowy, parasitic nothing, he becomes a substantial one. The process is close to that depicted in Donne's 'A Nocturnal upon S. Lucy's Day', in which the speaker is reacting, like Lear at the end, to the death of someone who was the whole world, the ground of his being, to him: 'If I an ordinary nothing were,' says the mourner, 'As shadow, a light, and body must be here'; he concludes, 'But I am by her death . . ./ Of the first nothing, the elixir grown.' In this speaker, love's art 'did express/ A quintessence even from nothingness': so is it with Lear.

Yet even that is not a pattern. At the lowest deep there is only suffering or joy, which may or may not be productive, only men enduring or not enduring pain or joy, only the Janus-character of life itself. There one can only speak of the stature of man as rendered titanic in relation to others by experience. 'The oldest hath borne most: we that are young/ Shall never see so much, nor live so long.' There, in the end, one can only maintain, 'Suffering is a privilege. What have you done to deserve it?'[26]

NOTES

1. For recent accounts, see H. A. Mason, *Shakespeare's Tragedies of Love: An Examination of the Possibility of Common Readings of 'Romeo and Juliet', 'Othello', 'King Lear' and 'Antony and Cleopatra'* (Chatto and Windus, 1970), pp. 165–226; and A. L. French, *Shakespeare and the Critics*, pp. 144–205. It is these recent revaluations of *Lear* which part of this chapter implicitly tries to answer.

2. References are to the Arden *King Lear*, ed. Kenneth Muir (Methuen, 1952).

3. See also S. L. Goldberg, *An Essay on 'King Lear'* (Cambridge, Cambridge University Press, 1974), p. 80, on Gloucester's later casting-off of Edgar: 'As with Lear, his desire for justice on Edgar is so savage that it clearly betrays the open wound underneath it.' Goldberg is however inclined to see this wound at a purely psychological rather than a metaphysical level.

4. For previous treatments of the disjunctions in *Lear*, see A. C. Bradley, *Shakespearean Tragedy*, pp. 257–58; Maynard Mack, *'King Lear' in Our Time* (Methuen, 1966), pp. 3–8, 49–80; Julian Markels, *The Pillar of the World: 'Antony and Cleopatra' in Shakespeare's Development* (Columbus, Ohio, Ohio State University Press, 1968), pp. 120–22; John Reibetanz, *The 'Lear' World: A Study of 'King Lear' in its Dramatic Context* (Heinemann, 1977), pp. 39–41. Bradley, Markels and Reibetanz leave the disjunctions as they are, seeing them either as 'exceptionally careless' (Bradley), or as expressions of a new 'technique of discontinuity' in Shakespeare's work (Markels), or as a means to striking dramatic effects (Reibetanz). Mack, however, argues that 'more of the play becomes intelligible and significant if a view of it is taken that relates its conventions to literary modes to which it is genuinely akin, such as Romance, Morality play, and Vision, rather than to psychological or realistic drama, with which it has very little in common' (p. 83). This attempt to make sense of the apparent discontinuities in terms of a deeper vision in the play is closest to the approach followed here.

5. *Shakespeare and the Critics*, p. 148.

6. Ibid., pp. 147–48.

7. I am thinking here of the kind of psychological account to be found in Goldberg, especially pp. 22–4, 70–1, 86–7, 115–17, where Cordelia is seen to be narrow and wrong in her refusal to give Lear sympathetic understanding at the beginning; Kent is taken as being too arrogantly righteous in his treatment of Oswald; and Edgar so concerned with his own moral standards before the human needs of his father, and so busy about his 'psychic self-preservation' (p. 116) that he takes on the disguise of the lowest to be immune from being brought lower.

8. Matt., 12, 30.

9. See also Mack, pp. 91–4 and Markels, p. 121.

10. French, pp. 163–67.

11. This would meet the contention of French, pp. 159–63, that Lear went of his own accord, and that subsequent implications in the play that he was shut out (III, ii, 63–7; III, iv, 17–18; III, vii, 62–3; IV, iii, 28–30; IV, vii, 31–40) are false.

12. See for example French, pp. 156–59. Contrast Mack, pp. 30–2.

13. See, arguing this, Mason, p. 183.

14. This can explain why Shakespeare did not keep to the sort of simple and obvious villainy that they possess in his sources. In Holinshed, after the love-test, Lear divides half the kingdom between his 'loyal' daughters, retaining half for himself. The daughters eventually oust

him from his share, and then keep him attendant on them while steadily reducing his entourage (no mention being made of any riotous behaviour by his knights) to the point of their father's utter misery. In the play source, *The True Chronicle History of King Leir*, Cordella's sisters are revealed from the start as plotting villains with a venomous hatred for her; and subsequently it is they who cause the quarrels with Leir in their houses, and attempt to murder him. Thus in neither case is insight, which brings a heightened sense of evil, asked of the audience.

15. Compare Mack, p. 93, 'Choice remains in the forefront of the argument, but its psychic antecedents have been so effectively shrunk down in this primitivized world that action seems to spring directly out of the bedrock of personality.'

16. Nevertheless it is symbolic of the natures of Lear's and Gloucester's 'original sins' that the one should appear to be punished mentally, the other physically. Similarly, Lear falls into a madness which is sanity, while Gloucester falls from a cliff which is not a cliff. But the difference of categories is not final, just as the difference of sins is not final: both mistook their good offspring and opted for the evil; and seen in another way, each suffers both physically *and* mentally—Lear in a physical storm which is also a storm in his mind, Gloucester from a blindness which also expresses both his past spiritual blindness and his present torment at the thought of it.

17. This is well expounded by French, pp. 167–205, though he believes that Shakespeare *meant* to portray Lear as evolving to a point of spiritual redemption simply, and that therefore the play is a partial failure. See also Mason, pp. 192–200, 223–25.

18. Ibid., p. 182.

19. Ibid.

20. French, p. 174; see also Mason, pp. 194, 196, 200–2, 207–8.

21. French, p. 184.

22. Mason, pp. 221–22.

23. The latter is almost arithmetical at one point, in the form of the reduction in the numbers of Lear's knights—but only so to show that arithmetic is here irrelevant.

24. See also Susan Snyder, *The Comic Matrix of Shakespeare's Tragedies: 'Romeo and Juliet', 'Hamlet', 'Othello' and 'King Lear'* (Princeton, N.J., Princeton University Press, 1979), ch. 4, pp. 137–79.

25. See e.g. I, i, 87–90, 159, 245; I, ii, 31–5; I, iv, 134–41, 195, 200, 202, 204, 239; II, iii, 21; III, ii, 38; IV, i, 9; IV, vi, 137, 170; V, iii, 308. On the 'nothings' in the play see also Sigurd Burckhardt, '*King Lear*: The Quality of Nothing', *Shakespearean Meanings*, ch. 8, pp. 237–59.

26. Nigel Dennis, *August for the People, A Play in Two Acts* (Samuel French, 1961), p. 47.

6

Macbeth

In *Macbeth* we begin with a division in the central figure which is steadily worn away to the point where it becomes external-ized in the difference between himself and his wife. The play is above all about isolation, isolation from the self, from society and from nature. The theme of alienation of the individual from the state is recurrent from *Macbeth* to *Coriolanus*.

What—to ask the central and probably most frequently debated question of this play again—what is it that brings Macbeth to slay his king? The readiest answer to this is that he is ambitious. Certainly, in the absence of any other clear motive, this is the one the audience will be most prepared to supply. It is the one that Macbeth himself once—though dismissively—offers, where he says that 'I have no spur/ To prick the sides of my intent, but only/ Vaulting ambition, which o'erleaps itself/ And falls on th'other' (I, vii, 25–8).[1] Yet there is never any account of what regal delights Macbeth hopes to gain from murdering Duncan, nor any characteriza-tion of him as an ambitious man, nor any analysis of ambition itself: all we have at one point (I, v, 16–25) is Lady Macbeth telling us at length that he is ambitious, as if in acknowl-edgment of the fact that this has not been demonstrated. If ambition is Macbeth's motive, it is at best left as an un-interesting datum: it is not fully established or attended to. In a play so replete with subtle spiritual analysis as this one, such an omission is to say the least surprising.

Nor can the source of Macbeth's impulse readily be traced to the supernatural solicitation of the witches. They promise as much glory to Banquo's descendants as to Macbeth, and Banquo is able to put all wicked thoughts behind him. We cannot say that it is the different facts which Macbeth is told that prompt him. The witches hail him first as what he is, Thane of Glamis, then as Thane of Cawdor, and finally as king. He cannot understand how he can be Thane of Cawdor since he believes that the present incumbent is both alive and still loyal to the king; we of course know that Cawdor is a condemned traitor. When Macbeth finds out that he is indeed that thane, he believes that the witches speak true, and more fully credits their prophecy regarding his eventual kingship. But this need not tempt him to action: since the second title came to him without any effort on his part, so may the crown, as he himself perceives—'If Chance will have me King, why, Chance may crown me,/ Without my stir' (I, iii, 144–45). Nevertheless he is also thinking of making himself king.

> Two truths are told,
> As happy prologues to the swelling act
> Of the imperial theme.
>
> (127–29)

Two truths: only the second required any supernatural knowledge, since Macbeth was already Thane of Glamis. This may show something of the megalomaniac's need to see his life as set in a ritualized, predestined frame, as part of some great cosmic purpose. The imperial theme is swelling only to Macbeth: in cold fact it is simply another item, disconnected from the others; to put it in terms of a pattern is to mask personal choice as necessity.

What follows in this speech is more revealing. Macbeth reflects, in the seesawing, 'divided' idiom characteristic of the play:

> This supernatural soliciting
> Cannot be ill; cannot be good:—
> If ill, why hath it given me earnest of success,
> Commencing in a truth? I am Thane of Cawdor:
> If good, why do I yield to that suggestion
> Whose horrid image doth unfix my hair,
> And make my seated heart knock at my ribs,
> Against the use of nature?

Macbeth seems here to be placing responsibility for his thoughts upon the witches. He says that their 'solicitation', as he puts it, is neither bad nor good: that is, he says what it is not, not what it is, which is precisely the burden of the eventual close of this speech—'nothing is, but what is not' (142). He also reveals a rather startling ignorance of what goodness and evil are when he sees becoming a thane as a good in the same moral terms that he sees killing the king as an evil—and of the latter he is in some doubt too, as he has to ask whether the hideous image conjured up by the idea of killing the king makes the idea a good or a bad one. We wonder, too, why he is asking whether the supernatural solicitation is good or evil, why it matters to him which it is, when he is yielding to a suggestion which he says he knows in soul and body to be horrible and unnatural. There seems a radical separation between Macbeth's mind and the true moral issues. The vision of the hair unfixing and the heart knocking is the most vivid thing in the speech, and seems to fascinate Macbeth: the way it is phrased—'I yield to that suggestion/ Whose horrid image doth unfix my hair'—gives the impression of Macbeth yielding not only to the suggestion but to the horrid image even while it repels him. He then tries to shake it off:

> Present fears
> Are less than horrible imaginings.
> My thought, whose murther yet is but fantastical,
> Shakes so my single state of man,
> That function is smother'd in surmise,
> And nothing is, but what is not.

We wonder how what has just been happening can be described as a horrible imagining rather than a present fear, since Macbeth has just spoken of some real intention to murder his king; and at the end of the speech, indeed, the distinction is lost, since nothing is present to him but horrible imaginings ('nothing is, but what is not'). What he is trying to do here is convince himself that he has not really been thinking of killing Duncan, but only imagining doing so: but then even at the moment of this thrusting-aside of intention, it becomes stronger, taking over his moral being.

The readiness with which Macbeth has responded to the witches, so that at a mere prophecy he is ready to contemplate the murder of his king, demands explanation. We have seen that the witches cannot be held directly responsible: they are only the supernatural solicitation of something in, or not in, Macbeth. We cannot on the other hand look outside the play for a Macbeth who has long been thinking of disposing of Duncan or advancing himself by crooked means; nor can we surmise his prior character. We have to take what we are given only: and what we are given is, at the outset of the play, a portrait of a loyal thane fighting for his king against an invader and a traitor, followed by a portrait of a man tempted to slay that king after meeting the witches. We do of course feel, when Macbeth accedes to the suggestions he finds in their prophecies and Banquo does not, that it cannot all be change, but the precipitation of some long-latent drive: yet there is no room for speculation on this, no textual evidence to go on. It is clear that the switch from honourable subject to potential regicide is meant to be striking, and that it cannot be explained away with 'ambition' or the witches.

Nor can we take Macbeth's wickedness as a datum, like Richard III's villainy or Lear's folly or Lady Macbeth's initial fiendishness, because we are asked to see him as changing from one state to another, and therefore to consider causes. There may be some case for feeling that the Macbeth who is made Thane of Cawdor at once takes on the treacherous attributes of the previous incumbent: certainly the notion of one sin overthrowing a whole social fabric which Shakespeare has used in numbers of previous plays is seen in what happens to Scotland and even its inhabitants after the murder of Duncan; and this idea of evil spreading and corrupting could be taken back to the first Cawdor's treachery. There is indication that Macbeth and (licensed) slaying go well together—he is 'Bellona's bridegroom' (I, ii, 55)—and therein that in time of peace he might be the readier for unlicensed violence. There is, also, at the beginning of the play, an insistence on sudden shifts from good to bad. The play opens with emphasis by the witches on the weather and its changes, and the battle is described in like terms:

> As whence the sun 'gins his reflection,
> Shipwracking storms and direful thunders break,
> So from that spring, whence comfort seem'd to come,
> Discomfort swells.
>
> (I, ii, 25–8)

135

The account of the struggle is one of fluctuating fortune. The sergeant reporting it left the battle uncertain, 'As two spent swimmers, that do cling together/ And choke their art' (ibid., 8–9). Then, recounting the struggle in a mixture of present and past tenses which obliterate sequence (7–23), he describes, first, the success of Macdonwald, then that of Macbeth, then the onslaught of the Norwegian king and finally the heroic resistance of Macbeth and Banquo (25–41). His story ends there, and Rosse enters to continue it, telling how he has come

> From Fife, great King,
> Where the Norweyan banners flout the sky,
> And fan our people cold.
>
> (49–51)

This suggests a Norwegian victory, and Rosse goes on to describe how hard an attack was mounted against the Scots: but in fact he has come to tell the king of the defeat of the enemy; foul, in short, is fair.[2] The motif of oscillation continues in Duncan's concluding comment on his sentence of the Thane of Cawdor, 'What he hath lost, noble Macbeth hath won' (69), and is heard again in Macbeth's first words, 'So foul and fair a day I have not seen.' The previous Thane of Cawdor was fair and yet foul: Duncan says, 'There's no art/ To find the mind's construction in the face:/ He was a gentleman on whom I built/ An absolute trust' (I, iv, 11–14). The battle, according to the witches, is 'lost and won'; and to them 'Fair is foul, and foul is fair' (I, i, 4, 11). All this is at least congruent with psychic instability in Macbeth himself, and suggests confusion of metaphysical opposites. Throughout the play there is insistence on the potential in any man for spiritual instability. Banquo himself has to plead, 'merciful Powers!/ Restrain in me the cursed thoughts that nature/ Gives way to in repose!' (II, i, 7–9), and later, as if corrupted by Macbeth's deed, 'May they [the witches] not be my oracles as well,/ And set me up in hope?' (III, i, 9–10); and the exiled Malcolm portrays himself a villain far worse than Macbeth, in order, so he afterwards claims to an unconvinced Macduff, to test the latter's moral character (IV, iii, 1–137)—Macduff remarks, in the idiom of 'opposites', that 'Such welcome and

136

unwelcome things at once,/ 'Tis hard to reconcile' (ibid., 138–39).

This, however, is only a vaguely-hinted metaphysical context to Macbeth's actions, a 'background' aspect of the evil in the play. And Banquo, if we except the thaneship of Cawdor, is in the same predicament as Macbeth, yet refuses the proffered suggestion. More is needed to explain Macbeth's assent to murder.

At the stage when Macbeth first meets the witches, his speculation on killing the king is largely unformulated, and he tries to put it aside in his 'If Chance will have me King, why, Chance may crown me,/ Without my stir' (I, iii, 144–45). But the impulse returns with Duncan's proclamation of Malcolm as his successor. Here Macbeth is engaged on what amounts to intellectual confusion, trusting the witches' statement that he will be king, but distrusting it in that he believes this will happen only if he makes it do so.

And as he describes the impulse, it is one to be carried out in isolation not only from the world, but from himself. It is to be a deed committed in ignorance, almost independently of volition:

> Stars, hide your fires!
> Let not light see my black and deep desires;
> The eye wink at the hand; yet let that be,
> Which the eye fears, when it is done, to see.
> (I, iv, 50–3)

He is to let the deed happen without acknowledging it, as if the hand, instructed by the will, thereafter had no connection with it and could be disowned (Macbeth is speaking of his own limbs as if they are hired murderers—like those he is actually to come to use): he is trying to cut off self from self, or as he says after he has murdered Duncan, 'To know my deed, 'twere best not know myself' (II, ii, 72); he is willing himself into a state of sleep, so that he may murder sleep. (So divided, his hands are later to pluck at his eyes (II, ii, 58), and horses are symbolically to rebel against man and devour one another (II, iv, 14 ff.).) Thus he writes his wife a letter telling her of the witches' prophecies and their accuracy so far—ostensibly so that 'thou might'st not lose the dues of rejoicing, by being ignorant of what grace is promis'd thee' (I, v, 12–14), but also, secretly from himself, so that she may apprehend that the crown must be secured by action. Thus, arguably, what Macbeth does in fact is tell his wife, who, he thinks, knows his true nature and wishes, that regicide is to be committed and that she is to give him the will to do it—and all in the belief that the letter is simply a curious piece of information; he gives the prompting to action to her without letting himself see that he does so. The time will come when it will no longer be that he refuses, but that he is unable, to see such actions for what they are; and this division of himself from himself will be expressed in his isolation.

What are we to make of his wife's characterization of Macbeth on her receipt of his letter?—

> I fear thy nature:
> It is too full o' th' milk of human kindness,
> To catch the nearest way. Thou wouldst be great;
> Art not without ambition, but without
> The illness should attend it: what thou wouldst highly,
> That wouldst thou holily; wouldst not play false,
> And yet wouldst wrongly win; thou'dst have, great Glamis,
> That which cries, 'Thus thou must do,' if thou have it;
> And that which rather thou dost fear to do,
> Than wishest should be undone.
>
> (I, v, 16–25)

(Again the seesawing, antithetical mode typical of the idiom of the play.) One would suppose that Lady Macbeth would have a real insight into her husband's nature, yet we have had no sense from Macbeth's reactions to the witches that he is in any way replete with the milk of human kindness. But what is additionally striking is that she states what she thinks is the truth about her husband no less than five different ways. This habit of repetition runs right through the play, always implying difficulty in defining anything clearly; the deed envisaged involves severance of the self from health and sense. Nor is it that Lady Macbeth says precisely the *same* thing. First Macbeth is portrayed as having too much goodness in him to do the wicked deed. Then she says that he is ambitious, but without the evil that should go with it—as if being ambitious were not in itself a step towards evil. Next

138

she says Macbeth wants eminence, but only with clean hands (the 'holily' implies not virtue so much as the ability to believe that one has done no vice). The 'wouldst not play false,/ And yet wouldst wrongly win' takes us nearer to Macbeth being prepared to do an evil act provided he can convince himself he is not implicated (precisely what he is setting about doing through the agency of his wife). Lastly, only fear, not any moral scruple, is described as keeping Macbeth from the deed. This speech shows the kind of erosion of moral categories which we are to see in Macbeth himself: neither he nor his wife really knows the nature of a moral act. The speech enacts not only the attempt by someone who does not understand it to grasp what conscience is, and the wearing down of moral behaviour to mere self-regard. More than this, it illustrates powerfully the *leitmotivs* of ignorance and division that run through the play. The witches equivocate; the battle is uncertain; Macbeth asks not to know himself; Cawdor's true nature is unknown; Macduff strangely deserts his wife; Malcolm presents himself to Macduff as a monster; the Birnam Wood that comes to Dunsinane is a disguised army, not a wood at all. And into it all instils itself the recurrently-mentioned darkness, obscurity and fog.

However, Lady Macbeth understands clearly enough the motive behind Macbeth's letter (later, when he is wavering, she demands, 'What beast was't then,/ That made you break this enterprise to me?' (I, vii, 47–8)): when he comes home she begins to manipulate him as he wishes. He can pretend that everything he says of Duncan's visit is perfectly natural, can seek to divide himself from his evil purpose so that his wife will be his prompter:

> *Macb.*   My dearest love,
>   Duncan comes here to-night.
> *Lady M.*   And when goes hence?
> *Macb.* To-morrow, as he purposes.
> *Lady M.*   O! never
>   Shall sun that morrow see!
>
>   (I, v, 58–61)

She remarks how 'Your face, my Thane, is as a book, where men/ May read strange matters': clearly Macbeth is letting

139

his desires slip; and when she tells him to put 'This night's great business into my dispatch' (68), he evades her only limply, 'We will speak further' (71); she, as he would wish, has the last word, 'Leave all the rest to me' (73). She has for the moment taken the burden of decision from him and he can partly conceal himself from himself. Indeed one could see the whole of Macbeth's journey as a search for peace, first by pretending that he is not responsible, and then by actively murdering all potential opponents.

Macbeth's subsequent soliloquy on the horror of killing Duncan is in effect an analysis of why he will do the deed.

> If it were done, when 'tis done, then 'twere well
> It were done quickly: if th'assassination
> Could trammel up the consequence, and catch
> With his surcease success; that but this blow
> Might be the be-all and the end-all—here,
> But here, upon this bank and shoal of time,
> We'd jump the life to come.
>
> (I, vii, 1–7)

The beginning is reminiscent of Hamlet's 'To be, or not to be' soliloquy, or even of Othello's 'It is the cause, it is the cause, my soul,/ Let me not name it to you, you chaste stars:/ It is the cause': there is similar non-specificity of language, a sense of blurring. This is seen also in the strange use of 'quickly' in the second line—a word which suggests guilty haste in the midst of posited freedom from further consequences ('If it were done'). This uncertainty is evident particularly in the way Macbeth goes on to say roughly the same thing twice more, and then rather confusedly. Thus the second attempt is in generalized language which somehow gives the impression of Macbeth playing with speculation and with words, particularly in the pun. The third effort is highly uncertain in reference: if he is asking that the blow may be the be-all and the end-all in this life, even though judgment may await it in the next ('We'd jump the life to come'), then it makes sense; but it also seems, in the use of 'this bank and shoal of time', that he is asking for the effects of the crime to be restricted to this world because otherwise he must fear the next. There is some irony in the fact that while Macbeth is asking for the deed to be divided from its metaphysical implications, he himself is cut off from clarity of thought, from the world of meaning and sense.

> But in these cases,
> We still have judgment here; that we but teach
> Bloody instructions, which, being taught, return
> To plague th'inventor: this even-handed Justice
> Commends th'ingredience of our poison'd chalice
> To our own lips.

Again he says roughly the same thing three times—and with increasing obscurity: in the first instance he seems to be concerned at the judgment that would return on him, but in the next two at the actual return of the deed upon him in the form of a reciprocal act. And still he has not used the singular personal pronoun: like Hamlet he seeks to sink the idiosyncratic in the typical and the oft-told—'in these cases,/ We still have judgment here'; and this again is part of his desire to hide himself from himself. The 'that' of the second clause seems the product of an only partially-formulated thought. As with the move from 'it' to 'assassination' to 'blow', there is a gradual increase of specificity in the progress from 'cases' to 'bloody instructions' to 'poison'd chalice', as of a man sidling up to the crime he has in view. It is clear that Macbeth has a species of insight into the consequences (though not the nature) of the projected crime, yet that awareness is stated so indirectly and blurrily that we feel that it is cut off from him, that he sees it with only the top half of his mind.

Macbeth's concern up to this point most simply is that his action should be attended with no consequences which would harm him personally. Yet now he switches to apparently more ethical considerations:

> He's here in double trust:
> First, as I am his kinsman and his subject,
> Strong both against the deed; then, as his host,
> Who should against his murtherer shut the door,
> Not bear the knife myself.

It is a curious rehearsal, suggesting that these thoughts are not instinctive, because they need such formulation. One's impression is not that Macbeth is describing his own feelings, but the way other people would feel about the deed—'If I do this then it will be open to condemnation in the following generally-agreed respects (and I will suffer moral repro- bation).' If this is moral scruple, it is so only at one remove. Further, the scruples that he does show, and the loyalties that he does acknowledge, are undermined by the fact that he has to mention them at all: for the one point that never strikes him is the sin of killing any man for himself, irrespective of any specific claims he may have to being spared. Macbeth does not consider murder in itself an evil, but only murder where some special allegiance is owed to the victim, or where he is of outstanding moral character—and this not because of these allegiances and excellencies considered in *themselves* either, but because of their impact on other people:

> Besides, this Duncan
> Hath borne his faculties so meek, hath been
> So clear in his great office, that his virtues
> Will plead like angels, trumpet-tongu'd, against
> The deep damnation of his taking-off;
> And Pity, like a naked new-born babe,
> Striding the blast, or heaven's Cherubins, hors'd
> Upon the sightless couriers of the air,
> Shall blow the horrid deed in every eye,
> That tears shall drown the wind.

This is little more (morally) than to say 'the death of this particular character will cause an almighty outcry from which I will suffer.' Duncan's meekness and virtue are nothing to Macbeth of themselves, but exist only, and with hallucinatory force, in relation to his experience of the horror with which the world will see and hear of their loss. The irony of the speech is that the man who asks that his act be without consequences is obsessed with consequences throughout: had Macbeth been aware of the horror of killing a man for himself rather than for what he meant, he would not so have been so. The imagery he uses is confused, o'erleaps itself like his ambition. Why should Duncan's virtues 'plead' rather than, say, 'roar', unless Macbeth has fallen into the imagery of the Last Judgment, whereby the virtues are conceived as pleading

142

before the bar of the Almighty? As with the 'bank and shoal of time', he has lost distinction between human and divine reactions. Morally it could be said to be damnable to slay Duncan, but Macbeth speaks not of this but of 'The deep damnation of his taking-off': the clash of the downward and upward movements suggests his own inability to see clearly. For a moment we are led to think of Duncan being damned, but then we see that the word 'damnation' ought to apply to Macbeth and a sense of sin, but in fact is largely a synonym for horror, and horror felt not so much by Macbeth directly here, but expressed by Duncan's virtues. Pity is likened to 'a naked new-born babe', but when Macbeth's mind pictures it striding the blast, he is moving towards a concept of outraged vengeance, and shifts to the notion of heaven's Cherubins as the broadcasters. Then he conceives of the winds as '*sightless* couriers', blowing the horrid deed in every eye; and speaks of these winds provoking tears which then drown them. Perhaps the simplest thing we can say here is that Macbeth has totally confused physical and metaphysical categories. Intellectually he seems lost—or rather blind, in the dark: again he has several attempts at saying the same thing. But the dominant points are clear enough—'trumpet-tongu'd', 'every eye'. (One recalls Volpone's 'To be taken, to be seen,/ These have crimes accounted been.') For Macbeth the act will be revolting out of other people's mouths: he has, as it were, located his conscience outside himself, in external opinion (which is why, to kill this conscience, he has to kill other people).[3] So dominant is his imagination, so acute his sense of this opinion, that he believes that if he murders Duncan everyone will know he did it. Thus, when temporizing with his wife after this speech, he argues that

> I have bought
> Golden opinions from all sorts of people,
> Which would be worn now in their newest gloss,
> Not cast aside so soon.
>
> (I, vii, 32–5)

The way Macbeth in fact behaves after his murder of Duncan makes this fear of exposure prove not far from the truth, but it need not have been so. Macbeth here thinks of becoming king as becoming unclothed, not dressed in borrowed robes.

The obvious question with Macbeth is how any man with so horrified a sense of the implications of killing Duncan should still wish to do so. Macbeth scarcely ever mentions what he could gain from doing so, or what tempts him: he sees his own 'vaulting ambition' as futile and self-defeating. Yet at the end of the very soliloquy in which he foresees the horror to others of killing Duncan, he is nearer to slaying the king than he was at the beginning. In the very act of envisaging so fully the ghastliness of the deed to others, he has imagined himself as having done it. When he now tells his wife, 'We will proceed no further in this business,' he does not give as his reason the horror of the act but the golden opinions of people, and therefore only postpones the matter a little, 'Not . . . so soon'.

Macbeth knows in his way that the murder makes no sense; yet he also knows that he will commit it, and more surely with every attempt to set out, like a dam against a flood, the reasons against it. For it is ultimately not reason, but blind refusal of the will—or plain love—which wins contests with temptation: reason may help, but it cannot be a substitute. As we have seen, the very fact that Macbeth sees the horror of the crime only in terms of consequences here shows that the act itself is no obstacle to him ('If it were done, when 'tis done'); it is the accusing voices that he thinks he hears in the murder chamber that cause him terror. Without blind refusal, loyalty, a grain in one's own character to go against—call it what we may—without these, mere reason and imagination are inadequate. The harder Macbeth tries to find reasons for not killing Duncan, the more he lays bare his lack of resources for true resistance. He thinks mostly of consequences to himself, or of other people's opinions; he repeats himself; the reasons he thinks of for loyalty to Duncan are reason, not loyalty; and his imagination is driven to a frenzy of terror by the fact that he knows it is inadequate to stop him. The resistance put up in this soliloquy is thus in direct proportion to the extent of Macbeth's yielding.

But yielding to what? To a metaphysic of evil, as has often been argued?[4] A recent critic suggests that there is in the play an independent force of evil, in part embodied in the witches, which sucks Macbeth in, and that the play has a Manichaean

144

vision whereby 'evil has the primacy of superior actuality. The feeling is that its capacity for destruction defeats that of goodness for reconstruction.'[5] There is truth in this: we certainly see some fascination for the vitality of evil in Lady Macbeth's 'unsex me here' soliloquy (I, v, 38–54); and later, though only after the deed, Macbeth is to display some primal pleasure at his involvement in evil (II, i, 49–56; III, iii, 40–4, 50–3). But here again, as with all the other potential reasons *for* Macbeth's action, there is insufficient clinching evidence. Much, for instance, has to be made by one commentator of Macbeth's supposed expression of a 'black contamination' as he meets his wife after his letter to her.[6]

The evidence is that in this play Shakespeare's main interest is less in Macbeth's positive motive—whatever that may be—for killing the king, than in the absence in him of a motive for not doing so. He is concerned with the fact that although Macbeth sees many reasons which would stay his hand, he still goes on; and he is concerned with the nature of those reasons, and what they reveal about him. In short, his moral analysis is preoccupied not so much with the ways in which Macbeth is a bad man as with the ways in which he is not a good one.

Thus Macbeth is shown as coming to the murder of Duncan more out of a lack in himself than out of any particular motive. Unlike Banquo, he did not have in him the capacity to resist the idea of killing the king. His crime is nurtured in negativity—he thinks of it in terms only of the reasons against it, and he can find nothing in him to oppose to it: its nature is summed up in his 'nothing is, but what is not'.

Lady Macbeth now pushes her husband from a position of half-hearted refusal to one of reluctant commitment. Macbeth is not uxorious: he is caught by her, as he unconsciously wished, in a position of exposure to her blandishments. It is not even as though, considered seriously, some of the blandishments could be very real to him. Her calling his scruples cowardice allows him, as C. C. Clarke has pointed out, to see the mere savagery in killing Duncan as courage.[7] Twice she insists that he broke the scheme to her before and cannot go back on it now, if he is not to be a mere coward: she rises to chilling violence in her assertion,

> I have given suck, and know
> How tender 'tis to love the babe that milks me:
> I would, while it was smiling in my face,
> Have pluck'd my nipple from his boneless gums,
> And dash'd the brains out, had I so sworn
> As you have done to this.
>
> (I, vii, 54–9)

This is on the evidence we have quite false: Macbeth never so swore. But in a sense he wants to believe he did, so that he can believe he made a positive decision to kill Duncan, rather than that he assented by yielding—hence perhaps her insistence on manliness at this point. Further, Lady Macbeth's image of the murdered baby would not seem a particularly heartening one—but it is an image of the strongest scruples giving way before a resolute vow. When she says, 'screw your courage to the sticking-place' (ibid., 61), we see that it is precisely that there is no sticking-place, no firm position from which to stop the slow slipping, that has been Macbeth's pain, and that it is this, of whatever moral character, that his wife has for the moment given him. Then, last, she gives him the assurance that she will take care of everything—even, it is implied, the murder itself. Macbeth is in a half-glad daze, willing to leave himself to her. She has talked of making the chamberlains drunk so that the murder may be committed, and then blaming them for the deed. Instead of asking her what motive could be given to the chamberlains for the murder, or how they could be supposed to fall asleep near the king after having done it, Macbeth simply repeats her idea as if she had not uttered it:

> Will it not be receiv'd,
> When we have mark'd with blood those sleepy two
> Of his own chamber, and us'd their very daggers,
> That they have done't?
>
> (75–8)

(Lady Macbeth too, excitedly repeats her idea (78–80).) She has now helped him over the border, 'I am settled, and bend up/ Each corporal agent to this terrible feat' (one is reminded of how his first thought of murder shook his 'single state of man' (I, iii, 140); now he has been reassembled). Not one of

146

his wife's reasons has counted in any final sense as a reason, just as with his reasons for not killing Duncan: they have simply acted as catalysts, speeding up Macbeth's move from just on one side to just on another, and he does not pay much attention to them in detail. His wife only has to sound powerfully convinced that the murder must be done, for him to become himself convinced more quickly than he would otherwise have done. In the end, reasons are nothing.

The deed is done, it would seem, for nothing. Insofar as he can find no basic human or other value in himself to set against it, Macbeth himself is nothing. (The absence of such a sense in him is highlit by contrast with Macduff's instinctively moral reaction to the murder, 'Most sacrilegious Murther hath broke ope/ The Lord's anointed Temple, and stole thence/ The life o' th' building!' (II, iii, 68–70).) And the product of such nothingness is obvious: as Macbeth instantly realizes, it gains nothing, 'Better be with the dead,/ Whom we, to gain our peace, have sent to peace' (III, ii, 19–20). The whole of his mind is now devoted to a longing for certainty in the midst of the uncertainty he has created for himself—the certainty of safety, of unopposed power, of fancied super-natural assurances. And there is the longing too for total concealment, the separation of the self from all other value, all other eyes, which Macbeth and his wife both show—'Come, thick Night,' 'Come, seeling Night' (I, v, 50; III, iii, 46). Macbeth's vacant deed, which emerges from no certain aim and which gives him less than he had, makes his life as meaningless as itself; and his severance from the real world and from sight makes him subject to delusions—whether in unquestioning acceptance of surface meanings, or in possible hallucinations (the air-drawn dagger, Banquo's ghost).

At first, after the murder, Macbeth has at once a longing for peace, and the irritated imagination which makes him remove such peace further than it might be through suspicion. He has, in a sense, lost his way, and can only lurch among a series of mutually exclusive choices:

> We have scorch'd the snake, not kill'd it:
> She'll close, and be herself; whilst our poor malice
> Remains in danger of her former tooth.

147

> But let the frame of things disjoint, both the worlds suffer,
> Ere we will eat our meal in fear, and sleep
> In the affliction of these terrible dreams,
> That shake us nightly.

(III, ii, 13–19)

The first line suggests further action against enemies; the second and third move towards a sense of powerlessness; then there is an over-violent reaction which in fact turns out to refer not to human enemies but to fears wrought by the workings of imagination (the jerk comes in moving from 'fear' in the fifth line, which we tend to read as a determination of action against enemies, to the notion of spiritual terrors in the sixth). If we read the last back into the preceding material we arrive at the strange meaning that Macbeth murdered Duncan to silence his imagination of doing so: to such spiritual confusion has he come. The fifth line says, 'we will [not] eat our meal in fear,' but the defiance is contradictory since they clearly already are; and the confusion is increased in the next lines, where Macbeth says he will never have his sleep disturbed and then admits that it is. Of course he really means that this will happen no longer, but as he puts it it sounds as though it both is and is not happening; here (presumably) the contradiction of the speech enacts the conflict between the will to peace and the constant disturbance of that peace in Macbeth's mind. Now he moves on to repeat the strange statement that he murdered Duncan to be at peace—that is, committed a deed bound to make conscience a burning brand, in order that conscience might be quenched:

> Better be with the dead,
> Whom we, to gain our peace, have sent to peace,
> Than on the torture of the mind to lie
> In restless ecstasy.

He knows now that he has lost, not gained peace. Now the only road to peace is through more murders, so that his spirit may be put to sleep through long brutalization. The paradox with him is that his sense of horror is at its most intense before he has done his first wrong. Now the peace of death attracts him; but, no sooner has he given utterance to this, than he shifts back to action and the project for murdering Banquo (ibid., 30 ff.). For the rest of the play suicide and murder alternately present themselves as solutions; and his essential position, as a man who gave up peace to gain it, is absurd. His senseless deed divides him finally from sense.

The confusion inherent in Macbeth's deed spreads out to affect others. Rosse says, speaking of Macduff,

> cruel are the times, when we are traitors,
> And do not know ourselves; when we hold rumour
> From what we fear, yet know not what we fear,
> But float upon a wild and violent sea
> Each way, and move.
>
> (IV, ii, 18–22)

Coming from his discovery of Duncan's murdered corpse, Macduff cries, 'Confusion now hath made his masterpiece!' (II, iii, 67). Good and evil seem to become indistinct from one another[8] as Macduff deserts his wife and Malcolm presents himself as a monster of iniquity. The fount is Macbeth himself, who does not know whether he seeks his own health or ill, only that he wants the peace of certainty:

> for now I am bent to know,
> By the worst means, the worst. For mine own good,
> All causes shall give way.
>
> (III, iv, 133–35)

The witches give him certainties which are really equivocations and uncertainties. But the curious thing about Macbeth —and this is consistent with the uncertainty and the nothingness to which he has committed himself—is that although he seems to care desperately, in another way he does not: although he seems to want, he also comes to a position of no want; and he has so divided self from self that he never sees the contradiction. He tries to keep what he has, without knowing what it is; equally readily he wishes to throw it away, without knowing what he will lose. There is no more reason for going on than for going back, 'I am in blood/ Stepp'd in so far, that, should I wade no more,/ Returning were as tedious as go o'er' (ibid., 135–37):

149

> This push
> Will cheer me ever, or disseat me now.
> I have liv'd long enough.
>
> (V, iii, 20–2)

He poses the possibility of gain or loss and lurches towards the latter, going on to say that it is hardly worth living out an empty life without honour or friends (22–8). Yet in a moment his mood changes, as he is told of the large army approaching against him: 'I'll fight, till from my bones my flesh be hack'd./ Give me my armour'; 'Send out moe horses, skirr the country round;/ Hang those that talk of fear.' And although Macbeth often in the last act speaks as though the assurances of the witches concerning his survival are crucial to him—'Till Birnam wood remove to Dunsinane,/ I cannot taint with fear,' ' "Fear not, Macbeth; no man that's born of woman/ Shall e'er have power upon thee," ' 'I will not be afraid of death and bane,/ Till Birnam forest come to Dunsinane' (V, iii, 2–3, 6–7, 59–60), 'swords I smile at, weapons laugh to scorn,/ Brandish'd by man that's of a woman born' (V, vii, 12–13), 'I bear a charmed life; which must not yield/ To one of woman born' (V, viii, 12–13)—despite these insistencies, there is a sense in which the promises of the witches do not matter to him. Though throughout the last act Macbeth thus insists on his insurance policy, and the discovery of its exclusion clauses is for him a momentary terror, he at the same time voices his sense of the emptiness of life and his readiness for death: 'I have liv'd long enough: my way of life/ Is fall'n into the sere, the yellow leaf' (V, iii, 22–3); 'I 'gin to be aweary of the sun,/ And wish th'estate o' th' world were now undone' (V, v, 49–50). Similarly, the man who is so often terrified at the thought of his own death can say, recalling the former great warrior of Duncan's battles, 'I'll fight, till from my bones my flesh be hack'd' (V, iii, 32); and no mention now is made of fear of the after-life. But for these perceptions and courageous acts in the midst of and after this cowering behind supernatural 'assurance' Macbeth would be without the increase of heroic stature that he gains in the last act: yet we cannot also fail to be aware that some of that very stature is as uncertain as his shifting attitudes—is itself the product of the meaninglessness that he actualized in his murder of Duncan.

For in the end, 'nothing is, but what is not' (I, iii, 142): the impossible—Birnam wood rising, the existence of a man not born of woman—comes into being to destroy Macbeth. And he himself answers unreason with unreason: though he said, 'Our castle's strength/ Will laugh a siege to scorn' (V, v, 2–3), he no sooner sees what he thinks is Birnam wood apparently approaching than he accedes to the portent and abandons himself to the destiny which has seemingly presented itself. We recall how formerly he thought to put his will *before* providential action by himself bringing into being the prophecy that he would be king. But, whether hubristic or slavish, he is still acting on his interpretation of fate—he is still doing what is an arch crime in Shakespeare's drama, setting his will in separation from providence. 'I pull in resolution; and begin/ To doubt th'equivocation of the fiend,/ That lies like truth' (V, v, 42–4). Finally stripped of the certainty he forfeited in regicide, he acts in unreason, 'Arm, arm, and out!—/ If this which he [the messenger] avouches does appear,/ There is nor flying hence, nor tarrying here' (ibid., 46–8).

The vision to which he has come is one of a total loss of meaning. He foresaw it, as he foresaw everything, at the murder of Duncan,

> from this instant,
> There's nothing serious in mortality;
> All is but toys: renown, and grace, is dead;
> The wine of life is drawn, and the mere lees
> Is left this vault to brag of.
> (II, iii, 92–6)

In killing Duncan he actualized the lack in himself of all sense, all value. Now he is at the plain fact itself. Told that the queen is dead, he reflects, 'She should have died hereafter:/ There would have been a time for such a word' (V, v, 17–18). He may be saying that she should have died at a time when he could have paid proper attention to the fact; equally he may be saying that she would have died some time anyway: either way he proceeds with a picture of life as a series of repetitions as empty as the ticking of a clock:

151

> To-morrow, and to-morrow, and to-morrow,
> Creeps in this petty pace from day to day,
> To the last syllable of recorded time;
> And all our yesterdays have lighted fools
> The way to dusty death.

The word usage destroys meaning as it denies it. In the first line the repetition establishes that in a sense there is no tomorrow, since all tomorrows are as today, and so too with all our yesterdays. The first two lines convey disgust, but at nothing in particular: Macbeth is not objecting to the pettiness of the pace (or preferring a more vigorous one), nor is he weary at anything, just weary. Time is collapsed in the shift from ultimate futurity to 'all our yesterdays'. The statement that 'all our yesterdays have lighted fools/ The way to dusty death,' is, as a statement of the universality of death, scarcely a perception at all even while it is presented as one: that death comes to all does not make death the ultimate fact of things save to those who are possessed by despair. The use of 'our' and the whole generalizing mode of the speech make it sound like a man summing up a perception common to all humanity: the fact that this is not really the case highlights Macbeth's isolation here.

> Out, out, brief candle!
> Life's but a walking shadow; a poor player,
> That struts and frets his hour upon the stage,
> And then is heard no more: it is a tale
> Told by an idiot, full of sound and fury
> Signifying nothing.

Here 'nothing is, but what is not' with a difference: it is not that nothing is everything, as in *Lear*, but that everything is nothing. It is remarkable that a speech which sounds so purposeful, so redolent with accumulated experience and insight, should actually convey so little. Repetitive as he has been since his first move to evil, Macbeth says the same thing—or gives voice to the same weariness at life—five times. The one image drifts into the other: the yesterdays that light fools lead to candles, candles to the shadows about them, shadows to the insubstantiality of play-acting, and play-acting to the play that it enacts. Each sentence slumps to an end in a tacked-on extra of six syllables starting a new line, 'The way to dusty death', 'And then is heard no more', Signifying nothing'; the sentences progressively shrink from five to three to two lines; and the juxtaposed '*ings* in the last line impose something of a grammatical identity between the two words, the participle and the noun, thus enacting the annihilation described. Metaphysically the speech can be seen to cover several categories of nothingness—of time, life, being and meaning—but there is no sense of categories, only of all things having settled to an inert desert.

Lady Macbeth's spiritual journey is in a sense opposite to Macbeth's.[9] When first she hears from Macbeth of the witches' prophecy and of Duncan's imminent visit she is at once absolute for the deed. Her speech of invocation of the powers of evil ('The raven himself is hoarse. . . .') is so imbued with resolution, so incandescent with triumphant purpose, that it seems not so much to envision a deed that will be done as to carry it out then and there—and this perhaps not least in the way that Lady Macbeth analogously murders her feminine self ('unsex me here'). To her, the king is already mere 'Duncan'. When on Macbeth's arrival she tells him,

> Thy letters have transported me beyond
> This ignorant present, and I feel now
> The future in the instant
>
> (I, v, 56–8),

we feel that for her there is in a sense no 'future' so far as the murder is concerned, for it has been made present, actualized now. Unlike Macbeth, she considers only the deed and how it may be effected without shrinking; for her, it is to be enclosed in time, by 'the blanket of the dark'. He, on the other hand, considers it only as done, imagining that the murderer will be obvious to all, and the horror that will result from the act.

Yet Lady Macbeth's unsexing is in fact very short-lived. The price she pays for the momentary white-heat to which she brings her purpose is that thereafter it steadily fades. But it is also simply a matter of spiritual fact, which produces ironically opposed journeys in Macbeth and his wife. By her refusing even to attempt to take account of the promptings of conscience and sympathy, these return to torment her. As early as the murder itself she is shrinking: 'Had he not resembled/ My father as he slept, I had done't' (II, ii, 12–13). Because she ignores the spiritual future it comes to plague her; he, on the other hand, foresees it with such force and thoroughness that it has diminishing power over him as it actually happens—to the point where he can say, 'I have supp'd full with horrors:/ Direness, familiar to my slaughterous thoughts,/ Cannot once start me' (V, v, 13–15). He begins 'weak' and ends 'strong', she vice-versa. She starts inhumanly, and ends with a burdensome awareness of renounced humanity; Macbeth begins as a man of conscientious scruples and then denigrates the status of man (for instance, likening men to dogs in addressing the murderers of Banquo (III, i, 90–100)), until he loses humanity altogether. Macbeth begins unable to wash his hands of his deed (II, ii, 59–62); Lady Macbeth so ends (V, i, 25–59). Her doom is to be static, her mind revolving continually about the regicide, reliving it. At the outset Lady Macbeth bids the 'Spirits' so conceal her crime that heaven cannot cry 'Hold, hold!'; Macbeth's last words are 'damn'd be him that first cries, "Hold, enough!" ' The return of humanity to Lady Macbeth shows that inhumanity is ultimately achieved by persistent refusals, not by one exalted moment or act. If Lady Macbeth starts with a bang and ends with a whimper, then given the different spiritual approach, Macbeth does the reverse. The 'good' that destroys Macbeth in the end comes from outside, in the form of an army.

For all the nothingness to which Macbeth's crime deservedly brings him, for all the pathetic evasions, moral vacancy and increasing inhumanity that characterize his journey into evil, this is not quite the whole truth about him, nor the sole determinant of our feelings towards him.[10] Macbeth is not, like Goneril and Regan, simply evil—for one thing, they lack his imagination. But more than this, Macbeth is often the most vital and purposeful character in the play. His own wife, slipping away from the sheer incandescence of her initial exultation in evil, heightens his own growing determination by contrast, giving it a certain positive force even at the moment we know it to be worthless. Shakespeare's view may be that evil has no real existence, that it is ultimately causeless, merely parasitic upon good, and leading only to a sense of the emptiness that it is, but as far as realization goes, it is the good characters who are shadowy, Macbeth substantial. In the context of the contrast with his wife, it is inevitable that, however futile his journey and empty the gains, Macbeth is going to come over as something of a heroic mental traveller. He sees everything before he acts, and yet does so: even at his weakest he is further on than she with her deliberate myopia. However stupidly evil the journey, he is the only person who makes one in the play. Lady Macbeth simply marks time; all the other characters become functions of a supposed metaphysic of good working through them. As the play's only consistently memorable character, there is a sense in which Macbeth even has the right to the Olympian tone of his 'To-morrow' speech; all the others are faceless shadows compared to him. And where Macbeth becomes increasingly steady in his evil, his opponents become more unstable in their good—Macduff leaving his wife, Malcolm portraying himself as a monster of iniquity (IV, iii); and in the end they even have to take on the lineaments of the unnatural, their army disguised as a moving wood, Macduff able to slay Macbeth because he is not 'of woman born'.

This lack of identity in the good is in part an index to the poverty of their characterization. Many of the scenes without the Macbeths suffer from feebleness of realization and writing: Shakespeare's inspiration only came truly alive with Macbeth. This—if we except *Timon*, written about the same time— makes the play unlike any other of Shakespeare's tragedies, where characters other than the central figure are vividly realized. In *Lear* Cordelia is strongly enough felt to be a credible source of renewal in the kingdom; in *Macbeth* we have to give the shrill, unsubtle rhetoric and psychological absurdity of the scene between Malcolm and Macduff, or the account of the healing powers of the English King Edward the Confessor a force they do not in themselves contain, if the ultimate destruction of Macbeth by the good is to be convincing at all. Indeed the truth is that the play is ultimately a monodrama:[11] Macbeth has destroyed himself before he is destroyed, and the armies sent against him are in this sense superfluous, shadows, as he says. But Shakespeare appears to have wanted a happy ending, the natural and health-giving replaced for the unnatural. At least, a part of him does, a part that is beginning to turn away from the vision of the tragedies to that of the late comedies; considered in terms of what is *said* to be restored, *Macbeth* ends more cheerfully than any previous tragedy of Shakespeare's. That part is however finally rendered impotent in this play because it exists at the level of assertion, not demonstration. What we feel much more strongly at the close is the force, at once empty and heroic, of Macbeth's defiance and refusal to yield himself a prisoner: 'Blow, wind! come, wrack!/ At least we'll die with harness on our back'; 'lay on, Macduff;/ And damn'd be him that first cries, "Hold, enough!"'

Macbeth, as has often been pointed out, is a play shot through with polarities—of light and dark, good and evil, fair and foul.[12] At the centre of the play is a man who divides himself first from himself and sense, and then from all society, living by absurd contradictions. The structure of the play mirrors these divisions: first we see Macbeth trying to silence the evil in himself, then the good; first his wife is strong in evil, then weak, while he is weak and then strong: the mode is that of the seesaw, expressing the antithetical nature of the world in which the characters move. Finally, Shakespeare himself is in part divided between total condemnation of Macbeth and admiration of him as a heroic villain. This last division of attitude is to recur in *Timon, Antony and Cleopatra* and *Coriolanus*.

NOTES

1. References are to the Arden *Macbeth*. ed. Kenneth Muir (Methuen, 1962).
2. Compare on this Terence Hawkes, *Shakespeare and the Reason: A Study of the Tragedies and the Problem Plays* (Routledge and Kegan Paul, 1964), pp. 132–33: Hawkes relates the account to the theme of divorced appearance and reality rather than to the issue of psychic and moral instability.
3. This would meet C. C. Clarke's contention that Macbeth is confused between horror and fear of exposure, the one being generated by his conscience and the other by the lower motive of self-preservation ('Darkened Reason in *Macbeth*', *Durham University Journal*, n.s. 22–3 (1960–62), 14–16).

4. G. Wilson Knight's account in *The Wheel of Fire: Interpretations of Shakespearian Tragedy* (1930), rev. ed. (Methuen, 1949), pp. 140–59, has been most influential; for a more recent statement, see Wilbur Sanders, *The Dramatist and the Received Idea: Studies in the Plays of Marlowe and Shakespeare* (Cambridge, Cambridge University Press, 1968), chs. 13, 14.
5. Sanders, p. 275.
6. Ibid., pp. 286–87.
7. Clarke, p. 16.
8. See also Clarke, pp. 15–16.
9. See also A. C. Bradley, *Shakespearean Tragedy*, pp. 366–79; Brents Stirling, *Unity in Shakespearian Tragedy*, p. 155.
10. See also the excellent account in Sanders, pp. 290–307. Sanders however maintains that this shows 'the capacity of the mature Shakespeare to encompass extremes of imaginative insight in the one aesthetic experience' (p. 292); yet to reconcile these opposites in his own mind he is forced to play down Macbeth's criminality (pp. 293–95).
11. See also Bernard McElroy, *Shakespeare's Mature Tragedies*, pp. 215–17.
12. See e.g. Stirling, ch. 9, *passim*; Hawkes, pp. 124–25; and G. I. Duthie, 'Antithesis in *Macbeth*', *SS*, 19 (1966), 25–33. On the 'paradoxical' medium of the play, see Sanders, p. 299.

7

Coriolanus

There seems real evidence that from the 'problem' plays onwards Shakespeare began to turn away from any sense that there could be a happy relation between the individual and society. The unanimity with which all his plays from *Hamlet* onwards have the themes of societal corruption or breakdown, or (later) renunciation of the state or of mankind as their central interest, is more than coincidence. *Troilus and Cressida* portrays a society destroyed by egotism and lust; *Measure for Measure* challenges the rule of law, the foundation of the state; *All's Well* assails the notion of social hierarchy in the unequal marriage of Bertram and Helena. The loneliness of Shakespeare's tragic heroes and their insights often go far further than those, say, of the protagonists of Greek tragedy, who rarely question the social fabric and beliefs by which they exist (though they may abuse them). Whatever else we say of the tragedies from *Hamlet* to *Coriolanus*, it is clear that their heroes are often in rebellion against the world or alienated from it, whether in Hamlet's disgusted 'How weary, stale, flat, and unprofitable/ Seem to me all the uses of this world!', Othello's isolation as the ignorant Blackamoor, Lear's 'Thorough tatter'd clothes small vices do appear;/ Robes and furr'd gowns hide all,' Macbeth's '[Life] is a tale/ Told by an idiot . . ./ Signifying nothing,' Antony's 'Kingdoms are clay,' or Coriolanus' 'I banish you!' In the late plays evil is portrayed as emanating from courts or cities—the incest of Antiochus or the treachery of Cleon and Dionyza in *Pericles*, the evil queen and her son at the court in *Cymbeline*, the jealousy of Leontes in his Sicilian palace in *The Winter's Tale*, the treachery of Prospero's brother while deputizing for him as Duke of Milan in *The Tempest*. All these plays involve a departure from the

158

court to nature: society is only restored to health when that nature is married to it, as Guiderius and Arviragus return in *Cymbeline* or Florizel and Perdita in *The Winter's Tale*.

We may also trace in all these plays a recurrent motif of 'doing dirt' on goodness: the Greeks and Trojans of *Troilus and Cressida* do not appear as the heroes Homer painted; the precise and upright judge of *Measure for Measure*, ironically named Angelo, turns out to be as sinfully lecherous as Lear's picture of justices, and the saintly Isabella is in reality heartless; Bertram besmirches his wife through his lechery; Hamlet abuses the gentle Ophelia as he himself, 'Th'expectancy and rose of the fair state', has been blighted, along with all things of value in Denmark, through Claudius' regicide. Othello turns against his pure wife Desdemona; Macbeth murders the good king Duncan and perverts a whole kingdom; Cordelia is at first cast out with calumny; Cymbeline is led by his wicked queen to distrust his daughter Imogen, whose fidelity is also tested and besmirched through the agency of her own husband Posthumus; and Leontes in *The Winter's Tale* destroys the paradisal friendship of himself, his wife and Polixenes with his sudden and destructive jealousy.

Timon of Athens, *Antony and Cleopatra* and *Coriolanus* are specifically about breakdown between the individual and society. Timon, betrayed when in want by his erstwhile parasites, quits Athens, and spends the last two acts of the play reviling its inhabitants until he dies; Antony increasingly turns away from Rome for Cleopatra, to the point of warfare with the forces of his native land and his subsequent death; Coriolanus, rejecting and rejected by Roman society, leaves the city and joins its Volscian enemies, to lead an army bent on Rome's destruction. In all these plays Shakespeare offers criticism of the protagonists for their isolation, but the social fabric is portrayed as uniformly unattractive, corrupt or mean. In *Timon*, a play whose possible incompleteness may imply greater self-revelation on Shakespeare's part, the indictment of the social order seems harshest. When our previous uncertainty as to the true nature of Timon's followers is removed when he runs out of money, our feelings against them are all the stronger. Further, Shakespeare seems quite prepared to go against the variety of life, and our previous sense of ambiguity,

159

by showing not one of the followers willing to lift a finger to help Timon: thus the judgment on them can be made quite total. The attitude to Timon seems uncertain: at first we are given no clear view of the moral nature of his liberality, whether self-indulgent or magnificent;[1] then after his fall we are alternately made to be repelled at the violence of his hatred of Athens and directed to detest the Athenians who come to him in hope of more gold. And if the misanthrope in Timon is in part condemned, it would seem that misanthropy is not, for he is allowed two acts in which to give vent to it.

With separation of their heroes from their societies their central preoccupation, these plays are essentially about division. They are full of the clash of irreconcilable opposites. *Antony* is built on the oppugnancy of Rome and Egypt, public and private, restraint and licence, land and sea, reason and passion, precision and inexactitude. Each of the opposites is at an extreme: Caesar's reason is coldly precise, Antony's passion chaotically unstable; as Octavia puts it, there is 'no midway/ 'Twixt these extremes at all' (III, iv, 19–20). The opposites in *Timon* are seen in the reactions of the protagonist, who shifts from the unqualified philanthropy of the first part of the play to the equally unqualified misanthropy of the second; his fellow-misanthrope Apemantus tells him, 'The middle of humanity thou never knewest, but the extremity of both ends' (IV, iii, 301–2). A similar irreconcilability governs the 'violent'st contrariety' of *Coriolanus*, with the opposition of extreme left- and right-wing political factions, and with switches from friendship to enmity and vice-versa in Coriolanus' relations with Rome and Tullus Aufidius.

Division also characterizes our response to these plays. This was not the case in an earlier play about division, *Troilus and Cressida*, for all the characters were ultimately seen in the same cynical light. But here it is a question of split sympathies. The heroes have all the force and grandeur available, and beside them society seems degraded and petty; yet at the same time we are made aware of the egoism or self-indulgence of their behaviour, or of the inadequacies in them that make them unable to accommodate to the changes of the world. Objectively there might seem no reason why these divided responses should not be able to coexist; but in practice that coexistence is

160

inherently unstable.

It is in *Coriolanus* that this motif of division finds the most sustained and highly-wrought expression; in *Coriolanus* too that we observe perhaps the most interesting of Shakespeare's struggles for impartiality in these plays.

In the Rome of *Coriolanus* we find none of those factors that can serve to bind the diverse phenomena of the world together and to make sense of them—no metaphysical value, no mind, no love. Menenius' early description of the workings of the state is in terms of the physical connectedness of all parts of the body in feeding: the kind of metaphysical sanction that (however inapplicable in that play) informs Ulysses' conception of universal order in *Troilus and Cressida*, is not present here.[2] We find, too, that 'spiritual' words such as 'noble' and 'honour' are steadily devalued through use in dubious contexts, as when Martius' son is called 'noble' for tearing a butterfly to pieces (I, iii, 67),[3] or when the citizens mockingly remark of Coriolanus, 'if he tell us his noble deeds, we must also tell him our noble acceptance of them' (II, iii, 8–9), or when Volumnia declares, 'I would dissemble with my nature where/ My fortunes and my friends at stake requir'd/ I should do so in honour' (III, ii, 62–4). When Coriolanus yields to the entreaties of his kin and spares Rome, he does not do so for Rome's people, nor for his native land, nor for his friends, but for his mother. And in that assent there is no sense that 'nature' in the full religious sanction that the word has in *King Lear* or *Macbeth* is operative; his relation to his mother is too strange and perverted for that in any case. We do not know that any of his mother's arguments persuaded him—whether the appeal to his care for his family or the prophecy of the everlasting shame that would befall him should he proceed. Our dominant impression is simply one of a previously immovable object overcome by an irresistible force: from birth Volumnia has fashioned Coriolanus as she wished and now we see her, as the only person who can, doing so again. And the overcoming, so local and personal in its cause, is only momentary: after Coriolanus has lifted the seige of Rome he is in no way altered; he is like a ball bounced off a wall, still itself, or, as he puts it to the Volscian lords, 'I am return'd your soldier,/ No more infected with my country's love/ Than when I parted hence' (V, vi, 71–3).

As for mind in the play, it is the belly, not the head, that is the authority in the body of Menenius' fable of the state: later we hear Volumnia describing how in battle Coriolanus will 'beat Aufidius' head below his knee,/ And tread upon his neck' (I, iii, 46–7), Menenius speaking of himself as 'one that converses more with the buttock of the night than with the forehead of the morning' (II, i, 50–2) and Coriolanus vowing not to apologize to the people lest 'by my body's action [I] teach my mind/ A most inherent baseness' (III, ii, 122–23). Throughout the play we have the sense of a dominant physicality.[4] The citizens and the patricians behave like warring atoms. The citizens have 'stiff bats and clubs' and the Roman state is portrayed to them by Menenius as a juggernaut 'whose course will on/ The way it takes, cracking ten thousand curbs/ Of more strong link asunder than can ever/ Appear in your impediment' (I, i, 68–71). War is seen only in terms of the impact of body against body. Coriolanus' sword is 'death's stamp', he strikes Corioles like a planet and when he returns against Rome he 'moves like an engine and the ground shrinks before his treading. He is able to pierce a corselet with his eye, talks like a knell, and his hum is a battery' (V, iv, 19–21). He has no time for stasis or tactics in war but is concerned only to be at the front of the action. It may be part of his preference for action rather than reflection that he cannot stand having his achievements later proclaimed in speech; and we might place in similar 'anti-mental' category his inability to recall the name of the poor man of Corioles who helped him (I, ix, 77–89). There are few soliloquies, those direct expressions of mental working, in the play. There is a peculiar stress too, on the body itself as something to be embraced or handled in *Coriolanus*. The primary evidence of Coriolanus' deeds is to be the mark of fresh wounds on his body, over which his mother and Menenius gloat, and which the Roman citizenry have to see and feel before they will support his becoming consul. Aufidius, newly Coriolanus' friend, says, 'Let me twine/ Mine arms about that body, where against/ My grained ash an hundred times hath broke,/ And scarr'd the moon with splinters. Here I clip/ The anvil of my sword' (IV, v, 107–11).

The dynamic of the play is quite mindless, the chance collision of bodies into unity or oppugnancy. About to offer himself to Aufidius, the banished Coriolanus declares:

> O world, thy slippery turns! Friends now fast sworn,
> Whose double bosoms seems to wear one heart,
> Whose hours, whose bed, whose meal and exercise
> Are still together, who twin, as 'twere, in love
> Unseparable, shall within this hour,
> On a dissension of a doit, break out
> To bitterest enmity: so fellest foes,
> Whose passions and whose plots have broke their sleep
> To take the one by the other, by some chance,
> Some trick not worth an egg, shall grow dear friends
> And interjoin their issues. So with me:
> My birthplace hate I, and my love's upon
> This enemy town.
>
> (IV, iv, 12–24)

This is ultimately to say that there is no motive for anything. Yet further, even as Coriolanus pronounces this principle, tried to make even this limited sense of his world, he falsifies the truth: it was not the dissension of a doit that made him leave Rome but a challenge to his whole being. And it is not the world, but merely himself who has brought about these changes: he has no right to Olympian generalizations from his very particular and personal case. The failure of his pronouncements here suggests that there is in fact no pattern or meaning in what has happened to him. This is to be a play in which the verdict on the hero's character (uttered by Aufidius) is not only ambiguous but fundamentally lacking in certainty:

> Whether 'twas pride,
> Which out of daily fortune ever taints
> The happy man; whether defect of judgment,
> To fail in the disposing of those chances
> Which he was lord of; or whether nature,
> Not to be other than one thing, not moving
> From th'casque to th'cushion, but commanding peace
> Even with the same austerity and garb
> As he controll'd the war; but one of these—
> As he hath spices of them all, not all,
> For I dare so far free him—made him fear'd,

> So hated, and so banish'd: but he has a merit
> To choke it in the utt'rance. So our virtues
> Lie in th'interpretation of the time,
> And power, unto itself most commendable,
> Hath not a tomb so evident as a chair
> T'extol what it hath done.
> One fire drives out one fire; one nail, one nail;
> Rights by rights falter, strengths by strengths do fail.
>
> (IV, vii, 37–55)

One of the possibilities, we are told, was behind what happened to Coriolanus, but the speaker does not know which. However, the fact that he gives the various alternatives equal possibility makes us more inclined to take them all as in some measure involved. It is not clear why Aufidius should insist, or how he should know, that only one was operative; and we are left to wonder how far Coriolanus would be morally 'freed' if the one cause were the more reprehensible one of pride. There is much shuffling back and forth by Aufidius at this point (45–8), producing an impression of self-contradiction. The succeeding statements are still more uncertain. First Coriolanus' merit is self-destructive (or, reading another way, it is such as to stop condemnation of him); then it is not that he is at fault but that the time in which he lived could not appreciate his virtue; then (characteristic of the hatred of staying seated in the play) power and worth are lost as soon as they are talked about; then—and here again we have an unconvincing general rule made out of the particular instance—it is virtue that destroys virtue. At the end of the speech we can make even less sense out of Coriolanus' history than before.

On the other rare occasions where we see mind at work in this play, it is in the service of falsehood, not truth. The prime instance is Menenius' fable of the belly.[5] To the citizens' complaint that in the dearth the patricians have been keeping the corn to themselves and making edicts against the poor, Menenius replies with an image of physical determinism, the operation of the healthy body: just as the food that is received by the belly is automatically distributed to the limbs, so the senators of Rome give the city's corn to the populace. The image is a false one in that the senators have the freewill to withhold the corn where the belly does not: but through its use Menenius hopes to hoodwink the citizens into a belief in the benign operation of the state. There is also deception in that the analogy depends on the actual distribution of food in the body where the citizens say they are not receiving any. At certain points the duplicity becomes particularly marked. Speaking as the belly, accused by the mutinous limbs of the body of being idle and 'cupboarding the viand', Menenius declares,

> 'Though all at once cannot
> See what I do deliver out to each,
> Yet I can make my audit up, that all
> From me do back receive the flour of all,
> And leave me but the bran.'
>
> (I, i, 141–45)

The citizens have not the wit to observe the potential deception present in no one being able to tell how much others are getting, nor to challenge that 'Yet I can make my audit up,' with its possible implication of juggling the accounts. The falsity would seem to be taken a stage further through the half-truth of the belly being left nothing but bran, that is, faeces, from the original corn: what is omitted is the fact that the belly itself needs flour in order to provide the energy to send out the food in the first place—and to dispose of the wastes returned to it. In a normal body the belly takes no more than its share: but, by falsifying the facts, by departing from the biological truths of his own image, Menenius opens up the possibility that the belly in this body—that is, the senators of Rome—takes much *more* than its share; false underestimation suggests a desire to conceal excess. For those with ears to hear (none of the multitude Menenius is addressing), this suspicion is further increased when Menenius says of the senators,

> Touching the weal o' th' common, you shall find
> No public benefit which you receive
> But it proceeds or comes from them to you,
> And no way from yourselves.
>
> (150–53)

Again, this is a truth designed to hoodwink: it may be true that the benefits the citizens receive come only from the

165

senators, but that still leaves open the question of just how much they do receive[6]—which is precisely the question with which they began: 'What authority surfeits on would relieve us' (15).

Later we again see mind directed to a perversion of the facts in the attempt of his mother and the patricians to persuade Coriolanus to appear reasonable and humble to the people, in order to secure his own and their ends. He is to speak in 'words that are but roted in/ Your tongue, though but bastards and syllables/ Of no allowance to your bosom's truth' (III, ii, 55–7). Coriolanus is concerned at the falsehood in this, but typically of this play, only insofar as the falsehood concerns himself, not as it relates to the people, nor indeed as falsehood pure and simple. He sees his body as having to become a physical lie,

> Away my disposition, and possess me
> Some harlot's spirit! My throat of war be turn'd,
> Which choired with my drum, into a pipe
> Small as an eunuch, or the virgin voice
> That babies lull asleep!
>
> (III, ii, 111–15)

He sees the perversion of his truth and mind involved however: 'I will not do't,/ Lest I surcease to honour mine own truth,/ And by my body's action teach my mind/ A most inherent baseness' (120–23).

Without mind, without objective value, the whole play is pervaded by division. The picture of Rome is of a mass of dangerously jarring egos, like the particles in an over-heated fission pile. The dearth has inflamed the citizens against the patricians; this in turn inflames Martius against the citizens; the tribunes the people secure to protect their rights are power-hungry and use their charges for their own ends; and as much as he provokes them the tribunes whip up the people against Coriolanus. There is a constant sense of imminent explosion in Rome, and the *leitmotif* of people striving to calm passions gone too far runs throughout—Menenius, trying to quiet the citizens at the start, and to soften Coriolanus' words and make excuses for him to the tribunes; he and Volumnia persuading Coriolanus to go and ask pardon of the citizens;

166

he trying and Volumnia succeeding in turning aside Coriolanus' purpose of attacking Rome.

There is no real love or togetherness between human beings in *Coriolanus*. Volumnia does not love Coriolanus as a person but as a thing which ministers to her own pride. When Virgilia, Coriolanus' wife, hears Volumnia say how she rejoiced at her son proving himself a warrior, she asks, 'But had he died in the business, madam, how then?': to which Volumnia replies,

> Then his good report should have been my son, I therein would have found issue. Hear me profess sincerely: had I a dozen sons, each in my love alike, and none less dear than thine and my good Martius, I had rather had eleven die nobly for their country, than one voluptuously surfeit out of action.
>
> (I, iii, 19–25)

Later we see Volumnia positively licking her lips in anticipation of the number of wounds Coriolanus shall have to show the populace (II, i, 141–55). It is she, not Coriolanus, who wishes him to become consul (II, i, 198–202). As for Coriolanus' fellow-patricians, Menenius and Cominius, the feeling that they have for Martius can only be one of rather awed admiration than love. On Coriolanus' side, friendship is spurned in his rejection of Cominius and Menenius before Rome, and even mother-love is scarcely present in the sense we are given of one will overcoming another in his submission to Volumnia.

At the other end of the scale we have the grand emotional cries of warriors greeting one another. Coriolanus, meeting Cominius in the field exclaims,

> Oh! let me clip ye
> In arms as sound as when I woo'd; in heart
> As merry as when our nuptial day was done,
> And tapers burn'd to bedward.
>
> (I, vi, 29–32)

Here there is a sense of perversion in thus comparing a passion between men that has been bred out of slaying, to the highest moments of their own experiences of creative heterosexual love. The same imagery is used by Aufidius later to express his delight at reconciliation with Coriolanus:

167

I lov'd the maid I married; never man
Sigh'd truer breath; but that I see thee here,
Thou noble thing, more dances my rapt heart
Than when I first my wedded mistress saw
Bestride my threshold.

(IV, v, 115–19)

In a sense the betrayal of the value of married love here implies the insecurity of this love also; and the grossness of the hyperbole underlines this.

Love is a giving, social act, but, despite the efforts of Cominius and Titus Lartius, there is little generosity present in the play. When Cominius tries to praise Coriolanus and give him a tenth part of the spoils of the victory over the Volsces, our attention is focused on Coriolanus harshly refusing rather than on Cominius offering: 'Pray now, no more. My mother,/ Who has a charter to extol her blood,/ When she does praise me, grieves me' (I, ix, 13–15); 'I thank you, general;/ But cannot make my heart consent to take/ A bribe to pay my sword' (I, ix, 36–8); 'I had rather have my wounds to heal again/ Than hear say how I got them' (II, ii, 69–70); 'I had rather have one scratch my head i' th' sun/ When the alarum were struck, than idly sit/ To hear my nothings monster'd' (II, ii, 75–7). Coriolanus will not be indebted to anyone: he is portrayed as essentially self-isolating and anti-social. He wins the town of Corioles on his own and continually sets himself apart from his supposed fellow-men in Rome to the point where he becomes actually exiled; and typically even when he is being banished by Rome he has the megalomania to say 'I banish you!' (III, iii, 123). His notion of government is solely exclusive, one of keeping the vulgar out (III, i, 129–60). And when it comes, in that one rare moment, to an act of generosity on his part, he has forgotten the name of the man he would reward (I, ix, 77–89).

The divisive landscape of the play is expressed in its imagery. There is a *leitmotif* relating to breakdown of communication. Just as co-operation among the various members of the body politic is lacking, so the play is pervaded by images of disease and of feeding gone wrong.[7] Coriolanus calls the people's affections 'A sick man's appetite, who desires most that/ Which would increase his evil' (I, i, 177–78). Later he says to the senators of the plebians, 'let them not lick/ The sweet which is their poison' (III, i, 155–56): here the notion of food common to all the body's members is challenged. Cominius speaks of war as a 'feast' and of participation in its butcheries as 'dining' (I, ix, 10, 11). Coriolanus claims that if the senate did not keep the people in awe they 'Would feed on one another' (I, i, 187). Menenius, faced by the people's hostility to Coriolanus, laments that Rome 'like an unnatural dam/ Should now eat up her own' (III, i, 290–91). This notion of cannibalism goes one step further in Volumnia's declaration after the exile of her son, 'Anger's my meat: I sup upon myself/ And so shall starve with feeding' (IV, ii, 50–1), with its reminiscence of Spenser's Envy.

There are also many images describing physical difficulty and obstruction. General atmospheric words in the play— 'musty superfluity' (I, i, 225), 'stiff' (I, i, 160, 240), 'dull' and 'fusty' (I, ix, 6–7), 'musty chaff' (V, i, 26)—convey a sense of the choked and the dry, and suggest a lack of fluid movement.[8] There are images portraying physical confinement: Volumnia wishes to 'unclog my heart/ Of what lies heavy to't' (IV, ii, 47–8); Cominius describes to the citizens 'Your franchises, whereon you stood, confin'd/ Into an auger's bore' (IV, vi, 87–8). Other images depict physical helplessness. Martius says to the citizens, 'He that depends/ Upon your favours, swims with fins of lead,/ And hews down oaks with rushes' (I, i, 178–80). Menenius describes the citizens as seeking to 'Tie leaden pounds to's [Coriolanus'] heels' (III, i, 311); and later tells the tribune Sicinius that there is as much hope of Volumnia's dissuading Coriolanus from his assault of Rome as there is of Sicinius being able to displace a cornerstone of the Capitol with one finger (V, iv, 1–6).

Disintegration is expressed in the frequent images of separated limbs. At best, as portrayed by Menenius in his fable of the belly, the body politic in the Rome of *Coriolanus* could only ever have been an aggregation of diverse parts, each member of the state making up one limb; the idea of the individual being able to subsume unity in himself, to be a microcosm of the larger whole, as we see it in *Lear* or *Macbeth*, is not present in this play. Nor, given the antagonisms of the play, and the perversion of Menenius' own image of the body, is the kind of organic unity implicit in the workings of the human body possible in the society of *Coriolanus*. What we have in fact is a condition where the limbs are at war with one another. Coriolanus demands that the senators 'at once pluck out/ The multitudinous tongue' (III, i, 154–55); the tribunes see him as a diseased limb which must be cut away. Coriolanus describes himself as warring against his own body in being humble to the people, 'A beggar's tongue/ Make motion through my lips, and my arm'd knees,/ Who bow'd but in my stirrup, bend like his/ That hath receiv'd an alms!' (III, ii, 117–20); he comes near to giving separate personality to his limbs. Indeed, so isolated do limbs become from one another that they can take on a life of their own, as when Coriolanus bids Menenius farewell and declares that his future behaviour will be no different from the past,

> *Menenius.* That's worthily
>   As any ear can hear. Come, let's not weep.
>   If I could shake off but one seven years
>   From these old arms and legs, by the good gods
>   I'd with thee every foot.
> *Coriolanus.* Give me thy hand.
>
>   (IV, i, 53–7)

The predominance of the limb imagery here forces double reference on 'foot' and 'hand' with peculiar effect.

Division and multiplicity in the play are also conveyed through the frequent use of numbers. Coriolanus' wounds are carefully enumerated by sevens, nines and twenty-fives (II, i, 148–54). Volumnia says she had rather eleven sons died nobly in action than one stayed at home (I, iii, 21–5). The citizens discuss the numbers they can enlist to speak against Coriolanus (II, iii, 209–10). Coriolanus says he could take on forty of the citizens single-handed and Menenius puts his own limit at two; whereupon Cominius says, 'But now 'tis odds beyond arithmetic' (III, i, 240–43). Coriolanus fuses limb and number imagery in cursing the tribune Sicinius, 'Within thine eyes sat twenty thousand deaths,/ In thy hands clutch'd as many millions, in/ Thy lying tongue both numbers. . . .'

(III, iii, 70–2). One of Aufidius' servants rates his master as worth six of Coriolanus (IV, v, 169); Coriolanus reverses this in his last words, 'O that I had him,/ With six Aufidiuses, or more. . . .' (V, vi, 127–28). Even conventional phrases take on added resonance in this context: for example Menenius' 'A hundred thousand welcomes' (II, i, 182), or his comment on Coriolanus to the people, 'Your multiplying spawn how can he flatter—/ That's thousand to one good one' (II, ii, 78–9); or his later, 'This morning for ten thousand of your throats/ I'd not have given a doit' (V, iv, 57–8). We may even say that in the struggle between Coriolanus and the people we see a mathematical battle of division against multiplication: the people are always seen as swarming and multiplying, and Coriolanus' sole desire is to divide himself and the senators from them, and ultimately himself from all people.

Take all the characteristics of *Coriolanus* so far outlined— the absence of metaphysics, mind and love, expressed in the dividedness and faction that pervade the play—and ask, why are things like this? In *Troilus and Cressida* or *Hamlet*, which in character most resemble this play, we could answer the question: a specific deed prior to the action of each of the plays, respectively the division of Helen from Menelaus and the murder of the king of Denmark by his usurping brother, has spread to produce dualism throughout their worlds. And in these plays the protagonists are continually asking why things are as they are—why there is discontent in the Greek army, why Hamlet cannot act—on the assumption that there is somewhere an answer. No such questions are asked in *Coriolanus*, no such initial blighting act is supposed. Rome, we are to think, is a settled condition of things, the only exceptional factor being the dearth, which is soon put right by the victory against the Volsces and the subsequent seizure of their corn: and the civil faction caused by the dearth only brings into the open oppositions which have always been present. What we have here is a picture of the political world as Shakespeare now sees it, and he sees it throughout the plays of this period. The divided nature of the play cannot now be explained internally: this is Shakespeare's vision of political reality; he has made things so.

Because of this, the question of human responsibility in

171

Coriolanus becomes peculiarly problematic. Who can blame people for behaving as they do when they live in a medium which makes them thus, when the author has formed them as he wishes? This issue is particularly prominent in the treatment of Coriolanus himself.

Undoubtedly Shakespeare asks us to consider the behaviour of Coriolanus, more than of other characters in the play, in moral terms. It is he, uttering nearly all the abuse and vilification of the play, who is continually contrasted with the normally quieter or more reasoned tones of almost all the other characters. Menenius, in the first scene has been trying to restrain the citizens from mutiny and reason them out of their rage: Coriolanus' first words when he enters thus sound additionally arrogant:

> What's the matter, you dissentious rogues
> That, rubbing the poor itch of your opinion,
> Make yourselves scabs?
>
> (I, i, 163–65)

His view of the people is utterly contemptuous, and as for their demands his initial solution is massacre, 'Would the nobility lay aside their ruth,/ And let me use my sword, I'd make a quarry/ With thousands of these quarter'd slaves, as high/ As I could pick my lance' (I, i, 196–99). At best we are made to feel that this is the same kind of lack of control that Menenius has been seeking to restrain in the citizens. And certainly the tone in which it is uttered is directed at making us blame Coriolanus for it. Throughout the play he is judged for being anti-social. We are to feel this even in his winning Corioles without help, in his refusal of gifts or praise, in his inability to submit himself to the people and in his eventual rejection of and by Rome. He becomes described as a monster, 'a lonely dragon' (IV, i, 30). But for him, Rome might be relatively at peace, and is so for a time when he is gone; he is the exception, the man who exacerbates feelings and polarizes loyalties into riot. And his continual insistence on the faults of others, his refusal ever to examine his own nature critically, drives us to do it ourselves: the more he blames society, the more we are inclined to blame him.

Nevertheless it is quite clear that Coriolanus is at the same

172

time the epitome of what, shorn of policy and the motive of self-preservation, every citizen of Rome would be;[9] and that that behaviour in turn is the product of the divisive medium of the play. Here Coriolanus is not to be held 'responsible'. The senators and upper classes of Rome exist for their own benefit—may indeed have starved the people to that end in the time of dearth; and the people, guided by their new-won authority in their tribunes, are out to gain for themselves more power and say in the affairs of Rome. In the deceptions of Menenius' fable of the belly lies an antagonism towards and disdain for the people as real as that of Coriolanus. The tribunes, also often contemptuous in their attitude to the people, have the desire to preserve their authority constantly uppermost in their minds (for example, II, i, 220–21, 242; III, i, 206–7). Ambition, self-preservation or both are the dominant motives of almost every Roman we see,[10] with the possible minor exceptions of Cominius and the 'gracious silence' of Virgilia, Coriolanus' wife. The imagery portrays a world of isolated and anti-social egos, and to this extent the tyrannical nature of Coriolanus is to be seen as Roman society with the mask off. He is here not to be marked out as more culpable than the other characters. Yet they themselves are not finally culpable either. For no act of choice on their part has made them behave as they do: they have been made that way by Shakespeare, and the whole idiom of the play is one where mind, value and the better impulses of the human heart cannot operate, and all things are essentially antagonistic to one another.

There is clearly a fatal cleavage in Shakespeare's attitude here: on the one hand he sees the characters as wholly powerless, and depicts the medium of the play as so divisive that men will inevitably be at odds; and on the other he tries to make them responsible for that divisiveness, he exacerbates our sense of their being personally answerable or reprehensible. Objectively, both positions need not be in conflict like this, inasmuch as an act can be both partly free and partly determined. But this is not the case in the world of *Coriolanus*, for the characters there are seen as existing in peculiarly limiting conditions which entail antagonism on them, and yet at the same time are made to seem entirely blameworthy. This dichotomy between determinist and judgmental positions is mirrored in Aufidius' speech on Coriolanus. The peculiar extremity of the opposition seems itself a product of the split, factional character of the play.

There is another problematic division in the play, stemming from this. It has often been argued that Shakespeare is politically impartial in *Coriolanus*, and certainly it has been possible for Marxists and Fascists alike to find satisfaction from it. Shakespeare puts the citizens' case of wrongful oppression by the patricians; and he also gives weight to Coriolanus' claim that not to keep the proletariat down is to invite anarchy (we should not forget either that much of what Coriolanus says expresses what the patricians feel but cannot say because unwilling to pay the price). *Coriolanus* speaks to us more directly perhaps than almost any other play in the Shakespeare canon, for the political issues it presents are perennial, affecting the prejudices of every man, and heightened and simplified to the point where divisive emotion takes over. No amount of showing the strengths and weaknesses of both sides alike is going, in this play, to prevent the watcher inclining to one side or the other, depending on his prior political sympathies, however sane, however moderate, however generous these may be. What is also important here is the degree to which Shakespeare felt the same pressures, and in what direction.

Despite his own efforts to remain impartial and judicious in the midst of this landscape of polarities, Shakespeare has given Coriolanus more complexity of character, more straightforwardness of dealing, and, however qualified, a degree of heroism and sheer imaginative and rhetorical force which, apart from his mother, is never reached by any other character in the play. In effect, the imaginative centre of *Coriolanus* lists towards its protagonist: he is conceived of as a Colossus.[11] Morally the picture of Martius entering Corioles alone to do battle is an emblem of the isolated ego: but we also experience it as an act of huge daring and ability. The descriptions of Coriolanus' behaviour in battle are repugnant, yet they have the attractiveness of brutal and efficient force also. However the victories are won, they are won amazingly, and by the kind of *blitzkrieg* methods which excite the

174

imagination. Nor can we find wholly egoistic Coriolanus' refusal to compromise and lie his way towards the gaining of the consulship. If it were a case of his being asked really to love the people, we might feel differently, but Menenius, Volumnia and the senators are concerned only that he should speak them fair, on the motives of self-interest which we have seen them demonstrate throughout (III, ii, 52–70). Martius' refusal has no more pride in it than it has the kind of nobility involved in Cordelia's rejection of her father's demand for the public display of her love: there is both arrogance, in his detestation of subjection to the vulgar, and grandeur in his hatred of policy; he is the only figure in the play who stands against compromise.

Coriolanus' rhetoric has simple, amoral power. He speaks openly the sentiments the patricians conceal and of which they fear the truth:

> This double worship,
> Where one part does disdain with cause, the other
> Insult without all reason: where gentry, title, wisdom,
> Cannot conclude but by the yea and no
> Of general ignorance, it must omit
> Real necessities, and give way the while
> To unstable slightness. Purpose so barr'd, it follows
> Nothing is done to purpose. Therefore beseech you—
> You that will be less fearful than discreet,
> That love the fundamental part of state
> More than you doubt the change on't; that prefer
> A noble life before a long, and wish
> To jump a body with a dangerous physic
> That's sure of death without it—at once pluck out
> The multitudinous tongue: let them not lick
> The sweet which is their poison. Your dishonour
> Mangles true judgement, and bereaves the state
> Of that integrity which should becom't,
> Not having the power to do the good it would
> For th'ill which doth control't.
>
> (III, i, 141–60)

No alternative is ever offered to this diagnosis: the tribunes only call Coriolanus a traitor for uttering it. The swelling cadences of the speech, the massive, if simple, certainty of

175

tone and analysis, has nothing to oppose it in the play.[12] We may call it 'rodomontade'[13] certainly; and it has all the questionable emotional and linguistic freedom available only to those who do not have to co-exist with their neighbours: but its analysis is the kind of truth beside which Menenius' fable of the belly as an image of benevolent cooperation can be exposed as a possibly sordid falsehood. More than this, this sort of speech further undermines any judicious impartiality Shakespeare tries to maintain in the play, for it calls directly on the prejudices of the audience. Those with left-wing sympathies will be drawn to detest it from their hearts rather than from the play, and those of the right will find themselves swept away by it. This is additionally so where, abandoning argument, Coriolanus resorts to the expression of primal hatred of the proletariat:

> You common cry of curs! whose breath I hate
> As reek o' th' rotten fens, whose loves I prize
> As the dead carcasses of unburied men
> That do corrupt my air: I banish you!
>
> (III, iii, 120–23)

But if the Right thus has a spokesman, the Left is given nothing by the play but a mere shrubbery of plebeian prose in which to locate its sympathies. The oratorical force of which Coriolanus is granted near-monopoly reveals further how despite the element of detached analysis in the play, Shakespeare's imagination is drawn to the side of his protagonist.

So divisive, so full of 'violent'st contariety' (IV, vi, 74) is the world of *Coriolanus*, that the protagonist gains in simple imaginative force what he loses in the judgments made on him. What, finally, we have in this play (as, it may be posed, to a lesser extent in *Antony and Cleopatra*) is not the judicious weighing of pros and cons in the hero, or an *understood* division of sympathy, but Shakespeare at war with himself. The conclusion and tragic effect alike are uncertain—'Let's make the best of it'; 'Yet he shall have a noble memory.' And what makes Shakespeare at times lean to Coriolanus is not only his own politics (if we may suppose that these are identifiable from the play) but the effect of his being caught between condemning his hero for egoism and portraying his behaviour

176

as the product of (ostensibly socio-political) determinism: while thus he is caught, judgment and sympathy go their separate ways.

In *Hamlet* and *Troilus and Cressida* an initial blighting act renders the sensibilities of the protagonists divided, so that they can no longer keep mind and body, thinking and acting, in tune. Here, we may say, something similar has happened to Shakespeare himself: his sensibility has become blighted until he can see the world as no more than 'an unweeded garden', and his faculties and vision have become divided against themselves. He, in short, has experienced in himself that dividedness which he was able previously to distance and dramatize in his characters. A recurrent and distinctive motif in *Antony and Cleopatra*, *Timon* and *Coriolanus* is the shifting of attitudes. *Antony* is pervaded by imagery of melting and of oscillating, and by changes of opinion and purpose in the protagonists; Antony's 'What our contempts doth often hurl from us,/ We wish it ours again. The present pleasure,/ By revolution lowering, does become/ The opposite of itself' (I, ii, 120–23), roughly sums up the continual process. In *Timon* the central character shifts from extreme love to equally extreme hatred of his followers. And in *Coriolanus* Martius makes enemies of his friends and friends of his enemies. It can reasonably be suggested from this that throughout these plays Shakespeare was unconsciously portraying his own shifting and divided judgment. For all these plays show uncertainty of sympathy on his part for the central figures; in all of them the protagonist is portrayed as a victim of his nature or his circumstances and yet is morally appraised; in all of them the political world is made so small and mean that the only place for the man of heroic spirit is outside it, and yet that spirit is also to be condemned as self-indulgent, petulant or anti-social.

A sense of immovability and helplessness pervades these plays. None of their protagonists can be said to develop spiritually. When Antony oscillates, he does so between the fixed poles of his own personality; and Timon's misanthropy is simply the inversion of his previous philanthropy. The heroes of earlier and later plays change for good or ill: Lear is driven mad and learns something of the nature of his evil,

Macbeth makes a spiritual journey into darkness, Leontes moves into and out of jealousy, and Miranda's innocence is educated. With Coriolanus, Antony and Timon, what we feel in their histories is a sense of *erosion*, of something static being worn away; and in each case the wearing is registered by the loss of power over people or realms outside the self, until by a process of shrinkage the self is all that is left. What these characters are is curiously bound up with what they have: and when they have nothing, their lives are ended. Nor do these figures learn anything about themselves: they always blame the outside world for their failures—Coriolanus the plebs, the patricians or Rome itself; Timon his erstwhile parasites, Athens, or even all humanity; and Antony the 'treachery' of Caesar or Cleopatra. They simply stay what they are, without thinking what they are, without any real mental life, until they are overwhelmed.

If we look over the whole of Shakespeare's plays after *Macbeth*, we can see a larger division, between these political plays on the one hand, and the late romances *Pericles*, *Cymbeline*, *The Winter's Tale* and *The Tempest* on the other. This division takes the form, once again, of a split between 'body' and 'mind'. We have seen how the landscape of *Coriolanus* is dominantly physical, and mind is rendered impotent or suspect; but there is similar emphasis on the physical in *Timon* and *Antony*. Timon buys love with things and finds that such love lasts only as long as the things; *Antony* is pervaded by a sense of the physical elements, whether of the earth that pulls one down, or of the fire and air by which one seeks to rise. In all these plays, whatever mental resolves the hero makes are reversed—whether it be Coriolanus' decision to attack Rome, or Antony's to leave Cleopatra. The heroes shift between opposed viewpoints—now for, now against Rome, now loving humanity, now hating it—but they never put the two positions together and compare them in one act of mind: they simply forget the one while they are the other. In the late romances, by contrast, there is much more scope for reflection, not least because of the large spans of time separating important doings. We are much more aware of the creations of mind: the magic of Prospero, the statue of Hermione, the skill of the doctor Cerimon in saving Thaisa in *Pericles*. In *The*

Winter's Tale we have a striking instance of purely mental working in the quite uncaused jealousy of Leontes. Leontes comes to perceive and repent his evil, as does Alonso in *The Tempest*. The 'physical' is defied in the resurrections of Hermione or Thaisa. The vision reached in *The Tempest* is of life as a dream, a mental state.

In *Antony* the cloud that refuses to retain a stable shape is the physical form of Antony himself (IV, xiv, 1–14); in *The Tempest* the 'cloud-capp'd towers' that dissolve (IV, i, 148–58) are the expressions of mind, and obedient to it. These differences, we may say, provide the contexts for the pessimism of the one group and the optimism of the other: body is intractable, but thought is free. But the fact that this polarity exists at all suggests that the vision of each group is on its own inadequate.

NOTES

1. There is not scope to demonstrate this here, but the reader is referred to the opposed critical views of Timon's liberality, neither of which finds unambiguous evidence in the text itself. On the one hand, with an antipathy for what they see as Timon's excesses are, for example, J. C. Maxwell, '*Timon of Athens*', *Scrutiny*, 15 (1947–48), 195–203; David Cook, '*Timon of Athens*', *SS*, 16 (1963), 83–9; L. C. Knights, '*Timon of Athens*', in '*Hamlet*' *and Other Shakespearean Essays* (Cambridge, Cambridge University Press, 1979), pp. 102–10, 117. On the other side, preferring to see Timon as bountiful, are G. Wilson Knight, 'An Essay on *Timon of Athens*', *The Wheel of Fire*, pp. 207–19; A. S. Collins, '*Timon of Athens:* A Reconsideration', *RES*, 22 (1946), 96–108; R. P. Draper, '*Timon of Athens*', *SQ*, 8 (1957), 195–96.
2. Theodore Spencer, *Shakespeare and the Nature of Man* (Cambridge, Cambridge University Press, 1943), p. 178.
3. References are to the Arden *Coriolanus*, ed. Philip Brockbank (Methuen, 1976).
4. See also on this Brockbank, pp. 46–9, though he tends to see mind as conjoined with body.
5. For previous accounts, see D. A. Traversi, *Shakespeare: The Roman Plays* (Hollis and Carter, 1963), pp. 208–10; David G. Hale, '*Coriolanus:* The Death of a Political Metaphor', *SQ*, 22 (1971), 197–202; Andrew Gurr, '*Coriolanus* and the Body Politic', *SS*, 28 (1975), 67.
6. See also Wilbur Sanders, 'An Impossible Person: Caius Martius Coriolanus', in Wilbur Sanders and Howard Jacobson, *Shakespeare's*

Magnanimity: Four Tragic Heroes, Their Friends and Families (Chatto and Windus, 1978), p. 141. For other falsehoods in the analogy, see E. A. J. Honigmann, *Shakespeare: Seven Tragedies; The Dramatist's Manipulation of Response* (Macmillan, 1976), pp. 179–81.

7. For previous accounts, see G. Wilson Knight, *The Imperial Theme: Further Interpretations of Shakespeare's Tragedies Including the Roman Plays* (Oxford University Press, 1931), pp. 176–81; Maurice Charney, *Shakespeare's Roman Plays: The Function of Imagery in the Drama* (Cambridge, Mass., Harvard University Press, 1961), pp. 142–63.

8. This is reminiscent of the medium of *Troilus and Cressida.*

9. Compare Kenneth Burke, '*Coriolanus*—and the Delights of Faction', *Hudson Review*, 19 (1966), 185–202; Larry S. Champion, *Shakespeare's Tragic Perspective* (Athens, Georgia, University of Georgia Press, 1976), pp. 230–38.

10. See also R. F. Hill, '*Coriolanus:* Violentest Contrariety', *Essays and Studies*, 17 (1964), 18–22.

11. On the force of Coriolanus as hero in relation to the other characters of the play, see also, e.g., H. J. Oliver, 'Coriolanus as Tragic Hero', *SQ*, 10 (1959), 53–60; Eugene M. Waith, *The Herculean Hero in Marlowe, Shakespeare and Dryden* (Chatto and Windus, 1962), pp. 121–43; Brian Vickers, *Shakespeare: 'Coriolanus'* (Arnold, 1976), esp. pp. 33–7, 57–60.

12. On the power and dominance of Coriolanus' rhetoric in the play, see also Joyce Van Dyke, 'Making a Scene: Language and Gesture in *Coriolanus*', *SS*, 30 (1977), 137, 138. Wolfgang Clemen, *The Development of Shakespeare's Imagery*, pp. 154–58, points out the wealth of glorifying imagery surrounding Coriolanus.

13. As does Norman Rabkin, '*Coriolanus:* The Tragedy of Politics', *SQ*, 17 (1966), 197.

8

The Late Romances

'There is a world elsewhere,' said Coriolanus on leaving Rome:
but in *Antony*, *Timon* and *Coriolanus* that world could not be
found save in death; rejecting or rejected by the state, the
protagonists could not in this life escape the city, but hung
around it in hatred or self-division. In the late romances—
Pericles, *Cymbeline*, *The Winter's Tale* and *The Tempest*—another
world, that of nature, seems to be reached, and if central
figures such as Cymbeline, Leontes or Prospero are still bound
up with the court or city, their children, who know nothing of
their wrongs, may bring home to the city a brave new world
of transforming nature. Such, at least, is the intended pattern.

With their movements over large time and space; their stress
on children, resurrection and rebirth; their possession of
presiding deities; their portrayals of chaste love putting down
lechery; their placing of old men and redemptive daughters at
their centres; their insistence on fruitful patience; their constant marriages of such opposites as nature and art, meanness
and nobility, discord and harmony, liberty and restraint,
mercy and justice, love and chastity: with all these, the late
romances form perhaps the clearest grouping among Shakespeare's dramas. One further feature, however, they all possess
which has not been much remarked, and that is the relative
lack of force with which they treat of evil.[1]

In certain features the romances are not radically different
from such 'middle' comedies as *A Midsummer Night's Dream* or
As You Like It. In *As You Like It* even the plot is similar to
that of *The Winter's Tale* and *The Tempest*: a duke has banished
a brother-duke, who is living in exile in the woods, and the
lovers-to-be eventually go there too. In *A Midsummer Night's
Dream*, Oberon and Puck are close to Prospero and Ariel of

The Tempest; the theme of imagination is central to both plays; the redolence of the former play with atmosphere of place also parallels the sheer vividness with which the island is realized in *The Tempest*; and the plays are of like brevity (paralleled in the Shakespeare canon only by the possibly shortened *Macbeth*). In all the plays there is a journey from city or court to country, and back again, with both contexts joined in the marriage of the lovers. Although there is rather more insistence on providence from a supernatural source in the late romances than on the 'luck' of comedy, the effect is much the same: it is not so much that in the late plays Shakespeare came by any increased faith in the efficacy of nature or grace in the world, only that this was for him 'another way of putting it'.

Indeed, although the romances have their own distinctive character, there seems no important sense in which we can say that they 'belong' spiritually after rather than before the tragedies, nor that they are in some way the apex of Shakespearean development. This claim runs counter to the 'evolutionary' view of Shakespeare's art which has become common critical currency: but it can be borne out by considering Shakespeare's treatment of evil in these plays. For while there is evidence that he tried to incorporate some of the harsh realism of his tragedies in the comic vision of his late plays, it can be shown that the comic element consistently emasculates rather than subsumes the tragic, confining the insights of these plays to those of the middle comedies. What is meant to be a condition in which the tragic element plays a part in and gives a deeper resonance to the comic, becomes one in which the latter engulfs and almost obliterates the former.

All of the late plays could be said to start with an unnatural act[2]—the incest of King Antiochus with his daughter in *Pericles*, the imprisonment of Imogen by her father in *Cymbeline*, the accusation of his wife and abandonment of his baby child by Leontes in *The Winter's Tale* and the supplanting and exile of Prospero from his dukedom of Milan in *The Tempest*—but these acts are seen as unnatural not so much in the cosmic and metaphysical sense that the word had in *King Lear* or *Macbeth*, but in the sense of being absurd and grotesque, of going against the grain of reality. Thus *The Winter's Tale* begins with a fulsome description of the long loves between Leontes and

182

Polixenes, against which the immediately sequent jealousy of Leontes has to be viewed; and Cymbeline is conceived of as temporarily deranged under the influence of his wicked queen rather than as evil in himself. Evil is sometimes given so slight a foundation for action as to seem inherently ridiculous: Iachimo's attempt on Imogen's virtue is carried out from no wicked motive, but simply for a wager. Often, too, evil is feeble: the wicked queen in *Cymbeline* who plans to kill Imogen with poison is tricked with a substance which causes only temporary unconsciousness, and Iachimo, burdened by guilt, is only too glad to confess his deception at the end. Much of the evil of *Cymbeline* indeed, is summed up in the name and nature of the queen's son, Cloten: a completely incompetent and brutish lover, he pursues Imogen from the court, only to be met and easily dispatched by Guiderius. Further, in both *Cymbeline* and *Pericles* the folk-tale patterning is strong and the characterization rather flat, so that evil is more often a stereotype than a felt reality.

In *The Winter's Tale* and *The Tempest*, however, there is more attempt to give evil some of the force and reality it has in the tragedies. The representation of Leontes in the former play is in contrast with that of Posthumus in *Cymbeline*. With Posthumus we are asked to believe that a man who can set on another to test the virtue of his wife for a wager is not the worse personally: his behaviour in tempting providence and suffering later under false evidence is, if anything, a function of the falsity and corruption at the heart of the play's world in the form of the wicked queen; his psychology and individual character are not centrally of concern. With Leontes, however, the psychology of the jealousy is of moment, and we are put in touch with his mind as he writhes under the influence of his suspicion. Further, the course of his jealousy is more realistically presented than that of Posthumus. Posthumus is portrayed as no sooner having heard Iachimo's 'proof' of having slept with Imogen than he believes him totally; all we have of his jealousy thereafter is a brief scene in which he reviles women and imagines the scene of Iachimo's success (II, iv, 153–86). Leontes' suspicions, however, are shown as developing from a little doubt, which, nagging, becomes a huge self-justified jealousy. He is torn at first between the feeling that all may be

183

well and his belief that it is not:

> This entertainment
> May a free face put on, derive a liberty
> From heartiness, from bounty, fertile bosom,
> And well become the agent: 't may, I grant:
> But to be paddling palms, and pinching fingers,
> As now they are, and making practis'd smiles
> As in a looking-glass; and then to sigh, as 'twere
> The mort o' th' deer—O, that is entertainment
> My bosom likes not, nor my brows.
>
> (I, ii, 111–19)[3]

Thus jealousy propagates itself. 'Affection! thy intention stabs the centre:/ Thou dost make possible things not so held,/ Communicat'st with dreams;—how can this be?—/ With what's unreal thou coactive art,/ And fellow'st nothing' (138–42). This process, and our admission to it, would by themselves make the growth of Leontes' jealousy very real.

Yet at the same time Shakespeare makes it thoroughly unreal: since nothing in Hermione's or Polixenes' behaviour gives grounds for it, and no one prompts Leontes, it comes from nothing. It is not a mere dramatic convention, a *donnée*, for Leontes himself at first reflects on its vacant origins and its possible absurdity, as do the other characters. Thus no sooner has he remarked, 'Inch-thick, knee-deep; o'er head and ears a fork'd one', than he goes on to say to his son Mamillius,

> Go, play, boy, play: thy mother plays, and I
> Play too; but so disgrac'd a part, whose issue
> Will hiss me to my grave: contempt and clamour
> Will be my knell.
>
> (I, ii, 186–90)

Under the strain of straining over nothing Leontes' language and imagery come to lack full force: he continues,

> There have been,
> (Or I am much deceiv'd) cuckolds ere now,
> And many a man there is (even at this present,
> Now, while I speak this) holds his wife by th' arm,
> That little thinks she has been sluic'd in's absence
> And his pond fish'd by his next neighbour, by
> Sir Smile, his neighbour: nay, there's comfort in't,

184

> Whiles other men have gates, and those gates open'd,
> As mine, against their will.
>
> (190–98)

His very sense of the disgraced part he is playing takes away from his conviction and his seriousness, and this is demonstrated in the curiously stupid first two lines of this passage and the light, domestic imagery of ponds, fishing, neighbours and gates. Again, where he speaks of the comforting bawdiness of the whole world—'be it concluded,/ No barricado for a belly. Know't,/ It will let in and out the enemy,/ With bag and baggage' (203–6)—his pleasure in the alliteration is irrelevant. His jealousy is ludicrous in the way he tries to wriggle, like a hooked fish himself, away from the pain it causes him by consoling himself with the thought that he is one among a host of cuckolds or even that he is privileged above others in not being deluded. We sense the absurd in Leontes' contorted syntax and ridiculous epithets when questioning Camillo:

> Was this taken
> By any understanding pate but thine?
> For thy conceit is soaking, will draw in
> More than the common blocks: not noted, is't,
> But of the finer natures? by some severals
> Of head-piece extraordinary? lower messes
> Perchance are to this business purblind? say!
>
> (I, ii, 222–28)

One can almost see him staring eagerly and writhing. This insistence on the baseless and ludicrous nature of Leontes' jealousy as much as on its reality takes away the edge of the latter. What Leontes does to Hermione is real enough, but at the same time, since his jealousy seems less than real (and, unlike Othello, he is constantly being told that he is wrong, which makes him look more of a fool), we begin to feel that whatever he does as a result of it must be finally unreal too. That in the event he loses Mamillius and not Hermione, Perdita or, finally, his friendship with Polixenes, indicates the limits of the gravity here (Othello lost everything). Antigonus sees that the court would be moved 'To laughter, as I take it,/ If the good truth were known' (II, i, 198–9). Leontes' jealousy is of so preposterously inflated a character that as soon as the

185

gods have revealed their anger at him in the death of his son, he loses his passion as suddenly as he gained it, believes his wife's faith and repents. The remaining 'evil' in the play, following on from the character of that of Leontes, is similarly comic while supposedly real. Antigonus is killed and eaten by a bear, and the ship that bore Perdita to Bohemia is wrecked and the sailors drowned, but most of this is reported in the comic idiom of a gibbering clown. And all this, it should be added, emerges not from the fact that the play is a comedy, but from its being a failed tragi-comedy.[4]

Given the nature of Leontes' jealousy we may accept that his first moment of repentance is absolute. Evil as portrayed in *The Winter's Tale* is more a blight that may visit mankind at random than something chosen by man. While we might accept in theory that the sixteen years during which Leontes remains convinced of the deaths of his wife and of Perdita are years in which repentance is confirmed and strengthened, that is not in fact our impression: indeed there is something of a hint of the old Leontes whose reactions are divorced from the facts in the comment of his spiritual tutor Paulina that he has 'paid down/ More penitence than done trespass' (V, i, 3–4). Despite this last point, the main purpose of the sixteen-year period seems to be to distance us from the evil done in the first acts. The play offers no answers to Leontes' behaviour: it only tries to make us feel that 'it will not happen again', and to make us suspend our knowledge that nothing that happens in the play can prepare one against such sudden, uninvited suspicion as that to which Leontes fell subject. In this way the evil that Leontes does in the first half of the play is in no way caught up and answered by the second half: it is simply swept aside, just as in the first half itself it was deficient in realization. The play is split at the sixteen-year gap into tragic and comic movements, and even where the tragic movement holds sway, its force is cancelled by comedy.

In *The Tempest* also evil is comically treated. A central instance is the scene (II, i) in which Antonio, Prospero's usurping brother, tries to persuade Sebastian to kill his brother Alonso, King of Naples. To Antonio's indirect blandishments Sebastian at first replies that he is talking in his sleep. Antonio bids him be serious, saying, 'I'll teach you how to flow,' to

186

which Sebastian responds, 'Do so: to ebb/ Hereditary sloth instructs me' (217–18).[5] Sebastian does now bid Antonio continue, but still mockingly: 'Prithee, say on:/ The setting of thine eye and cheek proclaim/ A matter from thee; and a birth, indeed,/ Which throes thee much to yield' (223–26). At this Antonio barely keeps his temper. When he goes on, preposterously, to say of Alonso's son Ferdinand, ''Tis as impossible that he's undrown'd/ As he that sleeps here swims,' Sebastian replies with an encapsulation of his moral listlessness, 'I have no hope/ That he's undrown'd' (233–34), meaning both that no hope is left of Ferdinand's survival and that he does not hope he will survive. Antonio struggles to energize this torpid evil—'O, out of that "no hope"/ What great hope have you!' When he asks Sebastian, 'Will you grant with me/ That Ferdinand is drown'd?' the latter laconically replies, 'He's gone.' Continually Sebastian mocks the orotund methods of solicitation used by Antonio. To the latter's elaborate description of Claribel, Alonso's daughter, as

> She that is Queen of Tunis; she that dwells
> Ten leagues beyond man's life; she that from Naples
> Can have no note, unless the sun were post,—
> The man i' th' moon's too slow,—till new-born chins
> Be rough and razorable; she that from whom
> We all were sea-swallow'd, though some cast again,
> And by that destiny, to perform an act
> Whereof what's past is prologue; what to come,
> In yours and my discharge
>
> (249–49),

Sebastian asks, 'What stuff is this! how say you?/ 'Tis true, my brother's daughter's Queen of Tunis;/ So is she heir of Naples; 'twixt which regions/ There is some space'; he makes Antonio work hard in his office of tempter. When Antonio proceeds finally to be quite explicit about murdering Alonso, Sebastian replies, 'I remember/ You did supplant your brother Prospero' (265–66). After this, and a glance at conscience, however, he briefly commits himself to Antonio's plan, though with perception of what has moved the latter on his behalf—namely, the hope of ending the annual tribute payable by Milan to Naples for assistance in the original supplanting of Prospero (287–89). But he seems to have a qualm, and while

187

he and Antonio talk further apart, Ariel enters to wake Alonso and Gonzalo: instantly the would-be murderers abandon their scheme. The whole plot thus appears, for all its villainy, abortive and absurd, and its agents comic.

A similar case obtains in the sub-plot of the play, where the ignorant Caliban tries to persuade the drunken comics Stephano and Trinculo to slay Prospero. (In itself the sub-plot is a mocking parallel to the main plot.) The pretensions of Stephano and Trinculo are as ludicrous as Caliban's cringings to them. As they approach Prospero's cell, Caliban bids them 'Do that good mischief which may make this island/ Thine own for ever, and I, thy Caliban,/ For aye thy foot-licker' (IV, i, 217–19). At this Stephano absurdly bids him, 'Give me thy hand. I do begin to have bloody thoughts'; but then Trinculo catches sight of the glittering apparel hung by Ariel on a line nearby—'O King Stephano! O peer! O worthy Stephano! look what a wardrobe here is for thee!'—and despite Caliban's warning against digressing for such 'trash' both do so and lose their purpose.

It is clear that in these late plays Shakespeare makes evil either remote and stylized, or in varying degrees lightweight, absurd or comic. If these plays are to be considered only as 'happy comedies' or wish-fulfilment fantasies, then this restricted admittance of evil, this curtailing of its force by authorial or providential means will be perfectly justifiable. But if they are intended seriously as a vision of the human condition, whether as it is or as it may be, then they are open to question. In *All's Well* and *Measure for Measure* Shakespeare once before tried to fuse the tragic and comic modes. The two were divided: the tragic was allowed full rein up to a point, after which the action was juggled to circumvent it and produce a happy outcome; thus in *Measure for Measure* Angelo was saved from the consequences of his treachery and Claudio from execution by two substitutions engineered by the absent-present Duke. It would seem that in the late plays Shakespeare tried to join the tragic and the comic more closely, but that here it is not the comic element which, as in the earlier plays, is unreal, but the tragic. Nor is the tragic vision of *Lear*, whereby man may be in part only a cosmic plaything and life meaningless and chaotic, ever canvassed in the late plays.

The vision of the tragedies—if we except *Othello*—is one of man alone in a universe of uncertain intelligibility, wherein choice is relatively free. In the late romances that choice is continually circumvented by a benign order. In *The Winter's Tale* evil is distanced both in time and space (we leave Leontes behind in Sicilia for much of the second part of the play); even the death of Hermione is removed by the art that makes a statue of her. This inhibition of evil comes to a pitch in *The Tempest*. Here, as in *Othello*, which could reasonably be termed its visionary antithesis, there is a recurrent imagery of 'free' and 'bound', reflecting the bondage to which Prospero subjects all on the island so that he and Ariel may be free.[6] While there is some thematic significance in the motif, particularly in the marriage of liberty and restraint portrayed in the union of Ferdinand and Miranda, it is so pervasive, descending even to minute particulars of how Caliban and other wicked people are to be 'pinched' or afflicted with cramps[7] as to seem ultimately not so much part of the meaning of the play as the unconscious expression by Shakespeare of his sense of the limitations imposed upon realism and evil in the play. The concept of freedom and bondage is not one particularly associated with old age; and it seems a strange one on which to insist in a play having to do centrally with justice and mercy: it would seem to be much more fitted to plays concerned with the theme of liberality, such as *Antony* and *Timon*, or of restriction, such as *The Merchant of Venice* or *Measure for Measure*. We have to suppose therefore that it issues from Shakespeare's uneasy intuition of his own manipulations, whereby evil is emasculated; just as in *Othello* its use reflects the contrived frustration of goodness. Some have claimed that *The Tempest* is realistic in that the evil Sebastian and Antonio remain unrepentant at the end:[8] but even if that were so, it is not their lack of regeneracy, but Prospero's forgiveness of Antonio and the powerlessness of his opponents which are emphasized; and their failure to repent would make the play no more realistic than those earlier comedies which left us at the end with an unreformed Don John, or Shylock or vengeful Malvolio while the good triumphed.

There is a sense in which the action of *The Tempest* can be said to occur inside Prospero's head. There are hints of the other romances being mental constructs, in the dissociative mode and marine idiom of *Pericles* and in the self-begotten 'mental' evil of Leontes in *The Winter's Tale*. But *The Tempest* is quite distinctive in dealing less with specifically supernatural action than with magical powers wielded by a human being and in having as setting one isolated place. We are thus continually aware of man the manipulator and, lacking the two or more places presented to us in the other romances, are without the certainty of objective reality. Prospero's past is described long-windedly enough (I, ii, 33–174), through his own mental recollection, and all his enemies are brought to him. At the end he cannot depart the island unless he has the help of the imaginations of his audience: there is in this sense no 'concrete' Naples to go to. Throughout the play not one of the antagonistic actions of the other characters is allowed to come to fruition: everything is made to fit with Prospero's wishes. There is stress on the right kind of mental attitude to be shown by the characters, especially in regard to wonder: faced by the creatures of the isle, the serene, comprehending admiration of Gonzalo is set against the fearful amazement of Alonso, the contemptuous acceptance of the absurd in Sebastian and Antonio (III, iii, 18–52), or the vulgar curiosity and mockery of Stephano and Trinculo (II, ii, 18 ff.); and equally, at meeting the people from the ship, the wondering and innocent delight of Miranda is in contrast with the ignorant credulity of Caliban (I, ii, 412–31; II, ii, 117 ff.; V, i, 181–84). The sense of Prospero as stage manager of a play is continually present, as is the notion of life as a dream:

> Our revels now are ended. These our actors,
> As I foretold you, were all spirits, and
> Are melted into air, into thin air:
> And, like the baseless fabric of this vision,
> The cloud-capp'd towers, the gorgeous palaces,
> The solemn temples, the great globe itself,
> Yea, all which it inherit, shall dissolve,
> And, like this insubstantial pageant faded,
> Leave not a rack behind. We are such stuff
> As dreams are made on; and our little life
> Is rounded with a sleep.
>
> (IV, i, 148–58)

Of course, the point here is that all life is a dream, and that to this extent reality itself is finally mental: but what we have to regard is that it is Prospero who is saying this. For someone living in a mental reality and habituated to making constructs out of the labours of his own thought, the likening of life to a stage or a dream must come naturally.

The characters sometimes seem to express different aspects of Prospero. Ariel and Caliban seem, like spirit and flesh, to represent the two halves of being. We find a reflection of the same dichotomy in Prospero's account of his earlier life in Milan, when he became a thinker, confined to his books, leaving his brother Antonio to be the 'do-er' in governing on his behalf. As Prospero's brother, Antonio could be seen as half of himself, as the unassimilable Caliban is on the island. In a sense, as Prospero partly sees, he himself 'begot' Antonio's original wickedness: 'I, thus neglecting worldly ends', he tells Miranda,

> in my false brother
> Awak'd an evil nature; and my trust,
> Like a good parent, did beget of him
> A falsehood in its contrary, as great
> As my trust was.
>
> (I, ii, 89, 92–6)

What is being suggested here is that the action of *The Tempest* may not 'actually' have occurred at all; and that in a sense the whole play can be viewed as a mental construct cut off from reality, as surely as we have seen how the reconciliations and resolutions which it reaches are divorced from any full sense of the evil in life.

Contemporary criticism of Shakespeare's late plays owes much to Lytton Strachey, who first argued that, far from being easily serene in these plays, Shakespeare retained a strong sense of the destructive force of evil. Strachey's point, however, was that the plays were broken apart by this, and that behind them we had a Shakespeare who was 'Half enchanted by visions of beauty and loveliness, and half bored to death; on the one side inspired by a soaring fancy to the singing of ethereal songs, and on the other urged by a general disgust to burst occasionally through his torpor into bitter and violent

191

speech'.[9] Later critics have been inclined rather to see Shakespeare's vision here as one which contains mutually jarring aspects of life in a larger harmony or *discordia concors*; and they have on their side the fact that in all these plays the central story is an act of destruction involving the scattering of the central characters followed by a process of coming together again in one place (if not *always* in one spirit) for repentance, forgiveness and marriage (restored or new). What has been suggested here is that the drive to 'synthesis' and 'reconciliation' in the late romances is quite *voulu*. Strachey was right to feel a sense of uneasiness in Shakespeare here, but mistaken to feel that it emerged from any strong sense of evil *within* the plays. If his statement has truth, it is rather in relation to the split between the insecure joys and beauties of the romances and the frequent pessimism of the political plays that precede them. In the romances Shakespeare is indeed trying to incorporate his sense of the destroying force of iniquity in a larger pattern, but what happens is that to do this he is driven to emasculate the evil. As reconciliations of contraries the late plays may work: but the contraries are not often very far apart. Shakespeare has not convincingly reflected or overborne the deep schisms that characterized his previous work; and the motif of irritation, disturbance and disquiet that runs through *The Tempest*,[10] possibly the last of these plays, seems further to expose his sense of this.

NOTES

1. Though see F. R. Leavis, *The Common Pursuit* (Chatto and Windus, 1952), pp. 176–77.
2. Charles Frey, 'Tragic Structure in *The Winter's Tale*: The Affective Dimension', in Carol M. Kay and Henry E. Jacobs, eds., *Shakespeare's Romances Reconsidered* (Lincoln (Nebraska) and London, University of Nebraska Press, 1978), p. 114, claims that 'in each Shakespearean romance a motive power of plot arises from the mind's fascination with familial taboo.'
3. References are to the Arden *The Winter's Tale*, ed. J. H. P. Pafford (Methuen, 1963).
4. See also Rosalie L. Colie, *Shakespeare's Living Art*, pp. 266–70.

5. References are to the Arden *The Tempest*, ed. Frank Kermode (Methuen, 1954).
6. See also Edward Dowden, *Shakspere: A Critical Study of His Mind and Art* (Henry S. King, 1875), pp. 419–20.
7. I, ii, 327–28, 330–31, 371; IV, i, 258–61; V, i, 74–7, 276, 286.
8. In any case there is no certain evidence that they do: see Larry S. Champion, *The Evolution of Shakespeare's Comedy: A Study in Dramatic Perspective* (Cambridge, Mass., Harvard University Press, 1970), pp. 172–73, 230–31, n. 13.
9. Lytton Strachey, 'Shakespeare's Final Period', *Books and Characters, French and English* (Chatto and Windus, 1922), p. 60.
10. Michael Goldman, *Shakespeare and the Energies of Drama* (Princeton, N.J., Princeton University Press, 1972), pp. 141–42.

9

Conclusion

Shakespeare's mind seems to have worked naturally with pairs, whether puns, identical twins or opposites; the sheer extent to which it does so marks him off from his contemporaries.[1] On the evidence we now have the interest would seem to stem from a tendency to dividedness in himself. At first in his plays the emphasis is more on likeness and reconciliation. The early comedies treat of division only to make a higher marriage, a *discordia concors*, out of it; the civil violence of the first history tetralogy eventually brings about the establishment of the Tudor line; the bloody struggle in *Titus Andronicus* between the protagonist and the perverted rulers of Rome may involve the death of Titus, but it also removes the vicious and restores the body politic to health. From the second history tetralogy however, through *Twelfth Night*, *Measure for Measure* and *All's Well*, attempts to heal divisions within the plays have diminishing success, until they are abandoned altogether and we move in spiritual landscapes shot through with irreconcilable discords. A further effort is made at reconciliation in the late romances, but fails. The development of the plays seems to be towards an increasingly fractured view of life.

The opposites which appear in the plays range from the recurrent motifs of division between mind and body or between men and women in love, to the more individual analysis of a man who divides himself from sense in *Macbeth*; and from the exploitation of psychological discontinuities as an imitation of a divided world in *Lear*, to the less intentional divisions of attitude in *Coriolanus* or *Timon*. There are also striking polarities between whole plays. In *Hamlet*, thinking about an action to be carried out ensures that it will not be performed; in *Macbeth*, thinking about a deed not to be carried out ensures that it will be; in the former, 'doing' is stopped by thought, and in the latter, thought by doing. In *Lear*, nothing becomes everything, and meaning is wrung out of despair; in *Macbeth*, everything becomes nothing, meaningless. *Coriolanus* and *Antony* are opposite in that where Coriolanus is unable to move, as Aufidius puts it, 'from th'casque to th'cushion', Antony cannot move in the reverse direction. The 'political' plays, *Coriolanus*, *Timon* and *Antony*, may be said to be concerned with 'body', where the late romances are informed by 'mind'. *Othello* and *The Tempest*, the only plays by Shakespeare set on islands, also have in common the possession of imagery relating to 'free' and 'bound': but where in *Othello* this imagery can be seen as reflecting the fact that events are manipulated to produce a tragic outcome, in *The Tempest* it similarly registers the engineering of a happy issue. And where in *All's Well* and *Measure for Measure* the happy ending arguably does not do justice to the serious issues raised by the plays, in the late romances it is the 'serious' side that fails to convince; the one has too much tragedy, the other too little. A certain one-sidedness of vision in Shakespeare is suggested by these contrasts, a readiness to see life from one exclusive angle and an inability to reconcile contrary views.

A broad overall movement in the types of polarity may be traced. Increasingly Shakespeare's plays deal more with divisions between the individual and the collective than with divisions between or within individuals: at first the divisions occur within society, but later the protagonist is more often cut off from the state. The extent to which this happens over all the later plays, despite the eventual restorations to social life depicted in the late romances, is striking, and suggests a pattern of withdrawal on Shakespeare's part. At the same time, throughout the portrayal of division in the plays, there is a gradual loss in dramatization. In *Hamlet* it is an act by Claudius, the slaying of his brother, which has split body from mind in Denmark: but the fact that the later political plays and romances are divided in the same terms points directly to Shakespeare. In the later plays the splits that appear are much less attributable to the needs of the plays: the divisions of attitude in *Timon* or the failure of reconciliation in *The Tempest* cannot be explained away in dramatic terms. The personal inference we can make from this is that dividedness increasingly dominated Shakespeare's vision to the point where it began to lose coherence.

The later plays are much more deterministic in their portrayal of discord. In *Hamlet* or *Troilus and Cressida* it is a voluntary act by one or more of the characters that causes division. But the world as seen in *Timon, Coriolanus* and *Antony* is inherently schismatic: arguably no character is finally to blame, for what he is expresses an environment which does not owe its nature to any single human act. Shakespeare does not analyse what makes these societies thus, nor does he propose any remedies: the compromises put before Cleopatra and Coriolanus, and accepted by Alcibiades in *Timon* are seen in at least a dubious light. The central characters remain unchanging, and change nothing outside themselves. The picture in these plays is much more 'objective' and despairing: the world divides societies and human responses, and there is nothing to resolve this save death. The late romances, which are an attempt to celebrate marriage rather than excoriate divorce, do not convince, because Shakespeare has not done justice to the sense of evil so dominant in the plays that precede them. Indeed, if one put them together with the plays from *Timon* to *Coriolanus* one could see the whole group as *Measure for Measure* writ large. Those who have in the past argued for a Shakespeare who becomes darker in mood throughout his work have a case.

Almost anyone writing today on Shakespeare, faced by these divisions in his plays, would prefer to say that he meant them, or that they are part of a dialectical or 'complementary' vision. With some of them it is possible to say this, and with two plays in particular, *Lear* and *Macbeth*, Shakespeare uses disjunctions and divisions to brilliant effect as the heart of the plays' meanings. But Shakespeare's interest in division comes ultimately from Shakespeare, and breaks others of his plays apart. We cannot explain away the increasing interest he shows in the theme: while the earlier vision of the breakdown between mind and body may have full explanation within individual plays, its recurrence does not. Nor is there any reason save bardolatry for so blandly accepting with the plays from *Macbeth* to *Coriolanus* that we either were meant to or even can reconcile condemnation and admiration in our attitude to the protagonists: we ought really to be asking why the same issue appears in all four plays, and why Shakespeare deals here with 'violent'st contrariety', with irreconcilable oppositions and points of view at extreme divergence. But then we ought to be asking a great many more questions of Shakespeare than we do—not out of iconoclasm, for that has not been the main object here, but to try to gain some sense of a man with certain interests, strengths, weaknesses and predilections, rather than some negatively capable Olympian behind the plays. If we do not, then we will continue to build walls at once protective and stifling around his work, perpetuating our own kind of division of Shakespeare from life.

NOTES

1. See also Robert Grudin, *Mighty Opposites: Shakespeare and Renaissance Contrariety* (Berkeley, Los Angeles and London, University of California Press, 1979), pp. 3–9.

Index